The National Co-ordination of EU Policy

The National Co-ordination of EU Policy
The Domestic Level

edited by

HUSSEIN KASSIM

B. GUY PETERS

and

VINCENT WRIGHT

OXFORD

UNIVERSITY PRESS

OXFORD

UNIVERSITY PRESS

Great Clarendon Street, Oxford OX2 6DP

Oxford University Press is a department of the University of Oxford.
It furthers the University's objective of excellence in research, scholarship,
and education by publishing worldwide in

Oxford New York

Athens Auckland Bangkok Bogotá Buenos Aires Calcutta
Cape Town Chennai Dar es Salaam Delhi Florence Hong Kong Istanbul
Karachi Kuala Lumpur Madrid Melbourne Mexico City Mumbai
Nairobi Paris São Paulo Singapore Taipei Tokyo Toronto Warsaw

and associated companies in Berlin Ibadan

Oxford is a registered trade mark of Oxford University Press
in the UK and certain other countries

Published in the United States
by Oxford University Press Inc., New York

British Library Cataloguing in Publication Data

Data available

Library of Congress Cataloging-in-Publication Data
The national co-ordination of EU policy: the domestic level / edited by Hussein Kassim,
B. Guy Peters, and Vincent Wright.
p. cm.
Includes bibliographical references and index.
1. Political planning—European Union countries. 2. European Union. I. Kassim,
Hussein, 1965– II. Peters, B. Guy. III. Wright, Vincent.
JN32 .N37 2000 341.242′2—dc21 00-027217
ISBN 0-19-829664-9

1 3 5 7 9 10 8 6 4 2

Typeset by Best-set Typesetter Ltd., Hong Kong
Printed in Great Britain
on acid-free paper by
Biddles Ltd Guildford & Kings Lynn

PREFACE

All chapters, except that on Portugal and the Conclusion, are substantially revised versions of papers presented at a workshop on co-ordinating EU policy held in Oxford in June 1998. We should like to thank the Warden and the Fellows of Nuffield College for their generous hospitality in accommodating us on that occasion.

We should also like to acknowledge the very considerable debt of gratitude owed to Stephanie Wright, who has administered the project from the organization of the workshop to the submission of the manuscript to OUP. All this has been achieved with her characteristic efficiency, and good humour. Amanda Watkins at OUP has been a sympathetic and helpful editor, offering encouragement at precisely the moments when it has been most necessary.

Finally, we should like to remember our co-editor, colleague, and friend Vincent Wright, who died on 8 July 1999. The June workshop saw Vincent at his best. His incisive interventions, stimulating provocations, and magisterial drawing together of themes were made with the lightness of touch and wit that were Vincent's trademark. He is greatly missed.

H.K.
B.G.P.

CONTENTS

NOTES ON CONTRIBUTORS

GIACINTO DELLA CANANEA is Professor of Administrative Law at the Faculty of Political Sciences, University of Urbino. He is the author of *Indirizzo e controllo della finanza pubblica* (1996) and has co-edited with Giulio Napolitano *Per una nuova constituzione economica* (1998) and with Jean Paul Costa *Public Administration and Human Rights* (1997).

HANS-ULRICH DERLIEN is Professor of Public Administration at the University of Bamberg. His research interest is on political bureaucracy and administrative elites.

HUSSEIN KASSIM is Lecturer in Politics, Birkbeck College, University of London. He has written on various aspects of European integration and the European Union. He is co-editor of *The European Union and National Industrial Policy* (1996) and of *Beyond the Market: The European Union and National Social Policy* (1998).

BART KERREMANS is Assistant Professor in International Relations and Senior Research Fellow of the Scientific Fund Flanders at the Catholic University of Leuven.

JOSÉ MAGONE is Lecturer in European Politics at the Department of Politics and Asian Studies, University of Hull. He has published extensively on southern European politics and the European Union. He is the author of *The Changing Architecture of Iberian Politics* (1996) and of *European Portugal* (1997).

ANAND MENON is University Lecturer in European Politics at the CEPES University of Oxford and Fellow of St Antony's College, University of Oxford. He is the author of *France, NATO and the Limit of Independence 1981–97* (2000).

IGNACIO MOLINA is a D.Phil. student at the Juan March Institute in Madrid. His doctoral research is an analysis of the nature and functioning of the Spanish executive, particularly during the policy stages of initiation and co-ordination.

WOLFGANG MÜLLER is Associate Professor in Political Science at the University of Vienna. He is co-editor of *Policy Office, or Votes?* (1999) and *Coalition Governments in Western Europe* (forthcoming).

THOMAS PEDERSEN is Associate Professor at the University of Aarhus. He is the author of *Germany, France and the Integration of Europe: A Realist Inter-*

pretation (1998) and co-editor of *The European Community in World Politics* (1993).

B. GUY PETERS is Maurice Falk Professor of American Government at the University of Pittsburgh. He is the author of *Comparative Politics: Theory and Method* (1998) and *The Future of Governing* (1996).

CALLIOPE SPANOU is Assistant Professor of Administrative Science at the University of Athens. She is the author of *Fonctionnaires et militants* (1991) and recent work includes 'European Integration in Administrative Terms: A Framework for Analysis and the Greek Case', *Journal of European Public Policy* (1998).

VINCENT WRIGHT was Fellow of Nuffield College, University of Oxford. He has written books on French government and politics, most notably on the French prefects and on the Conseil d'État, and has edited and co-edited several volumes on government and administration in Western Europe.

LIST OF FIGURES

LIST OF TABLES

ABBREVIATIONS

AC	Autonomous Communities
ASEM	Asia-Europe Meetings
CAP	Common Agricultural Policy
CDS-PP	Centro Democrático Social-Partido Popular
CEA	Committee for European Affairs
CFP	Common Fisheries Policy
CFSP	Common Foreign and Security Policy
CICE	Comissão Interministerial para as Comunidades Européias
CIPE	Comitato Interministeriale per la Programmazione Economica
CMAC	Conselho de Ministros para Assuntos Comunitários
COREPER	Committee of Permanent Representatives
DETR	Department of the Environment, Transport, and the Regions
DG	Director General
DGAC	Direcção-Geral para Assuntos Comunitários
DOP	Defence and Overseas Policy
DPE	Direction de la Production et des Échanges
DTI	Department of Trade and Industry
EAGGF	European Agricultural Guidance and Guarantee Fund
EC	European Community
ECJ	European Court of Justice
ECOFIN	Council of Economic and Finance Ministers
ECSC	European Coal and Steel Community
ECST	European Co-ordination and Strategy Team
EDC	European Defence Community
EEC	European Economic Community
EMU	European monetary union
ENA	École Nationale d'Administration
EP	European Parliament
EPC	European political co-operation
EPU	European political union
EU	European Union
EUDE	European Union Division External
EUDI	European Union Division Internal
EUDP	European Union Division: Presidency

EUROMED	Euro-Mediterranean Partnership
FCO	Foreign and Commonwealth Office
FO	Foreign Ofice
GAC	General Affairs Council
GDP	gross domestic product
GDR	German Democratic Republic
ICFP	Interministerial Conference for Foreign Policy
IEC	Interministerial Economic Committee
IGC	Intergovernmental Conference
ILO	International Labour Organization
JHA	Justice and Home Affairs
MAFF	Ministry of Agriculture, Fisheries, and Food
MCo	Ministry of Co-ordination
MEP	Member of the European Parliament
MFA	Ministry of Foreign Affairs
MNE	Ministry of National Economy
NUTS	nomenclature of territorial units for statistics
OECD	Organization for Economic Co-operation and Development
OPD	Overseas Policy and Defence
ÖVP	Österreichische Volkspartei
PCP	Partido Comunista Português
PM	Prime Minister
PP	Partido Popular (Popular Party)
PR	Permanent Representative
PS	Partido Socialista
PSD	Partido Socialdemocrata
PSOE	Partido Socialista Obrero Español (Spanish Socialist Workers' Party)
QMV	qualified majority voting
SCA	Special Committee for Agriculture
SCE	Service de la Coopération Économique
SEA	Single European Act
SEAC	Secretariado de Estado para Assuntos Comunitários
SEM	Single European Market
SGCI	Secrétariat Général du Comité Interministériel
SGG	Secrétariat Général du Gouvernement
SPÖ	Sozialdemokratische Partei Österreichs
SRI	Service des Relations Internationales
SSEU	Secretariat of State for the European Union
TEU	Treaty of European Union
UCD	Unión de Centro Democrático (Union of the Democratic Centre)

UKREP   United Kingdom Permanent Representation
VAT   value added tax
WHO   World Health Organization
WTO   World Trade Organization

Introduction

Hussein Kassim, B. Guy Peters, and Vincent Wright

The word 'co-ordination', when used in reference to the public sector, has positive connotations. Governments that are well co-ordinated are assumed to be more efficient, to have fewer conflicting and redundant programmes, and to utilize scarce public resources more rationally in achieving their policy goals. However, recent studies suggest that the level of policy co-ordination required to achieve all those positive ends is rarely achieved by any government (Hayward and Wright, forthcoming). Moreover, the prevailing climate of scarcity and distrust of government has imposed more pressures than ever on all European governments to co-ordinate. Achieving that degree of internal organization remains one of the perennial quests in the management of the public sector (Jennings and Crane 1994; Pressman and Wildavsky 1984: 113 ff.), an 'administrative Holy Grail' (Peters 1996: 295).

Entry into the European Union appears to impose even greater demands for co-ordination on its member states, adding new pressures and intensifying those that already exist. With EU membership, the domain of government action and responsibility has been extended. The complexity of decision making has increased and the policy stakes in many policy areas have been raised. As well as co-ordinating their internal policy-making activities, governments must be prepared to defend more coherent programmes at the EU level and also ensure that their proposals in Brussels and their actions in the national capital are compatible.[1] Further, given that there are economic and political resources to be gained from Brussels, national governments may believe that they need to present the best possible cases for their country in that arena, and that this can best be done through presenting a unified front against Brussels bureaucrats and the demands from other countries.

---

[1] 'Multi-level governance' also means that most national governments must be able to ensure co-ordination with regional governments as well as co-ordination within their own level.

The need to co-ordinate policy in response to EU membership may be a common stimulus, but, as the following studies make clear, the member countries have responded differently. Some, if not ignoring the need for co-ordination totally, have assigned rather low priority to that objective, while other countries pursue it actively. Still other countries pursue co-ordination with respect to Europe very much as they would co-ordination in any other policy area, treating Brussels as just another policy-making arena. Countries manifesting little interest in co-ordination appear to fear damage to delicate domestic coalitions, or they may believe that they have more to gain by playing multiple strategies in several arenas and seeing where they get the best deal.

For other countries, notably the United Kingdom and France, co-ordination has always been an important goal, and a great deal of time and effort is invested in ensuring that the government speaks with a single voice in Brussels. Some of this ambition to co-ordinate well is simply a product of the manner in which administration in conducted in these countries, but there are also more explicit motives. In particular Britain perceived a need for greater positive co-ordination during the period in which it was resisting very actively the continued expansion of the European project. The degree of ambition for co-ordination also varies with the degree of sectorization of policy making; in all countries there is some segmentation of policy, but strong interest groups with links to powerful ministries make attempts to impose co-ordination politically difficult.

Even when co-ordination is an important political goal, there are questions about how co-ordination should be achieved (Peters 1996). In particular, co-ordination can be driven from above, by the centre of government, or responsibility may be allocated to the lower echelons of the bureaucracy. There are always some issues that will be driven upwards in government, but there are also many can be resolved at an administrative level. The question is what choices are being made about which issues, and in which systems. Those choices may have something to do with the differential salience of European issues in the member countries.

Even if a government chooses to place the major focus of co-ordination activity at the centre, there is still a question about where that co-ordination should be located. One possibility is to place the activity in a specially designed organization, with the danger that this organization will have little real power, lacking any sort of base for that power. On the other hand, placing co-ordination in an existing ministry may simply continue and even reinforce existing rivalries and conflicts. And which ministry? The two usual options are foreign affairs and economics or treasury. Each option has its advantage and disadvantages, and governments must decide which values they wish to maximize, and which organizations they want to empower, when selecting the main locus of co-ordination for EU policy.

What follows is an examination of the co-ordination strategies on EU policy utilized in a number of European countries. The countries included in this book were selected to cover most of the important dimensions of variation among the member states: large and small, founding members and later comers, federal and unitary, north and south, etc. They also cover the gamut of levels of concern about co-ordination, with France and the United Kingdom at one end and Spain and the Netherlands appearing to be at the other. This volume provides an examination of the machinery that these countries have developed in their national capital (and perhaps in subnational capitals as well) to cope with the demands of EU memberships. A second volume, also to be published by OUP, will examine what these countries do in Brussels and, more specifically, the role of the permanent representations.

EU Membership and the Sources of Co-ordination Need

National governments have been faced with demands for co-ordination since the inception of the European Communities, but in the recent past, as Europe has grown in importance and complexity as a policy arena, it has become more important to 'get Europe right'. European policies have an increasing impact on citizens of the member states and the politicians in those countries find it more important to pursue the interests of those citizens (as well as their own interests) in that arena. Co-ordination is one way of more efficiently pursuing those interests in Brussels. As a result, European policies are becoming increasingly politicized. At one time EU matters were part of foreign policy and, while important, European policy making was something that happened far away from the national capital, was of only passing interest to the public and to politicians, and was handled almost exclusively by foreign ministers. The impact of the EU has, however, become more immediate and direct, and politicians find that they can influence voters by being effective in Brussels. In addition, effectiveness is generally perceived (sometimes mistakenly) as good positive co-ordination in an arena as complex as that of the European Union. In short, the need for co-ordination on the part of governments has grown increasingly urgent.

A set of demands and pressures that confront the member states and ground various co-ordination needs can be readily identified. First, there is the status of the EU as an authoritative policy-making system with the authority to impose binding obligations on the member states that are enforceable by the European Commission and the EU legal system with the European Court of Justice at its apex. Concerted action to define and defend a national position is called for, to ensure that EU policy outcomes are congruent, or at the very least not inconsistent, with national preferences.

The wide and growing competence of the Union in strategically important policy domains provides a second pressure on governments to co-ordinate domestically. At the outset, the EEC was responsible for core areas such as agriculture, competition, and external trade. With the signing of the SEA in 1986, the TEU in 1991, and the Amsterdam Treaty in 1996, its responsibilities have expanded to virtually every area of government activity. The adoption of the internal market programme heralded a period of activism at the European level that saw the Union assume primary policy-making responsibility in a wide number of fields, witnessed the creation of a framework and instruments for common action in domains of high politics, such as foreign and security policy, and justice and home affairs, and revitalized the Commission in the 1980s. The Union wields regulatory power in many areas of economic and social activity, enabling it to take action with far-reaching consequences for national actors, and has at its disposal substantial resources for redistribution in the shape of the European Aricultural Guidance and Guarantee Fund and the Structural Funds. The authoritative status of the EU and its reach create powerful incentives on the part of each government to ensure that its component parts act coherently in presenting national positions.

Beyond these general pressures lie more particular requirements that call for co-ordination by governments. The first concerns the six-month long presidency of the Council of the European Union which member states hold in rotation (Hayes-Renshaw and Wallace 1997; Westlake 1995). The responsibilities of the Presidency, set out in the treaties, in the Council's Rules of Procedure, and the documents defining the scope of the CFSP, are extremely demanding, and place a heavy burden on the national administration of the incumbent country (Bassompierre 1988; O'Nuallain 1985; Hayes-Renshaw and Wallace 1997). The presidency must chair the European Council and the Council of the European Union in all its formations and at all levels, and perform the varied functions of 'business manager', 'promoter of initiatives', 'package broker', and 'collective representative' (Wallace and Edwards 1976). The presidency has additional responsibilities regarding the CFSP: it represents the Council before the European Parliament and liaises in the Troika with previous and forthcoming incumbents. Not only must a successful presidency demonstrate political sensitivity and provide a purposeful, but neutral, chair, but it must also meet the formidable logistical challenges of scheduling and hosting meetings (for an idea of what is entailed, see Kirchner 1992; Ludlow 1993; Henderson 1998). Holding the presidency confronts the incumbent state with a severe test of its administrative capabilities and requires efficient national co-ordination in order to ensure that the Union is effectively represented and Council business properly conducted.

A second co-ordination need is generated by Intergovernmental Conferences (IGCs). These high-level summits have been convened with considerable frequency in the recent past—there have been four between 1985 and 1996—and are of critical importance for every member state. IGCs are the forum in which decisions concerning constitutional change are taken, all of which are likely to have far-reaching implications for member states. Negotiations are wide-ranging and complex, the pressure to secure a 'good deal' for domestic constituencies intense, and the stakes—political and economic— extremely high. In these conditions, national governments face a strong incentive to co-ordinate strategies and tactics: national negotiating positions must be clearly defined, and calculations made about what is and is not negotiable. Co-ordination between national representatives during the negotiations is also necessary.

The need to protect the national interest with respect to issues that have a high salience on the national agenda constitutes a third instance that calls for co-ordination. Agriculture in France, fisheries and budgetary contributions in the UK, state aid for regional development purposes in Germany, and structural funds in the Cohesion countries—Greece, Ireland, Portugal, and Spain— are issues that have assumed a symbolic status in domestic politics, and a stout defence must be mounted by national governments. In such high-profile areas, national governments need to ensure that positions can be developed, adopted, and defended rapidly, efficiently, and easily at whichever level—official, ministerial, prime ministerial—may be appropriate.

A final pressure derives from the increased national salience of EU policy. In some countries, such as the United Kingdom, and Denmark, EU membership has always been controversial. Both countries initially preferred the looser form of co-operation afforded by the European Free Trade Association (EFTA), and were latecomers to the Community. In the UK, the relationship with the Union has historically been construed in strongly instrumentalist terms, and supporters of integration have consistently—and misleadingly— argued that membership does not involve any threat to national sovereignty (Wallace 1997; Young 1998; Howe 1990; Lord 1992). Since accession, successive governments have felt compelled to emphasize the benefits that ministers have extracted from the UK's partners as a measure of success, thereby reinforcing the perception that the UK is playing a zero-sum game, and have adopted a defensive posture whenever developments imply the (further) forfeiture of sovereignty. Since the Maastricht IGC, 'Europe' has become an even more sensitive issue, as demonstrated dramatically by the 'No' vote in the Danish referendum, and by the 'siege' of the UK Parliament by Conservative Eurosceptics on the government back benches (Baker, Gamble, and Ludlow 1994).

The increased salience of EU policy since Maastricht has not, moreover, been limited to these late arrivals. In France, the negotiation of the TEU marked a watershed in the perception of European integration. Since 1992, and the referendum that took place in September, which produced a narrow victory for the ratification of the Treaty, greater concern has been expressed about the consequences of further integration for French sovereignty, and EU issues have become politicized (Flynn 1995; Menon 1996; Kassim 1997). In Germany, and the Netherlands, support for the European Union is no longer as widespread or unconditional as it was previously. The level of the national contribution to the EU budget became a major issue in both countries: in Germany, on account of the pressures arising from unification, and in the Netherlands as a result of becoming a net contributor for the first time after Maastricht.

European integration thus confronts national governments with strong incentives to co-ordinate action. These arise from the general characteristics of the EU, from specific duties and obligations incumbent on the member states, and from the politicization of European matters in domestic political life. However, the co-ordination of EU policy, and action is an extremely complex undertaking.

The Challenge of EU Policy Co-ordination

Although, as stated above, the EU is only one among many sources of co-ordination need confronted by national governments (see Hayward and Wright, forthcoming), it is certainly among the most demanding. The extended front across which the Union engages the member states, the permanence of their involvement, and the need for action at two levels—the domestic, and the European—impose particularly severe demands. These essential characteristics of the EU call for the creation and maintenance of complex systems of horizontal and vertical linkages on the part of each member state. Governments must take decisions about the aims of co-ordination, the appropriate structures and procedures for their delivery, and the allocation of responsibilities. Each level, moreover, presents its own particular requirements, involves different actors, and is subject to different, and often conflicting, pressures and conditions. Governments must satisfy the demands of domestic constituencies, while at the same time adopting positions that are negotiable in Brussels. These characteristics of the EU call for a 'co-ordination chain [that] extends from that within each ministry and inter-ministerial co-ordination (of both a vertical and horizontal nature) at domestic level, to co-ordinating the domestic-EU interaction and then to co-ordinating within Brussels' (Wright 1996: 149).

Institutional fragmentation also presents national governments with considerable difficulty. Power at the European level is shared between a multiplicity of institutions, and there is no single authoritative legislator (Scharpf 1994, 1996). Each institution is internally differentiated, has its own methods, procedures, and culture, exercises varying degrees of power, and commands different resources. Lines of division within the Commission, for example, run between the political level—the College of Commissioners and their *cabinets*—and the administrative level—the services, which in 1999 numbered twenty four Directorates-General, each with its own responsibilities and identity (Abélès, Bellier, and McDonald 1993). The Council of the European Union is also an extremely complex body. Its tripartite structure—working groups, COREPER and ministerial meetings—is differentiated along sectoral lines, its various bodies operate according to differing norms (Lewis 1999), and, with the decline of the General Affairs Council as a co-ordinator, there is a strong tendency towards fragmentation. Finally, the work of the European Parliament is carried out by its twenty committees, and its organization and procedures must be agreed by several party groups, which threaten continually to fragment along national lines.

Sectorization is an additional feature of the Union that renders national co-ordination problematic. Although an inherent characteristic of domestic policy making, 'the extent and nature of these problems in Brussels is of a different order' (Wright 1996: 130). First, the EU blurs the traditional distinction between foreign and domestic policy, and covers a range of different policy types. The main distinction is between polity issues, such as treaty reform, the power of institutions, external relations, and enlargement, and more technical areas that have traditionally been a matter of domestic concern. Further categories within the latter—regulatory, redistributive, and distributive—can be distinguished following Lowi (1964). Each policy type has a different logic and conflict potential, and demands a particular kind of expertise. Polity issues, for example, favour diplomats, while sectoral issues call for various technical experts. The construction of an integrated national system that draws together departments and officials with the relevant sets of experience and specialist knowledge is likely to be attended by institutional rivalry and tension.

Second, vertical linkages between decision-making arenas at the European level are strong, whilst horizontal connections are weak. Each area is governed by its own rules and procedures, and involves a different set of actors. The relative power of EU institutions varies from sector to sector, and policy processes, both formal and informal, tend also to be sectorally specific. Within each sector, regular interaction between the same set of actors can lead to a sense of shared identity, a distinctive culture, and a degree of introspection (Peterson and Blomberg 1999; Kassim and Menon 1996). Not only is there a real risk that contradictory objectives might be pursued by national officials working in different policy fields, but the possibility either that experts may follow specific aims that are not consistent with more fundamental national commitments or that, by a process of *copinage technocratique*, technical specialists may collectively escape the control of their governments is present.

Moreover, where policy is developed in discrete areas, and particularly where there are conflicts between sectoral networks, it becomes very difficult for a member state to define a national position. Complex trade-offs must be constructed and internally negotiated, which may well prove difficult where certain interests are likely to be losers.

The task of national co-ordinators is complicated by further distinctive characteristics of the EU. The most important of these are as follows (Wright 1996):

- high institutional and procedural density. The EU is a 'decisional maze' and 'overcrowded policy arena' (Wright 1996: 151–2). It encompasses not only the full panoply of European institutions, which include the European Council, the Council of European Union, the European Commission, the European Parliament, the European Court of Justice, and the Court of Auditors, but various intergovernmental committees, agencies, and other bodies. Relations between these actors are often not well defined, weakly institutionalized, and contingent.
- high committee volume. Business in Brussels is transacted in a wide array of intra- and interinstitutional groups and committees that become operative at various stages of the decision-making process. They vary considerably in terms of status, membership, and power. The best known are various consultative committees operated by the Commission and the comitological committees that enable the member states to supervise the Commission's exercise of its executive responsibilities.
- complexity and fluidity of procedures. The EU presents a bewildering variety of intricate decision-making processes and decision rules. In advance of the 1996 IGC, the Commission estimated that there were twenty-four combinations of legislative procedures—consultation, co-operation, co-decision, and assent—and Council voting methods— QMV, unanimity, simple majority—in operation (1995). The power of each institution in any particular circumstance largely depends upon the decision-making rules that apply in that instance, and each procedure establishes different incentives and requires differing winning or blocking strategies. Formal requirements, moreover, may be complemented, or even overridden by, conventions or informal codes of behaviour.
- lack of control over agenda setting. Individual governments at the European level have little formal power over policy initiation at the EU level. The Commission has a formal monopoly over the right to put proposals forward and, though the Council of Ministers (and the EP) may recommend that the Commission takes action, they cannot force its hand. The Commission can decide whether to act, and when, and it decides the

content of any proposal. Although it has been estimated that a substantial proportion of initiatives originate with national governments (Ludlow 1991), the fact that there are fifteen member states diminishes the ability of any one government systematically to shape the policy agenda. On the one hand, governments must constantly react to proposals tabled by other parties. On the other, such is the influence that can be had on determining the final policy outcome by shaping the agenda (Pollack 1996, 1997; Pierson 1996) that there is a strong incentive for governments to develop a proactive capacity, particularly with respect to issues that are salient on the domestic agenda. The decline of unanimity has in addition increased the importance of policy initiation, because member states can no longer simply veto proposals that they do not like.

- the weakness or absence of channels of co-ordination which are present at the national level. In the EU, national co-ordinators cannot rely on the channels provided by political parties, professional networks, policy networks, and patronage that at the national level enable them to overcome institutional fragmentation and sectorization.
- dependence on bargaining, networking, and coalition building. The multiplicity of actors and arenas together with the predominance of decision rules which do not permit a lone government to veto policy decisions, and a policy making culture that favours compromise, require member states to look for allies to either support or block the progress of proposals. Coalition building requires constant networking with potential partners and a continual awareness of strategic and tactical possibilities.
- the impact of the changing size of the Union. Enlargements require national governments to become familiar with the operating systems and styles of new members. In addition, the decision to enlarge and preparations for enlargement typically lead the existing member states to conduct exercises to establish the likely impact on economic sectors that are of strategic importance to the national economy and on the resources available for redistributive policy at the European level.
- an evolving agenda. Constant change in the scope of EU activities prevents national officials from relying on settled assumptions of good or appropriate policy, or on policy continuity over time.
- range of skills and resources. Effective operation in the EU requires linguistic skills, as well as technical, legal, and administrative expertise.
- administrative mismatch. The division of responsibilities between various Councils may not match the way in which competencies are allocated between national ministries. In these circumstances, EU business may need to be co-ordinated between different departments with different needs and cultures. Moreover, it may be the case that EU action is transacted in an area where competencies are shared between federal and

subnational authorities, where the state has no legal competence or where there is no relevant administrative authority.

These features make the co-ordination of EU policy extremely problematic for the member states, distinguishing it sharply even from demanding tasks of domestic co-ordination, such as the control of public expenditure or dealing with long-term unemployment, immigration, and law and order. EU policy making confronts governments with a challenge that is unique in terms of its scope and complexity.

Convergence and Distinctiveness

The growing importance of the European Union, interaction in Brussels within the same institutional framework, and the apparent need for well co-ordinated policy positions are common stimuli for the member countries, so a substantial degree of convergence in the salience of European Union policy making and in the structural and procedural means of implementing it might well be expected. Although there is evidence of a degree of convergence, national distinctiveness also persists. The mixture of responses represents the central part of the puzzle about co-ordination in the European Union, and perhaps about all aspects of EU policy making. We should expect convergence, given the need to work together within a common political structure, but we should also expect the persistence of well-established national political patterns. Why do we observe the particular mix of these two outcomes that we do?

Pressures for convergence

The dominant pressure for convergence arises from the fact that member states confront a similar environment and, in preparing and defending their positions in Brussels, face common challenges. The way in which governments pursue and represent their interests at the European level is strongly influenced by the institutional structure of the Union and its legislative processes. EU methods demand particular forms of participation in designated forums at defined moments. As governments must comply with EU rules, processes, and norms, it is in their interests to ensure that arrangements are in place domestically that will permit them to make the appropriate input.

A second pressure is mimicry and learning (Olsen and Peters 1996). Some countries appear to have been leaders in co-ordination and other countries may attempt to emulate their structures and procedures. This is especially true for countries just entering the EU that may feel the need to develop that co-ordination capacity quickly. By simply copying another country's mechanisms they can obtain this capacity 'off the shelf'. Countries will not tend to copy at random, however, and will tend to copy from countries with rather similar political structures, or with similar administrative styles (Olsen and Peters 1996). Even then, however, form may be copied more easily than substance, and the same machinery may be effective in one setting but not in another—a point made about Greece by Spanou in this volume.

Coercion is a third factor, identified in discussions of new institutionalism as a potential source of convergence between organizations (DiMaggio and Powell 1991). Clearly, in the context of the EU, force—coercion in the strong sense—is not a relevant concern, but EC law, its binding character, and enforcement by a system of courts with the European Court of Justice at its apex forms a weaker, but nevertheless powerful, coercive pressure. Treaty obligations and secondary legislation not only impose constraints on the freedom of action of governments, but may require action to be taken which otherwise would not have taken place or institutional machinery to be created. Subject to a common legal system, it would be surprising if there were no signs of convergence between the member states in the face of common obligations and restrictions.

Socialization, whereby national officials become 'gradually socialized into the shared values and practices of the EU system' (Harmsen 1999: 84; see also Haas 1958; Derlien in this volume; Kerremans 1996; Lewis 1998), is a further pressure. Leading to a 'gradual diffusion of those shared values within national administrative systems', an administrative culture may progressively develop producing over time the 'emergence of increasingly similar national structures and processes' (Harmsen 1999: 84). A number of authors have discovered a socializing logic at work in EU structures, including the Council (Kerremans 1996), COREPER (Lewis 1998), and the Commission (Christoph 1993), and it may be that frequent contact between national officials, their counterparts in other member states, and officials in the European institutions has spread common values among national administrations.

A final potential influence is a process of what Harmsen (1999. 84) calls 'optimization'. As governments face similar challenges deriving from membership of the Union, it can be expected that 'there will be a gradual convergence of national practices around the most effective solutions to those common problems' (Harmsen 1999: 84). National administrations will be 'driven by a logic of optimization to adopt increasingly similar processes and structures' (Harmsen 1999: 84). Harmsen criticizes the assumption that optimization is at work, which he contends underlies much of the literature on Europeanization, but the operation of such a mechanism is at least an empirical possibility.

Why continued national divergence?

While there are certainly common pressures for the homogenization of co-ordination machinery and procedures, there are also strong pressures for maintaining distinctive national patterns. Some of these represent adaptations to somewhat different political interpretations of EU member-ship, as well as differing political needs for co-ordination. Many, however, represent simply the persistence of national styles of policy making and administration (Richardson 1982), and important differences in national level politics. In some cases attempts to co-ordinate from the centre may be interpreted as threats to delicate political machinery for coping with regional and ethnic sensitivities, while in others the failure to do so would be taken as a sign of political weakness and/or incompetence. As we will now proceed to point out, there are a host of factors that appear to influence the style of co-ordination activity undertaken by a national government.

Policy Styles

One factor affecting the co-ordination activities of national governments at the domestic level is the national policy styles and ambitions. Any number of variables might be used to characterize these styles, but for EU policy making several factors appear to be of particular importance. One is whether the style in making policies tends to be 'bottom up' or 'top down'; that is, does the gov-ernment tend to act autonomously and then impose its decisions on social and economic actors, and subnational governments, or is policy the product of a long period of consultation and discussion (see, for example, chapters by Menon and Kassim, on the one hand, and by Derlien, Kerremans, Müller, and Pedersen, on the other).

Although increased consultation appears to be the standard in almost all national political systems, there are still marked differences in the degree of power and involvement of actors outside the centre of government in policy making. For example, even with New Labour, the British central government tends to act more autonomously than its counterparts in Denmark or Austria which must consult with their 'social partners' before acting. All of these coun-tries will co-ordinate, but they will do so in markedly different ways, and perhaps with very different success. The extreme case here may be Belgium where the two regions hold vetoes over national policy statements (see Kerremans, in this volume). Co-ordination in the smaller countries may be driven more by the perceived needs of the involved ministries and interests, rather than being demanded from central agencies (see Derlien and Müller, in this volume).

The above aspect of policy style may be closely associated with the degree of segmentation of policy making existing in a country. That is, are individual policy sectors permitted to make policy independently of other sectors, or are there strong demands for co-ordination from the centre? Is this true for domestic policy as well as for Europe? The more those centralizing demands are effective in shaping the policy-making process, the less capacity there is for 'bottom-up' forms of co-ordination among the actors involved, whether at home or in Brussels.

Another related factor in policy style is the extent to which a country regards itself as reactive or proactive with regard to EU policy making. Some countries, including France and Germany, have decided to take a proactive role in defining the agenda of the Union, and in shaping the ways in which policies are to be considered. Others have opted for a more passive or reactive role. This choice again may be occasioned by internal political divisions, or simply by the size of the country in question. Clearly a country with a more active role in defining the agenda will need, *ceteris paribus*, to have a more integrated policy perspective than will a country that mostly reacts to the initiatives of others. The latter type of country may be able to respond effectively to agenda items, and to work out a position after the fact, but find it difficult to co-ordinate proactively a new proposal. A final component of the policy styles issue is what role a country has been playing concerning the EU. We may distinguish between those countries that have been playing the positive role of 'locomotives' (Germany and France) driving the project forward, those taking a negative role as 'brakes' (Britain and sometimes Denmark) on action, and those acting more or less as 'spectators' (Greece and Portugal).

Both supporters of further integration and countries is a preference for intergovernmentism will have greater need for co-ordination, especially proactive co-ordination, than will the spectators. Given the power of the former, and the inertia that has been developing within Europe for further integration, the demands for co-ordination for the countries with more negative agendas in Brussels may be especially high.

Conception of Co-ordination

Another variable defining the differences among co-ordination strategies adopted at the national level is the very notion of co-ordination that informs national policy making (Metcalfe 1994; Wright 1996; Hayward and Wright, forthcoming). Some countries may believe that their programmes are well co-ordinated while observers from other political systems may consider them extremely disorganized. This difference may be a function simply of different ideas about what constitutes adequate co-ordination, and differences in what aspects of policy are considered crucial to co-ordinate. Some political systems focus on co-ordination primarily when making decisions, while others may be more concerned about co-ordinating the implementation of any decisions made.[2]

As well as the distinction between the co-ordination of policy making and co-ordination of implementation, there are also different ideas about the degree of positive co-ordination required. One conception of co-ordination may be that the role of the centre of government is to be sure that the government 'speaks with one voice' in Brussels, a perspective clearly held by successive governments in the UK government and France (see Kassim and Menon, in this volume). This is an active, and a difficult, conception of co-ordination. It requires making a decision, by imposition or by negotiation, that reconciles potentially competing societal interests and departmental views.

This positive style of co-ordination often creates clear winners and losers, and hence may generate political conflict. That is often the case when the common position for the government is selected 'from the top down'. On the other hand, the positive co-ordination may also create more legitimate policies, given that they would represent a decision by the government. The latter outcome may require a process of consultation and negotiation such as those typical of the smaller European democracies (see Müller on Austria and Pedersen on Denmark, in this volume). The process may be even more delicate when it involves not just societal interests but also subnational governments with their own sources of legitimacy, as it may in federal or quasi-federal systems.

In other cases, co-ordination may simply be filtering issues, ensuring that the issues that arise are dealt with by the appropriate organizations within government. The co-ordination machinery in this style of policy making is more a 'transmission belt' than it is a source of decisions or pressure. Relatively few choices are made by the central machinery in this style of co-ordination, so that political conflict is minimized in the process. An even more minimalist conception of co-ordination would involve simply the dissemination of relevant information about European issues among the participants in government about each other's activities. Agriculture might know what Environment was negotiating in Brussels, but would not have any ready means of forcing a consideration of their potentially conflicting interests in the policy area. Everyone would know what was occurring, but they might only know that contradictory policies were being pursued in different arenas.

[2] This distinction that may be related to the discussion of top-down and bottom-up perspectives on co-ordination, but it is certainly not the same thing. It is quite possible to be concerned about co-ordination of implementation from a centrist, top-down, perspective.

The nature of the co-ordination machinery and the co-ordination effort may also vary depending how the relationship with Brussels is conceived, and what ministry or ministries are central to the process. If the EU is considered largely a foreign policy issue dominated by the foreign affairs ministry then the informational model may be more likely, with the diplomatic service simply informing domestic actors of what is happening 'abroad'. If, on the other hand, the main actors are economic ministries or the chief executive's office there is likely to be a more active version of co-ordination, with a desire to align views and overcome bureaucratic politics to form a single national position.

Finally, the approach to co-ordination may depend upon the programmatic aims of the government in question. What does the government want? It is likely to invest much less in co-ordination if it is concerned primarily with monitoring what is happening in Brussels than if it is more actively concerned with driving the process of integration forward, or alternatively concerned with slowing it as much as possible. In the former scenario all that is required is noting agenda items and perhaps giving ministries or social actors an early warning on likely changes in EU policy. The latter conception will involve a much more activist role for central government actors.

Likewise, simply stressing co-ordination as a means of avoiding political disasters, or at least being able to avoid blame for the disasters, requires a very different level of commitment to co-ordination by politicians than does attempting to generate real policy coherence. The former stance implies monitoring and only reacting when there is clear danger of a political mishap; the substantive, rather than political, dimensions of problems appear less relevant (Bovens et al. 1998). The latter stance requires at least the same level of monitoring, as well as a greater attempt to create common policy stances and a reduction of conflict among the bureaucratic actors involved.

Political Opportunity Structures

The degree of investment in, and the type of approach to, co-ordination of EU policy at the national level will also depend upon the political opportunity structure within the country. Although it comprises some unique challenges to the existing governmental order, the EU is to some extent just another bundle of political issues that must be processed within that political order. Thus, to understand what co-ordination outcomes are likely, or even possible, it is necessary to understand the political structures that will make the co-ordination decisions.

One of the crucial political factors, already alluded to, is the salience of EU issues on the domestic agenda. For some countries, notably Denmark and the

UK, EU issues may be highly delicate issues that provoke intense political debates that divide the parties and the public. In others, the EU may have become simply another part of the political environment, and the issues arising from Brussels are accepted as little different from purely domestic considerations. To some extent, the longer a country has been a part of the EU the more likely the salience of the issues is to have diminished, though this does not apply to all cases as French sensitivities about agriculture and Dutch resentment at the increase of their contributions to the Community budget testify, Likewise, countries that tend to perceive themselves as net beneficiaries of membership are less likely to generate contentious domestic politics out of EU matters. Everything else being equal, we would expect co-ordination in countries where EU issues are salient to be more important, but also perhaps more difficult to achieve.

The party system and the relationship of parties to the cabinet are also likely to influence the capacity of a political system to co-ordination of EU policy. On the one hand, the more parties there are in the parliament, the more likely it will be that there are a number of difficult stances on EU policies that will have to be factored into the decisions. On the other hand, most countries with multi-party systems have developed mechanisms for building consensus, something that more adversarial two-party systems tend to lack (Lijphart 1984). The party system may present special difficulties when one or more parties focus on the EU as a central issue, as some minor nationalist and regionalist parties have done.

A fragmented party system may be expected to produce a more fragmented executive, and this is often the case. Again, however, many multi-party systems, especially those of the smaller democracies, have a well-developed capacity for compromise and to co-ordinate. The party system is not, however, the only variable affecting the capacity of the political executive to co-ordinate effectively. Some of this capacity stems from ideas about the executive, such as, for example the notion of *Kanzlerdemokratie* in Germany, which accords a privileged position to the Chancellor in policy making. As more cabinets accept a more powerful role for the Prime Minister then co-ordination capacity should be increased. The major problems with co-ordination appear to arise in multi-party systems without consensual norms and in which the Prime Minister is not accorded a dominant position, as is the case in Italy (see della Cananea, in this volume; see also Hine n.d.).

Even if the cabinet is capable of creating coherent action there may be co-ordination difficulties if the legislature is also involved in EU policy making. The major instances here are in the Scandinavian countries, especially Denmark (see Pedersen, in this volume). These arrangements do not create 'divided government' as in fully presidential systems, but they do provide yet another 'veto point' in the policy process and hence another need to compromise and to negotiate over a common position. Even if there are not partisan differences over policy there may be sufficient institutional jealousy to create difficulties if the parliament is an active player in the co-ordination exercise.

Co-ordination problems can increase if there are still other actors involved in the process. As noted already, interest groups are more powerful players in some systems than in others, and when making a common policy in an EU policy debate involves getting the interest groups to agree co-ordination issues may become very thorny. The issues that require the most co-ordination are also likely to be those that affect the most diverse interests and hence the ones where reaching agreement may be more difficult. As with multi-party governments, however, those countries (Austria and Denmark in particular) that tend to involve interest groups the most also have developed patterns of accommodation and negotiation that make reaching the agreements more feasible than in most other political systems.

As well as involving interest groups, some political systems also require the involvement of subnational governments in making EU policy. Germany, for example, has granted a much greater role to the *Länder* during the past several years, to the point that they are involved directly in some EU discussions (see Derlien, in this volume). Belgium's case is even more extreme, with the two regions having virtual veto powers over any position that the central government might want to take in EU discussions (see Kerremans, in this volume). Spain constitutes a third with its model of asymmetric federalism, where some regions are more assertive than others (Molina, in this volume), while in Austria the *Länder* have been unable to reproduce with respect to European matters the role they play in domestic policy making (see Müller, in this volume). As regional demands increase and regional issues become more relevant, as they appear to be doing, then the need to involve subnational governments will affect the capacity of all governments to cope with EU policy making.

Administrative Opportunity Structures

The final factor to be considered in this discussion of the factors affecting the co-ordination of EU policy at the domestic level is the nature of public administration in the political system. There are a number of factors to be considered here, including the simple question of the competence of the administrators and their interest in producing a coherent set of policy proposals. Even in the industrialized democracies of Europe those factors are not evenly distributed, and administration in some countries is manifestly more professional and more concerned with co-ordination than in others.

In all the systems we are examining the administrative system plays a major role in creating policy coherence. Final decisions may rest with politicians, but those decisions are prepared and shaped by administrators. As well as their competence, there is also a question about how many are involved in the process. Some systems attempt to create coherence by involving all the relevant actors directly, while others attempt to do so with a much smaller number of participants who are empowered by the senior politicians. These differences in numbers generally reflect the norms about participation in the respective political systems, as well as the perceived need for information about the specifics of policy.

Administrative systems are also more or less integrated and centralized in the several political systems in the European Union (compare, for example, the UK with Greece as discussed by Kassim and Spanou respectively, in this volume). In some systems there is, at least at the top of the civil service, a single cadre that has shared relatively common experiences (in government and outside) and find it important to continue to be able to work effectively with one another. In other administrative systems there are a number of internal divisions that shape careers and create rivalries, and competition over 'turf' and policy. Those divisions may be horizontal (*corps* in France, *cuerpos* in Spain) or vertical (departmental) but in either case the internal divisions may make coherence more difficult to come by.

In addition to their internal manifestations, these internal divisions in the bureaucracy may be associated with linkages to societal interests that will exacerbate the differences existing within the administration itself, and also exacerbate the problems of creating coherent policy positions. Some form of linkages of administration to societal interests is encountered in all countries, but the question is how closely these institutions are linked, and whether there are any mitigating factors. As well as being linked to networks of interests at home, administrative organizations may be linked to networks in Brussels, a linkage that may either enhance or minimize the co-ordination capacity of national administrators. On the one hand, the linkages may be to sectoral interests at the European level, perhaps further minimizing the interest in co-ordination (see Mazey and Richardson 1993). In other instances the linkage may be to other European actors that are more concerned with increased integration and policy coherence, rather than with the protection of segmented policy interests.

In short, EU policy making is becoming sectorally significant, more politically salient, and more complex, and has set up convergent pressures for greater and more effective co-ordination. However, these convergent pressures continue to be mediated by national needs, ambitions, and capacities which are, in turn, shaped by domestic political and administrative opportunity structures.

The construction of European entity may be gathering apace, but dealing with that entity reveals the tenacity of nationally rooted factors—perhaps the major theme of this collection of essays.

References

Abélès, M., Bellier, I., and McDonald, M. (1993), 'Approche anthropologique de la Commission Européenne', unpublished report for the Commission.

Baker, D., Gamble, A., and Ludlow, S. (1994), 'The Parliamentary Siege of Maastricht', *Parliamentary Affairs*, 47/1.

Bassompierre, G. de (1990), *Changing the Guard in Brussels: An Insider's View* (New York: B Praeger).

Bovens, M. A. P., t'Hart, P., and Peters, B. G. (1998), 'Conclusion: Types of Policy Failure', in P. Gray, *Policy Disasters in Western Europe* (London: Routledge).

Christoph, J. B. (1993), 'The Effect of Britons in Brussels: The European Community and the Culture of Whitehall, Governance, 6/4: 518–37.

DiMaggio, P. J., and Powell, W. W. (1991), 'The Iron Cage Revisited: Institutional Isomorphism and Collective Rationality', in W. W. Powell and P. J. DiMaggio (eds.), *The New Institutionalism in Organizational Analysis* (Chicago: University of Chicago Press).

Flynn, G. (ed.) (1995), *Remaking the Hexagon: The New France in the New Europe* (Boulder, Colo.: Westview).

Haas, E. B. (1958), The Uniting of Europe (Stanford, Calif.: Stanford University Press).

Harmsen, R. (1999), 'The Europeanization of National Administrations: A Comparative Study of France and the Netherland', *Governance*, 12/1: 81–113.

Hayes-Renshaw, F., and Wallace, H. (1997), *The Council of Ministers* (London: Macmillan).

Hayward, J. E. S., and Wright, V. (forthcoming), *Governing from the Centre* (London: Macmillan).

Henderson, D. (1998), 'The UK Presidency: An Insider's View', *Journal of Common Market Studies*, 36/4 (Dec.), 563–72.

Hine, D. (n.d.), 'The Co-ordination and Implementation of Italy's European Community Policy', unpublished mimeo.

Howe, G. (1990), 'Sovereignty and Interdependence. Britain's Place in the World', *International Affairs*, 66/4.

Jennings, E. T., and Crane, D. (1994), 'Co-ordination and Welfare Reform: The Quest for the Philosopher's Stone', *Public Administration Review*, 54: 341–8.

Kassim, H. (1997), 'The European Union and French Autonomy', in special issue of *Modern and Contemporary France*, ed. Vincent Wright, 5/2 (May), 167–80.

—— and Menon, A. (1996) (eds.), *The European Union and National Industrial Policy* (London: Routledge).

Kerremans, B. (1996), 'Do Institutions Make a Difference?' Non-institutionalism, Neo-institutionalism and the Logic of Common Decision Making in the European Union', *Governance*, 9/2: 216–40.

Kirchner, E. (1992), *Decision-Making in the European Community: The Council Presidency and European Integration* (Manchester: Manchester University Press).

Lewis, J. (1998), 'The Institutional Problem-Solving Capacities of the Council: The Committee of Permanent Representatives and the Methods' of Community', Cologne: Max-Prack-Institut für Gesellschafts forschung, Discussion Paper 98/1.

——(1999), 'Administrative Rivalry in the Council's Infrastructure: Diagnosing the Methods of Community in EU Decision-Making', Paper prepared for the Sixth Biennial ECSA International Conference, 2–5 June 1999, Pittsburgh.

Lijphart, A. (1984), *Democracies* (New Haven: Yale University Press).

Lord, C. (1992), 'Sovereign or Confused? The "Great Debate" about British Entry to the European Community Twenty Years on', *Journal of Common Market* Studies, 30/4.

Lowi, T. J. (1964), 'American Business, Public Policy, Case Studies and Political Theory', *World Politics*, 16/4, 677–715.

Ludlow, P. (1991), 'The European Commission', in R. O. Keohane and S. Hoffmann (eds.), *The New European Community* (Boulder, Colo.: Westview Press).

——(1993), 'The UK Presidency: A view from Brussels', *Journal of Common Market Studies*, 31/2.

Mazey, S., and Richardson, J. J. (1993), *Lobbying in the European Community* (Oxford: Oxford University Press).

Menon, A. (1996), 'France and the IGC', *Journal of European Public Policy*, 3/2.

Metcalfe, L. (1994), 'International Policy Coordination and Public Management Reform', *International Review of Administrative Sciences*, 60: 271–90.

Olsen, J. P., and Peters, B. G. (1996), *Learning from Experience: Lessons from Administrative Reform* (Oslo: Scandinavian University Press).

O'Nuallain, C. (ed.) (1985), *The Presidency of the European Council of Ministers* (London: Croon Helm).

Peters, B. G. (1996), *Managing Horizontal Government: The Politics of Co-ordination* (Ottawa: Canadian Centre for Management Development).

Peterson, J., and Blomberg, E. (1999), *Decision-Making in the European Union* (London: Macmillan).

Pierson, P. (1996), 'The Path to European Integration: A Historical Institutionalist Analysis', *Comparative Political Analysis*, 29/2 (Apr.), 123–63.

Pollack, M. A. (1996), 'The New Institutionalism and European Community Governance: The Promise and Limits of Institutional Analysis', *Governance*, 9/4 (Oct.), 429–58.

——(1997), 'Delegation, Agency and Agenda Setting in the European Community', *International Organization*, 51/1: 99–134.

Pressman, J. L., and Wildavsky, A. (1984), *Implementation*, 2nd edn. (Berkeley and Los Angeles: University of California Press).

Richardson, J. J. (1982), *Policy Styles in Western Europe* (Hemel Hempsted: Allen & Unwin).

Scharpf, F. W. (1994), 'Community and Autonomy: Multi-level Policy Making in the European Community', *Journal of European Policy*, 1/2: 219–42.

Scharpf, F. W. (1996), 'Negative and Positive Integration in the Political Economy of

European Welfare States', in G. Marks, F. W. Scharpf, P. C. Schmitter, and W. Streeck (eds.), *Governance in the European Union* (London: Sage).

Wallace, H. (1997), 'At Odds with Europe', *Political Studies*, US: 677–88.

——and Edwards, G. (1976), 'European Community: The Evolving Role of the Presidency of the Council', *International Affairs*, 52/4: 535–50.

Westlake, M. (1995), *The Council of the European Union* (London: Cartermills).

Wright, V. (1996), 'The National Co-ordination of European Policy-Making: Negotiating the Quagmire', in J. Richardson (ed.), *European Union. Policy and Policy-Making* (London: Routledge).

Young, H. (1998), *This Blessed Plot: Britain and Europe from Churchill to Blair* (London: Macmillan).

1

The United Kingdom

Hussein Kassim

The case of the United Kingdom presents two paradoxes. The first opposes the UK's reputation as an 'awkward partner' (George 1994) to the efficiency of its co-ordination system (Bender 1991, 1996; Wallace 1996; Wright 1996). On the one hand, the UK is considered to be 'at odds with the theory and practice of integration' (Wallace 1997), behaving more like a third party negotiating with the European Union than a member of it. Its relationship with Europe has been one of 'missed chances' (Denman 1996). It joined the European Communities begrudgingly at the third attempt, and has remained at best a 'semi-detached' participant ever since (George 1992). On the other, the UK system for EU policy co-ordination has attracted widespread admiration. Practitioners and observers are generally agreed that UK representatives are well briefed, that officials 'sing from the same hymn sheet', and that the government's position is presented with clarity and precision (Armstrong and Bulmer 1996; Bulmer and Burch 1998; Buller and Smith 1998; Butler 1986; Edwards 1992: 74; Menon and Wright 1999; Schmidt 1996). Its flexibility (Wallace 1996: 65), capacity for rapid action, and the high quality of its interventions have drawn praise. Emile Noël rated it the best among the member states,[1] and 'its efficiency has been confirmed by research findings of the European Institute of Public Administration in Maastricht' (Spence 1995: 364). France has learned from it (Lequesne 1993), and newer member states have attempted to emulate it.[2] Moreover, it has an impeccable record in implementating EU legislation. The second paradox highlights a contradiction

I should like to thank the two former Secretaries of State and the officials in Whitehall, Edinburgh, and Brussels who agreed to be interviewed on a strictly non-attributable basis as part of the research for this chapter. Interviews were conducted during 1998 and 1999 in the Cabinet Office, the Foreign and Commonwealth Office, the UK Permanent Representation, the Ministry of Agriculture and Food, the Department of Trade and Industry, the Home Office, the Scottish Office, and the Northern Ireland Office.

[1] *Financial Times,* 19 Oct. 1987.
[2] Interview in Brussels with Swedish official.

between the UK's reputation for administrative efficiency and the view that it has been ineffective in securing favourable policy outcomes at the European level. This clash is surprising, since, as Menon and Wright (1999) observe, '[i]ntuitively, we would expect that effective policy making potentially enhances policy outcomes and influence over the outcomes at the European level'.

This chapter attempts to reconcile these conflicting views. It offers an examination of the UK system for co-ordinating EU policy, explains the UK's response to the challenges posed by membership of the EC/EU, and discusses the actors and mechanisms involved. It argues that the 'contradiction' between the efficiency of the system and UK scepticism is only apparent, and, indeed, that the UK's co-ordination strategy is partly explained by its attitude towards European integration (first paradox). It contends, moreover, that the contrast between the UK's administrative efficiency and (alleged) policy failure (second paradox) must be treated with caution (Menon and Wright 1999). The UK may not have secured desirable policy outcomes in all areas, but its record has been far from negative, and it can boast a number of important successes. In addition, the link between administrative efficiency and policy effectiveness is not as straightforward as it may appear. As Wright (1996) has argued, effectiveness is conditioned by a number of factors, and any proper assessment must take into account policy ambition, type, and issue.

The chapter proceeds in four parts. The first section considers the UK's interpretation of the co-ordination need generated by EC/EU membership. The co-ordination ambition is outlined and explanatory factors discussed. The organization, structure, and operation of the co-ordination system are discussed in the second part of the chapter, which examines in detail the relationship between central actors and the line ministries, the division of labour and responsibility, and the formal and informal channels of communication. The third section assesses the effectiveness of UK co-ordination within the wider context of the relationship between administrative efficiency and policy success. The final part concludes that the UK's system for co-ordinating EU policy has been shaped more profoundly by pre-existing institutional structures and values (Harmsen 1999) that characterize the domestic polity than by the demands generated by membership of the Union, but that the influence of both imperatives is apparent.

The Co-ordination Ambition and the UK Political System

A distinguishing feature of the UK system is the existence of an explicit, well-defined co-ordination ambition, which is not limited to avoiding mishaps or contradictory actions (Wright 1996: 148) but aims at the overall steering of policy. Crystallized as the mission statement of the European Secretariat, the goal of the system, as well as its various parts, is:

to ensure that for any EU activity or proposal . . . agreement is reached on a UK policy in good time, taking account of identified UK interests and advancing or at least protecting those consistent with overall Government policy with realistic objectives taking account of the interests of other members of the EU and that the policy agreed is followed through consistently during negotiation, and put into effect once decisions have been taken in Brussels.[3]

This formulation is based on an assessment of the requirements of EU membership that reflects fundamental principles, practices, and norms underlying the UK system of government, the strong centralization of the UK polity, and the importance assigned to government unity.

Foremost among these principles is the doctrine of collective responsibility which governs the operation of cabinet government in the UK (Burch and Holliday 1996; Dunleavy and Rhodes 1990) and, in its support, the work of the UK civil service (Dunleavy and Rhodes 1990; Wallace 1996). The principle holds that decisions made by the Cabinet have been agreed by all its members. It follows that any minister dissenting from policies taken in cabinet should resign from the government. Collective responsibility encompasses collegiality in the making of decisions and unity in their implementation.[4] The principle has survived, even though the dramatic expansion in the scale and complexity of government responsibilities since 1945 has led to the development of a dense network of cabinet committees and subcommittees to ease the burden. Few decisions now are taken in full cabinet (Hennessy 1986).[5]

Whitehall's administrative procedures have been organized to support the requirement for horizontal and vertical co-ordination presupposed by collective responsibility. As decisions are taken in the name of all ministers, the administration is responsible for ensuring that for any item of business all interested departments are consulted. Procedures and working practices are oriented towards developing a unified position that all departments can defend. The Cabinet Office plays a central role in monitoring how issues are progressing, taking steps where co-ordination is necessary, and organizing

---

[3] Quoted from presentation given by former member of the European Secretariat, Oxford, Dec. 1994. See also Bender (1991, 1996) and Butler (1986).

[4] As Helen Wallace has commented (1996: 62), '[g]overnment is supposed to act in a unified way. . . . Departments do not have rigidly defined and demarcated spheres of responsibility . . . Hierarchies there may be, but divergences are not supposed to be perceptible.'

[5] Decisions taken in these committees that bring together ministers or officials from the relevant areas are considered to be Cabinet decisions, even though the full Cabinet may never discuss them. See Hennessey (1986) for detailed discussion of the UK Cabinet.

meetings where differences cannot be resolved by informal means. The system has generated a distinctive administrative culture of norms and values which support information-sharing, instinctive consultation, and cross-departmental contact, and a spirit of mutual trust, group loyalty, and corporate endeavour (Christoph 1993; Bulmer and Burch 1998; Wallace 1996). Moreover, the UK administration, even after the implementation of the 'Next Steps' programme and agencification, is distinguished by the homogeneity of the higher civil service. Loyalty is directed towards Her Majesty's government rather than to an administrative corps as in France or Spain or to individual departments. The tradition of neutrality and the absence of political patronage also contribute towards the reinforcement of a broad corporate identity.

Vertical co-ordination in the UK civil service is assured by the principle of ministerial responsibility. Ministers lay down policy guidelines that civil servants are to follow.[6] Officials carry out their work in accordance with these general instructions, but in the case of large policy issues, where a change in policy direction may be necessary or where conflict arises with another department that cannot be resolved at official level, the minister may need to be consulted for specific guidance. According to the principle, ministers are deemed to be responsible for the action of officials in their charge. As Wallace (1973: 252) has observed: 'The British administrative tradition lays much stress on the responsibility of Ministers for actions undertaken by their civil servants, and on the anonymity of civil servants acting on behalf of their Ministers.'

The strong centralising pressures exerted by collective responsibility and the UK's politico-administrative culture are reinforced by six additional factors:

- the unified political executive (in contrast, for example, to France's bicephelous system);
- the tradition of single party government;
- the fusion of legislature and executive;
- executive dominance of the legislature;
- the unitary state;
- the absence of social partnership.

The wider features of the UK polity only partly explain, though, why the UK has such a well-defined co-ordination ambition. The anxiety felt by a late-comer to a well-established club was no doubt an important factor. However, the UK's attitude towards membership of the EC/EU and the terms of the political and popular debate about the relationship has also been crucial. As

[6] As one former civil servant, quoted in Edwards (1992: 76), has observed: 'The British have an obsession with consistency which I think stems from the nature of our politics. Ministers must say the same as civil servants, civil servants the same as Ministers.'

Helen Wallace (1997) has argued, the need for Britain to join the Communities was justified to the British public on strongly instrumental grounds. The symbolic reasons for European integration repeated by politicians in other countries are rarely cited in the UK debate, even by its strongest supporters. Moreover, the impact on UK sovereignty was not properly addressed at the time of accession, neither has it been subsequently (Wallace 1997; Lord 1992; Young 1998). The inevitable adjustments and constraints on national action brought by membership have been downplayed with leading politicians arguing as recently as the debate over Maastricht that national sovereignty was not being eroded. On the one hand, this has led to a tendency in the UK to construe membership in strictly cost–benefit terms, putting pressure on successive governments to deliver 'what is good for Britain'. On the other, each further step along the path of integration is interpreted as a dangerous threat to national sovereignty. Unlike other member states, there is no positive consensus about the value of Union membership either amongst political and economic elites, or among the wider public.

The UK's cautious approach, rooted in history—the imperial past, victory in two world wars, the unconquered isles—and culture—the myth of the island nation, its global vocation, the link with the Commonwealth, the special relationship with the USA—as well as commitment to an Anglo-Saxon, rather than a Rhenish, model of capitalism, has played an important part in shaping the UK's co-ordination ambition.[7] The UK's wariness about membership and the caution with which it regards the European project explain the adoption of a system designed to ensure that UK interests are carefully safeguarded. It is in this sense that the contradiction between the UK's co-ordination strategy and its reputation as an awkward partner, as construed by the first paradox outlined above, is only apparent. Both are rooted in a fundamental defensiveness and a deep anxiety about the UK's participation in Europe. As Derlien argues in this volume, 'marvellous EU policy co-ordination may be an artefact produced or nurtured by politicians wanting to demonstrate their concern for the national interest to an anxious electorate'.

UK Co-ordination: Actors, Structures, and Procedures

The UK's co-ordination system shares many of the characteristics of the wider Whitehall system—a factor that has contributed significantly to its efficient operation. The objective of achieving a unified position, and procedures and mechanisms for ensuring horizontal and vertical co-ordination are evident in

---

[7] This list is drawn from Wallace (1997). For detailed discussion see Young (1998). For a controversial account, see Denman (1996).

both. Moreover, the administrative norms and values that characterize White-hall have been projected into the UK's management of EU matters.

The UK introduced relatively few innovations at the time of its accession (Bulmer and Burch 1998). This partly reflected the fact that contact with Brussels was long-standing and that institutional mechanisms had already been created to manage its relations with European institutions. In addition, a co-ordination machinery, albeit of a limited form, had existed since the UK made its second application in 1967. A European Unit had been set up in the Cabinet Office to oversee the negotiations. This was the forerunner of the European Secretariat, now at the centre of UK policy co-ordination.[8]

In preparation for entry, a strategy was set down for co-ordination, which has remained largely unchanged since. The Prime Minister, Edward Heath, and the Secretary of the Cabinet decided that each department should itself deal with Community matters in its particular area of responsibility (Edwards 1992). Technical experts in the ministries were to take the lead in formulating the UK's position and be responsible for consulting other departments. The role of overall co-ordination was entrusted to the European Secretariat in the Cabinet Office, with important roles also given to the Foreign and Commonwealth Office (FCO) and to the UK Permanent Representation (UKREP). The European Secretariat assumed responsibility for ensuring that the all interested parties were consulted and that as and when necessary a UK position was defined. 'Light co-ordination' was mixed with a 'large measure of departmental initiative' (Bulmer and Burch 1998: 10).

Line ministries

Individual ministries play a crucial role in the UK co-ordination system. With the expansion of EU competencies, virtually all Whitehall departments and many agencies handle work that has a European dimension. An important distinction, however, must be drawn between the technical ministries that take the lead for policy in their area of responsibility and the territorial departments that have interests in a range of sectoral areas, are involved in the process of interdepartmental co-ordination—often extensively as, for example, in agriculture and fisheries—but do not take the lead in any field (Armstrong and Bulmer 1996; Bulmer and Burch 1998).[9] Ministries of both types, though, have established units to co-ordinate European activities internally. The precise responsibilities and operation of these units is a departmental matter, and arrangements vary from ministry to ministry, though in

[8] The European Secretariat was downgraded by the Labour government, 1974–79 (see Edwards 1992).
[9] This was the case at the time of writing, but has attered since the creation of the Scottish and Welsh assemblies.

most cases the lead role is left to the technical experts in the relevant division. Officials are expected to maintain contacts with their counterparts in other member states, the appropriate section of the UK Permanent Representation, and officials in the EU institutions, especially the European Commission. This communication is not monitored by the internal co-ordination units, although officials must observe standing instructions and protocol conventions.

The differences between departments reflect the history of EU involvement, the proportion and spread of departmental work that is EU related, and the opportunities that the EU offers for the pursuit of departmental objectives. In the Ministry of Agriculture, Fisheries, and Food (MAFF), for example, EU business has a high profile and has enhanced the standing of the department in Whitehall. Participation in the CAP enabled it to develop and conduct its own foreign policy (Buller and Smith 1998: 173, 177). In departments where Union involvement is relatively new by contrast, EU business may be regarded as an intrusion or diversion (Buller and Smith 1998), or treated as peripheral. The mark of ministers, both Europhile and Eurosceptic, is important, and the imprint of departmental cultures is also evident, in internal procedures and the division of labour. In the Home Office, responsibility is concentrated in the hands of EU specialists and dossiers move up the line, whereas in the Treasury 'every team that deals with a particular policy domestically deals with it at an international and European level' (Treasury official, quoted in Buller and Smith 1998: 179) and the hierarchy is relatively flat, with desk officers in some cases reporting directly to ministers. These differences have an impact on personnel management, recruitment, training, and placement practices.

Internal departmental arrangements for the management of EU business have an obvious importance in a system where line ministries take the lead in policy formulation. They are also significant because power is not distributed evenly between departments. The Treasury, for example, does not play a central role in EU policy co-ordination, but its horizontal responsibilities make it an important interlocutor of every spending department. Some departments, moreover, have a monopoly over technical expertise which may make it difficult for other actors to challenge their positions, while others are expert in manipulating the Whitehall machine. The discussion below is limited to the Ministry of Agriculture, Fisheries, and Food (MAFF), the Department of Trade and Industry (DTI), the Home Office, HM Treasury, and the territorial ministries.

MAFF

MAFF's involvement in EU business is long-standing, stretching back to the time of accession, and extensive. Due to the volume of agricultural business and its technical complexity, officials fly out from London to attend Council meetings. European work is concentrated in the European Union and Livestock Group in the Agricultural Crops and Commodities Directorate, which handles the product regimes under the Common Agricultural Policy (CAP).[10] Although experts in the technical divisions within the Group take direct charge of policy, Union-related work is overseen by EU Division. EU Division is subdivided into four units dealing with agrimonetary policy, agricultural policy in general, the financial aspects of CAP, and procedural and institutional questions, such as relations with the European Parliament and comitology. A fifth was added in 1997 to prepare and manage the UK presidency's organization of agricultural policy, and was duly disbanded in July 1998.

EU Division performs five main functions. First, it is responsible for co-ordinating the work of the Group. While not directly supervising the work of technical experts in the product regime divisions, it ensures that relevant interests are consulted (including, for example, the territorial interests represented by the Northern Ireland Office, the Scottish Office, and the Welsh Office), is informed about the progress of dossiers, oversees implementation, and must give its authorization for financial operations. It also provides advice and expertise. Second, EU Division takes direct charge of general policy issues concerning the CAP. There are two formal co-ordination mechanisms: a weekly meeting of the Committee on Agriculture, which is chaired by the head of the EU Division (a Grade 5 ranking official) and which meets weekly to discuss the agenda of the forthcoming meeting of Special Committee on Agriculture—the Council body equivalent to COREPER in the agricultural sector; and a monthly strategy meeting, chaired by the deputy secretary of the Agricultural Crops and Commodities Director (a Grade 2 ranking official). Officials from the UK Permanent Representation attend the latter, where the approach for the upcoming Agriculture Council is agreed.

Within Whitehall, EU Division maintains contact with other ministries with an interest in the CAP—a third role. Besides the territorial ministries, the Treasury is an important interlocutor, as are the DTI and the FCO, and to a lesser extent the Department of Health and the DETR. These contacts are usually managed informally on a bilateral basis or, where a more formal exchange is required, in interdepartmental committees chaired by the European Secretariat (see below). Furthermore, EU Division is responsible for contributing the CAP element to the development of cross-sectoral policy. In the Agenda 2000 exercise, for example, it was responsible for developing the UK's position on CAP reform. Responsibility for institutional matters is a fourth function. This includes supervising the system of parliamentary

---

[10] Divisions deal respectively as follows with: Beef and Sheep; Milk, Pigs, Eggs, and Poultry; Livestock Quotas.

scrutiny (see below), managing relations with the European Parliament and, when the UK holds the Council presidency, organizing meetings and planning the agenda. Finally, EU Division prepares and delivers briefings to officials and ministers prior to meetings in the Council, and, like the co-ordination units in other departments, is a centre of intelligence and information gathering. It is typically headed by a senior official with long experience in European matters, who has contacts in Brussels in the Agricultural Section of the UK Permanent Representation and with detached national officials in the European Commission, as well as with officials in other member states. He or she is also likely to be connected to wider, informal networks in the Whitehall 'village'.[11]

DTI

The extent of MAFF's immersion in EU business is matched by the DTI. DTI ministers attend at least six technical Councils on a regular basis (Internal Market, Industry, Energy, Research, Consumer Affairs, Telecommunications) and occasionally participate in the General Affairs Council and Social Affairs, while no fewer than seventeen of the thirty-one chapters of the *acquis communautaire* highlighted in negotiations for EU enlargement fall within the DTI's remit. Although the DTI has been regularly reorganized by successive administrations and shuttled between Europhile and Eurosceptic ministers, a degree of continuity was preserved in its European policy. Since the mid-1980s, EC/EU policy has been consistent with the DTI's agenda of internationalizing and multilateralizing free trade (Buller and Smith 1998: 174).

Co-ordination for EU matters is the responsibility of the European Directorate located within the Trade Policy Division. The European Directorate's sixty staff are organized into five units, with responsibilities for the single market, state aid, industrial policy, energy, and enlargement respectively. Its functions and *modus operandi* are similar to those of EU Division in MAFF, but the range of policy areas for which it bears the responsibility for co-ordination are somewhat broader. First, the European Directorate co-ordinates internal work on EU matters. Like its counterpart in MAFF, it does not closely scrutinize the work of each official in the technical divisions, but it does act as a troubleshooter, intervening when policy implications are out of step or when problems arise with other departments. Second, the European Directorate is the lead division within Whitehall for UK policy on the single market, including competition policy and state aid, and all aspects of EU action concerning industry. These are major responsibilities which involve

---

[11] More than one senior official spoke of the importance of informal relationships with officials of similar rank and similar, often overlapping European experience, in departments across Whitehall.

considerable co-ordinating effort inside the DTI, and continual contact with other ministries. The Directorate also provides expertise and advice on these areas. Third, the European Directorate co-ordinates DTI thinking on constitutional and institutional reform, playing, for example, a major role in developing the UK's position at Intergovernmental Conferences, and is responsible for formulating the ministry's contribution to exercises such as Agenda 2000. Finally, it provides information for officials and briefings for ministers attending Council meetings.

Home Office

In contrast to MAFF and the DTI, where involvement with the Community has been long-standing, Europeanization is a relatively recent phenomenon for the Home Office. Its main area of involvement is Justice and Home Affairs (JHA), where the Home Office takes the lead in Whitehall, though it also handles other disparate elements of business under the first pillar, such as data protection, European voting systems, health and safety, and British summertime. Co-ordination is managed within the Home Office by the EU and International Unit. A small body of about fifteen staff, which was slightly expanded during the UK presidency in 1998, the Unit is responsible for preparing officials and ministers for meetings of the JHA Council and meetings of the K4 Committee. It also takes the lead on horizontal issues, co-ordinated the department's input into the Amsterdam IGC, and is responsible for formulating the UK's policy on the JHA elements of enlargement.

The Treasury

Although it lacks a formal co-ordinating role,[12] the Treasury exercises a strong influence on EU policy. Its involvement in European business has evolved significantly since 1973, as a result, initially, of the controversy surrounding the UK's contribution to the budget, and later, of economic and monetary union. Not only is it in constant bilateral contact with many line ministries on the spending implications of sectoral policies, but it also takes the lead on macroeconomic issues, finance, and the budget.

The Treasury was slow to create a specialist unit for the internal co-ordination of EEC-related business. European issues were originally managed by a section within International Finance Division. Then in 1982, the European Community Group (of Divisions) was established as part of Overseas Finance, although its role was relatively limited. Technical experts took primary responsibility for matters with a Community dimension as part of

---

[12] This situation contrasts with the years following the signing of the Treaty of Rome when the Treasury was the central co-ordinator in Whitehall for UK relations with the EEC. See Bulmer and Burch 1998: 601–28.

their routine responsibilities. The Banking Division of Financial Institutions and Markets Group, for example, assumed responsibility for Community proposals for a banking directive, while the Industry, Agriculture, and Employment Group handled the expenditure aspects of the CAP (Edwards 1992: 81). In the absence of formal mechanisms, co-ordination took place in 'village communities' within the Treasury (Sir Leo Pliatsky, cited in Edwards 1992: 81), which brought officials together informally.

The European Community Group gradually centralized the co-ordination of EC business and took direct charge of issues, such as the UK budgetary contribution, reform of Community policies, and financial and economic policies, such as the single European market and EMU. In 1994, however, this approach was abandoned in favour of a return to a more fluid approach and responsibility was devolved once again to the technical experts. Two groups located in the International Finance Directorate assumed responsibility for overall co-ordination (interviews). The European Co-ordination and Strategy Team (ECST), similar to its counterparts in MAFF and the DTI, is a centre of expertise, offering advice to the technical experts. It prepares officials and briefs ministers for meetings of ECOFIN, and it takes the role in general policy matters, such as the reform of economic policy and employment. Financial issues, the annual budget, and future financing, under Agenda 2000, on the other hand, are co-ordinated by EU Finance. Both groups take a 'light touch' approach to co-ordination (interviews), reflecting the Treasury's distinctive administrative culture and managerial style.

Interdepartmentally, the influence of the Treasury is strongly felt through the operation of EUROPES, a mechanism for ensuring overall financial control over European expenditures. EUROPES creates a strong incentive for spending ministries to take a critical approach to Commission initiatives that involve extra spending by requiring that any department that agrees to a UK contribution deducts an equivalent sum from its departmental budget. As Dowding remarks, EUROPES 'has decreased Whitehall enthusiasm for the EC, given that civil servants' own pet schemes may have to be casualties of the commissioners' pet schemes' (1995: 139). The effect is to forge an alliance between the Treasury and spending ministries in EU negotiations (Bulmer and Burch 1998: 618–19).

While the controversy over the budget pushed the Treasury to the forefront of relations between the UK and Europe in the early 1980s, Economic and Monetary Union and the Delors White Paper have further enhanced its position since the late 1980s. Even if the UK's attitude has been generally sceptical, as demonstrated by the opt-out negotiated at Maastricht, action at the European level in macroeconomic policy has brought the Treasury to centre stage. The Treasury's involvement in preparations for the third stage of monetary union and ECOFIN's expanding agenda have further strengthened its position.

Territorial ministries

The three territorial ministries, the Scottish Office, the Welsh Office, and the Northern Ireland Office, occupy a curious position in the EU policy-making process. Although they participate in co-ordination,[13] they do not, as noted above, take the lead in any area of policy and depend on the sectoral departments in Whitehall to take their interests into account. Any differences tend to be resolved at this level, but where serious problems arise, as they did with BSE, issues may be passed on for arbitration by the Cabinet Office.

All three territorial ministries have EU co-ordination units that take responsibility for horizontal issues, including institutional issues such as comitology, enlargement, and Agenda 2000, and management of the UK presidency, while sectoral matters, notably, agriculture, regional, and environmental policy, and, in the case of Scotland, fisheries, are handled by the relevant technical departments. The creation of these units is relatively recent. In the case of Scotland, for example, the establishment of the European Central Support Unit, which later became the European Affairs Unit, followed a review conducted in 1990–1 aimed at strengthening Scottish input into EU policy making. It was accompanied by a concerted effort to develop European expertise and to secure better representation of Scottish interests by improving the placement of Scottish Office officials in the UK Permanent Representation and in the Commission. The creation of Scotland Europa as an information office in Brussels also took place at this time.

In addition, the precise functions and responsibilities of the territorial departments—and consequently, the scope for differences with Whitehall ministries—vary considerably, reflecting differences in their competencies, political, legal, and administrative traditions, and economic interests. With respect to the first, for example, the Scottish Office has wider responsibilities than the Welsh Office. Concerning the second, Northern Ireland has its own administration and civil service, while Scotland has a different legal system from the rest of the UK. With regard to the third, Scotland has a particular interest in fisheries, since it accounts for nearly two-thirds of the UK catch, and both Northern Ireland and Scotland are important producers of beef, and not as dramatically affected by BSE as herds in England. These differences are likely to become sharper after devolution,[14] although the aim of arriving at a single UK perspective and the emphasis on presenting a unified position is set to remain the same since UK relations with the European Union has been designated a reserved area.

[13] Ministers and officials, for example, attend departmental and interdepartmental meetings, and may participate in some policy areas in Council meetings in Brussels. For example, it is not unusual for the Scottish minister to attend the Fisheries Council.

[14] In the case of Scotland and Northern Ireland, for example, departments of the devolved executives are to sign concordats with Whitehall ministries detailing the procedures for the co-ordination of EU issues.

The actors at the centre

Responsibility for the central co-ordination of UK policy lies with the European Secretariat, the Foreign and Commonwealth Office, and the UK Permanent Representation. Each performs a distinct function, and their interlocking partnership is a distinguishing feature of the UK system. Although not generally involved in the routine process of co-ordination, the Prime Minister also has a crucial role in EU policy making.

The European Secretariat

Based in the Cabinet Office, the European Secretariat is charged with overall responsibility for the co-ordination of the UK's EU policy and 'provides the permanent core of core executive co-ordinating activity' (Wright 1996: 156). The decision to entrust this function to the Cabinet Office reflected a more general shift of central co-ordination responsibilities within Whitehall away from the Treasury to the Cabinet Office (Bulmer and Burch 1998). It also guaranteed proximity to Number 10. In contrast to other member states where this function was exercised by the Foreign Ministry (see, for example, Cananea and Petersen in this volume), and perhaps learning from their experience, this task was not entrusted to the FCO. A ministry with departmental interests over a wide range of issues could not also be an impartial co-ordinator. To avoid the possibility of a conflict of interests, responsibility was instead vested in a more neutral body.

The European Secretariat is one of four units in the Cabinet Secretariat. (The others are Economic and Domestic, Overseas and Defence, and the Constitution Unit). It is a small, compact unit with a staff of twenty-four. Officials are secondees from other departments, and a third are Fast Stream administrators. The three senior posts positions are held by high-ranking civil servants: the Head of the European Secretariat is usually a Grade 2 official, the deputy Grade 3 and the third official Grade 5. The Head and Deputy come from the MAFF, DTI, or the Treasury, but not usually from the FCO, while the number three, responsible for overseeing the Common Foreign and Security Policy, is typically seconded from the Foreign Office. The high rank of its senior staff ensures that the Secretariat is able to obtain access to experts and gives it authority to intervene in other departments.

Besides the routine Cabinet Office duty of centralizing and circulating all relevant documents, the European Secretariat performs five main functions. Its principal task is to oversee and manage interdepartmental co-ordination. Although the lead division in the line ministry is responsible for deciding how to handle a particular issue, the European Secretariat makes sure that other departments with an interest are consulted and participate in determining the UK's approach. The progress of proposals is monitored by the European

Secretariat's five or six desk officers (counsellors), each of whom surveys a number of policy areas and keeps in close touch with the technical experts in the lead department, as well as with the UK Permanent Representation. It intervenes on a fail–safe basis, where difficulties arise or when it needs to ensure that departments have properly considered risks, opportunities, and possible tactics (Bender 1996). According to a former head (Bender 1996), intervention is typically prompted in three ways: 'confession', where the lead department admits the need for co-ordination with another ministry with a peripheral interest; 'tip-off', where a department with a peripheral interest complains that its views are not being taken sufficiently into account by the lead ministry; and 'copper's nose', where the European Secretariat suspects that appropriate consultation is not taking place.

When intervention is deemed necessary, the European Secretariat attempts in the first instance to resolve difficulties informally—over the telephone or in ad hoc meetings involving officials from the departments concerned. These meetings are minuted, but no papers are distributed. Should differences persist, recourse is taken to more formal procedures and a meeting of the sub-committee on European questions is convened (see Fig. 1.1 for list of members). This committee, which is a subcommittee of DOP, the Ministerial Committee for Defence and Overseas Policy, has a tripartite structure (Bulmer and Burch 1998): it meets at official level as EQ(O),[15] at senior official level as EQ(O*), and at ministerial level as (E)DOP (formerly OPD (E)). Most issues are resolved in EQ(O) and 'there is most often no need for collective ministerial consideration, since officials consult ministers before and after meetings' (Bender 1996). Where an issue is of sufficient importance, the lead department will inform the minister who will write to his or her colleagues (Bender 1996). Meetings of EQO and EQO* are organized, serviced, and chaired by the European Secretariat, while the Foreign Secretary presides over (E) DOP.

EQO is not only concerned with policy and negotiating tactics. A sister committee, EQO (L), co-ordinates legal advice across departments (Bulmer and Burch 1998). EQO (L) is chaired by the legal adviser to the Cabinet Office, a post created in 1982 when legal advice was centralized in the Cabinet Office following a merger of the Lord Chancellor's Office with FCO legal officers. This is the forum where the legal aspects of implementation are discussed and infraction cases brought against the UK are considered. Another sister committee, EQO (P), is where matters relating to personnel are discussed.

A second function of the European Secretariat is to ensure coherence and consistency with existing government policy, and to offer guidance on horizontal issues, such as subsidiarity and budgetary discipline (Bender 1996: 1). It may also intervene where it considers that the course of action favoured by

---

[15] EQ(O) is a subcommittee of the Overseas and Defence Committee.

Terms of Reference: 'To consider questions relating to the United Kingdom's membership of the European Union and to report as necessary to the Ministerial Committee on Defence and Overseas Policy (DOP)'

Secretary of State for Foreign and Commonwealth Affairs (chairman)
Deputy Prime Minister and Secretary of State for the Environment, Transport, and the Regions

Chancellor of the Exchequer
Secretary of State for the Home Department
Secretary of State for Education and Employment
President of the Board of Trade
Secretary of State for Transport
Leader of the House
Minister of Agriculture, Fisheries, and Food
Secretary of State for Scotland
Secretary of State for Defence
President of the Council
Secretary of State for Northern Ireland
Secretary of State for Wales
Secretary of State for International Development
Lord Privy Seal
Attorney General
Parliamentary Secretary—Treasury
Minister of State—Foreign and Commonwealth Office
Minister for Trade and Competitiveness in Europe
UK Permanent Representative to the EU
Minister without Portfolio
Other ministers as business dictates

Fig. 1.1. Membership of the Ministerial Subcommittee on European Questions, (E) DOP

Source: UK Government Home Page:http://www.open.gov.uk/co/cabcom/eu.1.htm

the lead department threatens to establish a technical or legal precedent that may be undesirable. The co-ordination of the UK position on major policy issues is a third task. The European Secretariat conducts cross-departmental exercises to develop policy on major horizontal issues, such as the Delors White Paper, Trans-European Networks, and Agenda 2000, which cut across the responsibilities of a number of ministries. It also conducts 'stocktaking' on particularly important issues. A fourth function is supervision of the system of parliamentary scrutiny. The European Secretariat ensures that departments meet their obligations under the procedure, informing the scrutiny committee of both Houses of Commission proposals, and preparing

and supplying explanatory memoranda to accompany them within the designated ten-day limit.[16] Finally, the European Secretariat acts as consultant and
adviser, offering information about EU institutions, procedures, legislation,
and protocol.

The head and deputy head of the European Secretariat are extremely
important figures in the UK system of EU policy co-ordination. With routine
business left largely in the hands of the desk officers, the senior officials serve
the Prime Minister and Number 10, keeping in close contact with the PM's
Private Secretaries, the Policy Union, and the PM himself. The head of the
European Secretariat attends cabinet meetings and briefs the Prime Minister
in person on EU matters, particularly those which are sensitive, as well as
offering advice on strategy and tactical options. He also participates directly
in high-level negotiations, including European Councils and IGCs. At Amsterdam, for example, the then head of the European Secretariat, Brian Bender,
was a Personal Representative of the Prime Minister. Moreover, as EU business has become less legislation-centric, both senior officials are increasingly
involved in cultivating and maintaining contact with their counterparts in
other EU member states. Particular efforts have been directed towards the
Prime Minister's Office in France and the Kanzleramt in Germany. A range of
bilateral initiatives with a number of member states have been launched since
1997 as part of a wider strategy to exchange views on particular subjects, to
learn from other member states, and to improve understanding among its EU
partners of the position taken by the UK on issues it regards as important.
The head and his deputy have played a leading role in these actions.

Despite its small size and without undertaking detailed supervision of
the process unlike its French equivalent, the SGCI (see Lequesne 1993;
Guyomarch 1993; Menon in this volume), the European Secretariat plays a
key role in the UK co-ordination system. Located at the centre of the Whitehall 'village', it makes use of wide range of informal and formal mechanisms
to effect co-ordination with a light touch. Its role is generally procedural in
that, while it ensures that co-ordination does take place, it 'bludgeons only
occasionally' (Bender 1996: 3–4), and leaves important work to other departments. As Wright notes (1996: 156), the European Secretariat 'has proved
highly competent in reacting quickly to emergencies in providing overarch-
ing framework for departments'. The recent review of the Cabinet Office conducted by Sir Robert Armstrong offered a similarly positive endorsement
(Bulmer 1998; see also Wallace 1996: 64).

The Foreign and Commonwealth Office

The FCO occupies a central position in the UK's EU policy-making system,
even if its relative importance has been in decline since accession. The Foreign

---

[16] Departments are also responsible for supplying similar information to UK MEPs.

Secretary is responsible for defining European policy as part of the UK's foreign policy, though his—all Foreign Secretaries have so far been men— ability to do depends on Number 10's interest in EU matters and the extent to which the PM's views on Europe coincide with his own. The Foreign Secretary accompanies the PM to meetings of the European Council and IGCs, attends the General Affairs Council, and takes the lead in diplomatic relations with the UK's European partners. The Foreign Secretary is assisted by a secretary of state for European affairs. As well as deputizing for the Foreign Secretary, the minister of state plays an important part in high-level EU negotiations, bears a special responsibility for diplomatic relations with other European states, both inside and outside the Union, and has a leading role in managing the presidency when the UK's turn comes around.

Both the Foreign Secretary and the minister of state have Whitehall-wide responsibilities for co-ordination. The former presides over (E) DOP, the ministerial- level (sub-)committee, to which EQ(O), the official-level committee, reports. The minister of state chairs two committees. The first is MINICOR, which brings together junior ministers from Whitehall departments and is intended to ensure co-ordination at a political level. The second, responsible for party-to-party questions, provides a forum for discussing New Labour's relations with other European parties of the centre-left.

At senior official level, the Economic and EU Director is an important figure both inside and outside the Foreign Office. One of five Deputy Under-Secretaries in the FCO, the Economic and EU Director is not involved in day-to-day business, but is charged with thinking strategically about the UK's European policy in medium- and long-term perspective. He takes a special interest in issues which are particularly sensitive for the UK, such as EMU, and becomes involved sporadically on the front line as is required. He was called upon, for example, during the 1998 UK presidency, to participate in negotiating the launch of a major initiative in transatlantic trade and regulation. The Economic and EU Director is also the line manager of the UK Permanent Representative in Brussels with whom he is in daily contact.

A more 'hands-on' role is played by the Director for Europe. As well as accompanying the Foreign Secretary when abroad on EU business, the Director manages the FCO divisions dealing with European policy. Responsibility is divided between three divisions—European Union Division Internal (EUDI), European Union Division External (EUDE), and European Union Bilateral relations (EUB)—while a fourth—European Union Division Presidency (EUDP)—is created when the UK holds the EU presidency. The divisions report to the Director for Europe who takes overall charge of EU policy. A specialist division in a different chain of command is responsible for the CFSP.

The functions performed by these units reflect the general responsibilities of the Foreign Secretary in European policy and the specific role in co-ordination entrusted to the FCO. EUDI has four main tasks. First, desk officers shadow the progress of technical dossiers through EU legislative processes, and contribute a Foreign Office perspective, based on the UK's wider international and diplomatic objectives. Second, officials in the division keep the Foreign Secretary abreast of developments in the EU. Third, the division takes the lead in Whitehall on broad issues, such as IGCs, Agenda 2000, and institutional reform. In close association with the European Secretariat, it organizes cross-department co-ordination on these matters. Fourth, EUDI is responsible for operating the communications infrastructure connecting London with Brussels and other European capitals. It processes the telegrams that carry correspondence to and from UK officials, and transmits the negotiating briefs and instructions for UK representatives attending EU meetings (Bender 1991: 18). Bilateral contacts are important for keeping the UK informed about the opinions of other member states and for seeking allies for negotiations in the Council. The Foreign Office relays advice to the rest of Whitehall about what positions it considers to be negotiable in the light of this intelligence.

EUDE, by contrast, is closer in terms of its functions to divisions in the line ministries. It takes the lead in defining UK policy in its area of responsibility, namely, the EU's external relations. Typically, this includes issues such as EU enlargement, development policy, relations with Turkey, and EUROMED. The work of the division is carried out in co-operation with the geographical departments of the FCO. Similarly, the CFSP Division, responsible to the Political Director, is the lead department in common foreign and security matters.

As the competencies of the Union have broadened, an increasing number of Whitehall departments have developed their own European expertise and have brought their technical specialisms to bear in the development of UK policy. Moreover, the spread of new technology has undermined the centrality of the communications infrastructure operated by the Foreign Office. Furthermore, the position of foreign ministries which was formerly underpinned by the special responsibility of the General Affairs Council (GAC) for the co-ordination of the various technical councils has been undermined by the decline in the status of that body. Nonetheless, the FCO remains a core actor in the making and co-ordinating of the UK's EU policy.

The UK Permanent Representation

The UK Permanent Representation (UKREP) has its origins in the four-person delegation to the European Coal and Steel Community (ECSC) in Luxembourg, established in 1955, which was expanded into the UK Delegation to the Communities three years later (Wallace and Wallace 1973; Bulmer and Burch 1998). UKREP conforms to the same organizational model as the other Permanent Representations (Hayes-Renshaw and Wallace 1997: 219). It is headed by a Permanent Representative of ambassadorial rank who is a career diplomat. The Permanent Representative is assisted by a Deputy, who, in the case of the UK, usually has a background in the DTI or the Treasury. Officials work in sections whose areas of responsibility mirror the separation between the various Councils.[17] As with other member states, officials are recruited from both the foreign ministry and home departments. This ensures that the Permanent Representation not only has the services of skilled negotiators, but also has the technical expertise necessary to conduct negotiations in Council working groups. In the case of the UK, the balance between diplomatic and technical officials, struck at the time of accession and reflected at the highest level, was intended to prevent UKREP from deteriorating into 'a set of baronies working to home departments' (interview).

UKREP performs a number of generic functions. It provides a base for national negotiators, defends the national position, interacts with the EU institutions, the Council presidency, and the representatives of other member states, maintains links with the media, and provides the main negotiators for meetings of the Council (Spence 1995: 362), though in sectors, such as transport, where work is highly technical, or in agriculture, where meetings are extremely frequent, officials fly out from London. However, UKREP differs from its counterparts in several important respects. Not only is it among the largest (Hayes-Renshaw and Wallace 1997), but its role in the national system and its relationship with the capital mark it out from other Permanent Representations. First, UKREP is highly proactive. It is expected to monitor closely the activities of the Directorates General of the European Commission and to alert the national capital of impending or possible legislative action. The intelligence gathered in Brussels and communicated back to London enables the UK to intervene in the policy process at an early stage. Officials in UKREP are well aware that early intervention in the initial technical phases of the policy process, ideally before the Commission has even prepared its own draft, and in the form of a written text in treaty language, is the most effective way of influencing the final outcome (Hull 1993; Schmidt 1996: 231–45; interviews 1998).

Second, UKREP keeps in constant touch with Whitehall. Desk officers are encouraged to report all useful information to the home departments, and to keep the European Secretariat and the Foreign Office informed of developments within the EU institutions and all meetings involving UK officials in Brussels. A standing instruction requires that meetings be reported to the FCO

---

[17] In 1998, these dealt with Agriculture and Fisheries, Social, Environmental and Regional Policy, Economic Affairs, Finance and Tax, Industry and the Internal Market, External Relations, Development and Trade Policy, Justice and Home Affairs, and Institutions. Desk officers within each section take responsibility for specific sectors and their work is supervised by counsellors, who head each section.

and copied to ministries within the relevant 'frame' within twenty-four hours (interviews). This system backs up domestic co-ordination by identifying where departments have strayed from agreed positions. It also provides an early warning system that sounds the alarm where UK officials have adopted positions in working groups that are likely to leave the UK delegation isolated, as well as a signalling the need for a rapid response where changes in Council discussion necessitate a further round of discussions at home.

Third, UKREP contributes directly to determining the UK's position on matters of EU business. Commission proposals, accompanied by a report on the operational consequences and advice on which positions are negotiable, are transmitted to London and the relevant embassies in EU member states. UKREP officials, moreover, attend meetings in Whitehall, where they provide information on the other member states and offer input on what positions are likely to be negotiable in Brussels. It is, furthermore, established practice for the Permanent Representative to return to London every Friday for a meeting at the Cabinet Office to discuss forthcoming sessions of the Council business. Also present are teams from the Foreign Office, the Treasury, and other ministries with an interest in the subjects under discussion. The meetings settle instructions on tactics and seek further work on issues which are judged to have been inadequately prepared (Bulmer and Burch 1998: 15). As a major element in fulfilling the 'objective of securing an early, agreed cross-departmental European policy position', the Friday morning meeting is a 'feature which sets the British governmental machinery apart from most of its partners in the EU' (Bulmer and Burch 1998: 15). The importance of these sessions is emphasized by a former Permanent Representative, Sir Michael Butler, who notes that the meeting also gave him an opportunity to speak to the Prime Minister and the Foreign Secretary (1986: 115). In comparison with other member states, Germany, for example, (see Derlien in this volume), the Permanent Representative and his officials are trusted and respected in Whitehall, and regarded as part of the team, even if their advice may not always be welcome.[18]

The Prime Minister

Though not involved directly in routine co-ordination, the Prime Minister's role in EU policy making is crucial in matters of 'high politics'. As the European Council has become increasingly institutionalized, and IGCs more frequent and the EU a salient domestic political issue, the PM is continually involved in EU business, particularly in regard to major initiatives, such as EMU, as well as matters of high political sensitivity, such as the budget,

---

[18] This play on words involves the phrases 'Ständiger Verrater' ('Permanent Traitor') and 'Ständiger Vertreter' ('Permanent Representative').

institutional reform, and elements of foreign policy. Even where these matters fall under the responsibility of the Foreign Secretary or the Chancellor, the PM can take charge. The example of the Madrid Summit in June 1989, where the position adopted by the Margaret Thatcher was not supported by her Foreign Secretary or her Chancellor, demonstrates the short-term ability of the PM to overrule her most senior colleagues (Howe 1994; Lawson 1992; Thatcher 1993). Indeed, in the latter half of the 1980s, Number 10 became a permanent presence in EU policy, substantially displacing the Cabinet Office (interviews).

Intervention by the PM in technical matters is usually rare, although the PM is briefed regularly on EU developments and the progress of controversial issues by the Head of the European Secretariat. Alternative sources of information and advice are also available to the PM. These included the Policy Unit, the PM's Private Office, and the PM's personal foreign policy adviser. PMs have their own (changeable) preferences about which provides the best advice. Occasionally, very important EU questions are discussed in OPD, the cabinet committee responsible for Defence and Overseas Policy, which is chaired by the Prime Minister (Bender 1996). Also, in some cases, where routine technical matters become politicized, the PM may become directly involved or take personal charge. This occurred with the BSE crisis, where strategic decisions were taken at Number 10. Much depends on the PM's personal style, but also on the wider political context. For example, John Major's slim majority in the House of Commons enabled a vociferous group of backbench MPs to strengthen the hand of Eurosceptic ministers in the cabinet and to compel the government to adopt a nationalist position on important issues. The PM subsequently became more closely involved in the detail of European policy than his predecessors had been.

Since the Labour Government came into office in 1997, the Prime Minister has taken an active lead in European policy. Considerable emphasis has been placed on improving and building relations with other member states in an attempt to build up goodwill after the ill-feeling generated by its predecessor. The Policy Unit has played a leading role in this endeavour, particularly in trying to strengthen relations with governments of the left in Germany, France, and Italy.

The role of Westminster

Parliament is involved in the co-ordination of EU policy, but as with national legislatures elsewhere in the European Union—with the exception of the Danish Folketing (Norton 1996; Pedersen in this volume)—its influence is limited. Since the UK's accession, many existing parliamentary procedures have been used in an attempt to exercise general control over government and ministers, and thereby officials, through the principle of ministerial responsibility: in EU matters oral and written parliamentary questions are tabled, EU matters raised in Prime Minister's Question Time, debates held, and select committees may examine EU-related matters pertaining to the responsibilities of their department (Bozdan 1991: 4).

In addition to these general methods for scrutinizing the executive, the two Houses have developed special procedures and mechanisms. In the House of Commons, the arrangements were based on the recommendations of the reports prepared by a specially appointed select committee, chaired by John Foster MP. In particular, a select committee, the 'scrutiny committee', was established by the House to examine Commission proposals and to inform the House whether issues of legal or political importance were raised. The government agreed that proposals should be accompanied by an explanatory memorandum, prepared by the relevant government department, within ten days of their receipt and that it would not give its assent to any proposal recommended for debate by the select committee until that debate had taken place. In addition, the government agreed 'to keep the committee informed above developments in the Community . . . to make oral statements to the House after all Council meetings, to hold six monthly debates on EEC matters generally and to set aside time for other debates during the course of the year' (Leicester 1997: 2).

Since the SEA, three sets of changes have been made to arrangements in the House of Commons to enable it to deal with the increased volume of business.[19] First, the terms of references and remit of the Scrutiny Committee were expanded, empowering it to examine any document published by Community institutions, not only legislative proposals.[20] Second, the unsatisfactory arrangements for debates on Commission proposals were altered (Bozdan 1991: 6), so that from the 1990–1 session, documents recommended for further consideration by the House have been referred to one of two European Standing Committees, unless the House otherwise decides. Each Committee consists of thirteen members, who are nominated for a full session. Third, whereas general debates in the House had been based on retrospective six-monthly white papers, *Developments in the European Community*, they were from 1990 to be more general and to be held before meetings of the European Council.

A select committee was also established by the House of Lords, but rather than limiting its role to that of alerting the rest of the House to matters which required full discussion, it was allowed to prepare reports on any area of Community business. Since the early 1970s, the committee has evolved,

---

[19] Many of the modifications follow the recommendations of the inquiry conducted by the Select Committee on Procedure in 1989.

[20] See Standing Order No. 127.

and work is now carried out in five subcommittees, each concentrating on specific areas.

Although both Houses are routinely involved in the policy-making process, procedures have been improved, and the House of Commons has periodically been the focus of national attention on EU issues, the influence of Parliament on the formation of the government's EU policy is limited. Partly, this reflects the high barriers to involvement arising from the level of technical knowledge needed to understand EU business. However, it also results from features of the scrutiny system itself. The committees in the House of Commons have became severely overloaded. The Scrutiny Committee has borne the brunt of the increase in the volume of paper produced by EU institutions. As Graham Leicester observed, '[i]t was originally envisaged that there might be some 300 scrutiny events a year, but in practice the number was closer to 700 in 1974–75, and stands today at around 1200' (1997: 3). The Committee typically considers fifty documents at its weekly meeting, and the two European Standing Committees are also overworked.

Moreover, in many important cases, information is provided to the Scrutiny Committee too late to be properly considered. This is attributed by the Committee to the 'unpredictability of Council agendas, the late production of proposals and other documents by the Commission, the preparedness of the Council to take items and short notice, and the slow transmission of documents' (cited in Leicester 1997: 3). Although the government has tried to ease the problem by providing unnumbered explanatory memoranda, which report the content of Commission proposals as they move through the EU's legislative process, the situation remains unsatisfactory.

Furthermore, the principle of scrutiny reserve at the heart of the system has not been closely followed. By its undertaking, in a Resolution of the House in October 1980, that it would not adopt a final position on any legislative proposal that was still subject to scrutiny or awaiting consideration by the House, the government committed itself to maintaining executive accountability in relation to the action of ministers in the Council. However, it has become increasingly difficult to meet this commitment, not only because the proposal constantly changes during Council negotiations, but also due to the European Parliament's greater involvement in the EU policy process. The complexity of EU processes notwithstanding, the principle of scrutiny reserve has been limited by the government's tendency to adopt a position without waiting for Parliament. It has been estimated that this applies to one fifth of business (Dowding 1995: 146).

Despite the extremely high reputation of the reports prepared by its Select Committee, arrangements in the House of Lords have not escaped criticism. In spite of their quality, it has been argued that the reports have little, if any, influence on government policy (Leicester 1997: 2–3). This is an important objection, given that only twenty documents per year are published and that their production consumes two-thirds of the resources available for all committee work in the House (Leicester 1997).

Many of the problems of the system of scrutiny reflect underlying weaknesses in the position of Parliament (Norton 1996). First, as Armstrong and Bulmer (1996) have noted, the UK Parliament is a 'talking parliament' rather than a 'working parliament'. Greater importance in Westminster is attached to plenary debate than to committee work, which distinguishes the UK from other advanced capitalist democracies. Second, the House of Commons is institutionally and, for the most part, politically dependent on the government. The government controls the agenda of the House of Commons and must approve organizational changes. Moreover, the mechanism of party discipline in a system where the powers of executive and legislature are fused and where single party government is the norm for the most part acts to reinforce the dependency of the UK Parliament.

The UK System of Co-ordination: An Assessment

Evaluating the effectiveness of the UK system of co-ordination requires investigating its efficacy in three areas: its domestic operation; its functioning at the European level; and its influence on EU policy outcomes. With respect to the first of these, the UK has generally been effective: a national position is developed where and when necessary, interested parties in Whitehall are consulted, consistency with domestic policy is achieved, and EU rules and regulations are implemented effectively. The smooth running of the system is due principally to its 'fit' with the wider polity, which its objectives and *modus operandi* embody, reflect, and project. Specifically, these include the unitary structure of the state, its fundamental constitutional principles (collective responsibility, ministerial responsibility), the unified executive, and its entrenched political traditions (centralization, single party government), administrative practices (neutrality, non-political appointments, information sharing), and administrative culture (mutual trust, corporate identity). The impact of devolution on the functioning of a system predicated on the existence of a unitary state could be very significant.

The emergence of a European cadre in the higher reaches of the civil service is also an important factor (Bulmer and Burch 1998: 6). A large number of officials in senior positions have had a long involvement with EU issues and have typically served in Brussels, either in the UK Permanent Representation or more rarely in the European institutions. In addition, many ministries such as MAFF and the DTI encourage 'recycling' though European jobs. These ministries are particularly adept at posting officials in the UK Permanent Representation or as detached national experts in the European Commission. This penetration by departmental networks of strategic outposts in Brussels permits ministries to ensure that their interests are effectively represented and that they are kept informed about developments on the 'front line'. However, the importance ascubed to evoling European expertise, to assisting officials in building a career anchor around the EU, and to creating networks in Brussels is department specific. With respect to the latter, the devolution of responsibility and budgeting for personnel and training to departments has in practice not been conducive to the even development of European expertise across Whitehall. Some ministries run in-house training programmes, send officials to the Civil Service College, or encourage younger officials to pursue a European career path, but there are no central arrangements, and in many departments individuals are left very much to themselves in making their career choices.

Despite its efficiency, the UK's centralized co-ordination strategy is not without its weaknesses. As Wright has argued (1996: 161), centralized systems are likely to be dysfunctional where the centre is 'divided', 'paralysed', or 'inept'. Under the second Major administration, the centre betrayed indications of all three. The government acted at times like an unstable coalition, split between Euro-enthusiast and Eurosceptic ministers (Wallace 1996, 1997; Forster 1998; interviews with former ministers). Its room for manœuvre was limited by a combination of its narrow majority and the actions of a vociferous minority on its back benches, which led to the adoption of highly questionable tactics on issues, such as voting rights in the Council in 1994. The strong salience of 'Europe' in the domestic politics, moreover, created a tendency for EU-related matters to become politicized, in which case, as Menon and Wright (1999) have observed, issues were removed from the consensual, routine, and sheltered arena of Whitehall to the central political arena, so that co-ordination by experienced, technical experts was replaced by crisis management from the political centre.[21] This was the case, for example, with the BSE crisis, which, as it became more problematic for the Major government, was managed directly from Number 10.

In its operation at the European level—the second important area for consideration—the UK system is also generally effective. In terms of the four dimensions identified by Vincent Wright (1996: 162–3), the UK scores highly. The global ambition of its co-ordination strategy, which lead it to be especially sensitive to policy developments that may extend the competencies of the Union or increase expenditure, requires that UKREP officials in particular keep a careful watch over the Directorates General of the Commission and are alert to the possibility of new initiatives. They also maintain relations with the *cabinets* of the UK Commissioners, and increasingly with MEPs. Although

---

[21] The same point was put rather more graphically by an interviewee: 'What's the point in having Rolls Royce machinery if the car is being driven by a lunatic?'

it has been argued that the UK is disadvantaged by its under-representation in the middle ranges of the European Commission—a trend which has continued despite efforts by the European Secretariat, the introduction of the European Fast Stream and the pressure exerted by the UK for reform of the *concours*—there is little evidence to suggest that the quality of its intelligence gathering has been negatively affected. Indeed, the UK's ability to anticipate new EU legislation is much respected (Schmidt 1996). With respect to its capacity to shape the EU policy agenda, the UK is considered to be a particularly 'good downstream lobbyist for economic matters' (Wright 1996: 162; Hull 1993). Its effectiveness lies in its appreciation of the need to intervene at the earliest possible moment and at a technical level. This contrasts with France, for example, which tends to act late and to target the political, rather than the technical, level of decision making (Schmidt 1996: 231–45). Early action is critical in the EU since it is estimated that about 80 per cent of the text finally agreed upon will have remained unchanged from the original draft. In both anticipating legislation and lobbying, the UK is strengthened by its relatively open relationship with private interests (Mazey and Richardson 1993; Menon and Wright 1999). Unlike in other countries, where the private sector is kept at arms length by the state, the UK encourages the exchange of information between and the co-ordination of lobbying by government officials and interest group representatives. Its domestic policy style offers an advantage in operating in the pluralist policy environment that Brussels has become. Finally, in both the translation of European legislation into national law and its implementation at street level, the UK's machinery works very efficiently. Irrespective of the view that the UK takes on the substance of a directive, transposition and implementation proceed smoothly, reflecting deeply entrenched values.

Again, however, the picture is not wholly positive. First, the EU decision-making arena presents unfamiliar challenges to UK officials. UK civil servants are schooled in a tradition of neutrality, and are used to single party government and an adversarial party system. They do not necessarily adapt easily to the EU's policy environment which is characterized by accommodation and consensus building. Also, UK officials tend to be pragmatic, and less adept than officials from other member states at 'presenting points of national interest in *communautaire* vocabulary' (Buller and Smith 1998). Moreover, their counterparts in working groups may well not be career civil servants with technical expertise, but political appointees, closely allied to political parties back home and with greater negotiating flexibility based on that additional element of authority (Christoph 1993). Second, the lack of language skills among UK civil servants is disadvantageous. The shortage of foreign language speakers can affect coalition-building possibilities and may help to explain why the UK typically tends to form alliances with northern member states rather than those from the south (Bulmer 1998). Lack of skills in this area may limit the capacity of the UK to influence the policy process in important policy areas.

The third difficulty relates to the centralized strategy adopted by the UK. The UK places a premium on defining a single position agreed by all interested parties. However, this may not be best suited to the EU setting, which involves a multiplicity of actors, negotiating continuously over a wide range of issues at different levels, where decision making is fluid, and which is characterized by a policy style that is 'bargained and consensual' (Kassim and Wright 1991). As insiders have acknowledged (Bender 1991; interviews), the UK may be disadvantaged by its lack of flexibility where a position meticulously crafted in Whitehall must be unpicked to keep in the game when negotiations are fast moving. More generally, as Derlien argues forcefully in this volume, the UK system which requires *ex ante* co-ordination of all policy matters regardless of salience is likely to prove counter-productive, since it leaves little room for recurrent multi-issue bargaining and the informal norm of reciprocity at the European level. A reputation for awkwardness or intransigence may be the result, leading other member states to find ways of circumventing the UK and to exclude it from further integrationist projects.

The UK's success in shaping policy outcomes at the European level is a third area that must figure in any assessment of its effectiveness. Returning to the second of the two paradoxes outlined at the beginning of the chapter, it has been argued that there is a 'contradiction' between the UK's (well-deserved) reputation for administrative efficiency at the domestic and the EU level and its (allegedly) poor record in influencing Union policies. However, this conflict is more apparent than real for two main reasons. First, the assumption that underlies the contrast, specifically that efficient co-ordination by a member state should guarantee its policy effectiveness at the EU level, is mistaken. Policy outcomes in Brussels result from the complex interaction of a multiplicity of factors, of which the ability of a member state to make clear and prosecute its own interests is but one. Success depends to a very large extent, for example, on the substance of national preferences with respect to any particular issue and how close they are to those of the other member states and of the Commission, on the prevailing policy climate, on the input of the European Parliament, and on the mobilization of interest groups. Second, as Menon and Wright (1999) have argued, '[m]any of the studies that criticise Britain for its European policies confuse popularity in Europe, the ability proactively to shape the agenda of "integration" and institutional outcomes, with success in shaping substantive policy outcomes. If attention is paid to the latter, a very different picture emerges.' Empirical investigations of the impact of EU action on the member states (see, for example, Kassim and Menon 1996; Forder and Menon 1997) have found that the UK has been particularly successful in securing favourable policy outcomes in the area of economic policy.

Its influence was especially notable in the development and implementation of the single market programme, where it advanced a pro-competition agenda. Drawing from its own experience of privatization and liberalization, and wishing to promote the interests of UK businesses and firms used to competitive pressure, it contributed significantly to the market-building process. It played a leading role in shaping many of the sectoral regimes of which the single market is composed. It is somewhat ironic, for example, that one of Margaret Thatcher's most outspoken Eurosceptics had the idea, whilst transport minister, to use the Community as an instrument of national policy to multilateralize air transport liberalization (Kassim 1996). More broadly, Francis McGowan has commented on the UK's successful export of its regulatory model to Brussels.

The UK's influence in EU economic policy can partly be ascribed to the UK's effective co-ordination and lobbying efforts. However, the coincidence of its neo-liberal ideology with the convergence of preferences of other member states, notably France and Germany, as well as with the Commission, was clearly also very important. UK policy was congruent with what Wright (1996: 163) has called the 'constitutional principles' that underlay the single market programme. With respect to other policy types, such as constitutional and institutional reform, and in other areas, notably, social policy, the UK has been markedly less successful in shaping policy outcomes in line with its preferences. According to this third criterion, the UK's record has been mixed, but it is not without its successes and is certainly not blank as is sometimes alleged. The relationship between the UK's administrative efficiency and its effectiveness in securing favourable policy outcomes is less clear-cut than that construed by the second paradox described above.

Conclusion

This brief account of the UK system of EU policy co-ordination endeavours to resolve two paradoxes that arise in relation to the UK case. In so doing, it inevitably has implications for a wider debate about the impact of European integration on the member states and the factors that determine national arrangements for managing EU business. One view holds that membership of the Union has inevitably led, not only to similar policy outputs at the European level, but also to structural convergence between the administrative systems of the member states (Rometsch and Wessels 1996). From this perspective, it follows from the fact that the EU-15 are exposed to similar demands and that the member states interact within a common political system that a process of convergence is underway (Wessels and Rometsch 1996; Wessels 1997). This is hypothesized as the outcome of one or more of four forces: socialization, where officials working together in EU institutions, are inculcated with common values, which they then propagate within national administrations (Kerremans 1996; Harmsen 1999; Wessels and Rometsch 1996; Wessels 1997); optimization, according to which, subject to similar co-ordination needs, member states converge around the most efficient administrative model (Harmsen 1999; Conclusion, this volume); mimicry, where member states 'learn' lessons from each other in how best to confront the challenges produced by EU membership (Peters, this volume); and/or imposition, by which means the Union compels national governments to adopt similar procedures and mechanisms.

The opposing approach contends that there is no evidence of convergence; rather a pattern of national differentiation prevails (Metcalfe 1994; Harmsen 1999; see Conclusion, this volume). The demands for co-ordination generated by the EU are genuine and powerful, but they are mediated by pre-existing structures and values in each of the member states. These provide the reference points for institutions as they respond to external challenges (March and Olsen 1984, 1989; Olsen 1997). In terms of national EU policy, it is expected that domestic arrangements are likely to be reproduced.

It is typically thought that the two perspectives are mutually exclusive (see Harmsen 1999, for example). However, the UK case, like others considered in this volume, demonstrates the effects of both imperatives.[22] On the one hand, the UK political system has undoubtedly been affected by the demands made by Union membership. The strengthening of the office of Prime Minister domestically can, for example, at least partly be attributed to functions that heads of government are required to perform by the EU in the European Council and at IGCs, as well as the profile that they command in Union business (Moravscik 1994).[23] On the other, the impact of domestic structures and values on the system of EU policy co-ordination is clearly apparent. UK arrangements bear the imprint of a cultural scepticism about European integration, as well as an administrative and political opportunity structure that supports centralization and unity of purpose.

References

Armstrong, K., and Bulmer, S. (1996), 'United Kingdom', in D. Rometsch and W. Wessels (eds.), *The European Union and Member States* (Manchester: Manchester University Press).

[22] See the Conclusion to this volume for a fuller account than space permits here.
[23] As Menon and Wright (1999: 46–66) observe, UK rhetoric in support of greater democracy at the European level coexists with executive ascendancy over parliament in EU matters at the national level.

Bender, B. (1991), 'Whitehall, Central Government and 1992', *Public Policy and Administration*, 6/1: 13–20.

—— (1996), 'Co-ordination of European Union Policy in Whitehall', text of a lecture given by Brian Bender, Head of the European Secretariat, at St Antony's College, Oxford, on 5 Feb. 1996.

Bozdan, P. (1991), *The House of Commons and European Communities Legislation*, Factsheet No. 56, House of Commons Public Information Office.

Buller, J., and Smith, M. J. (1998), 'Civil Service Attitudes towards the European Union', in D. Baker and D. Seawright (eds.), *Britain for and against Europe* (Oxford: Clarendon Press).

Bulmer, S. (1998), 'End of Award Report', unpublished manuscript.

—— and Burch, M. (1998), 'Organizing for Europe: Whitehall, the British State and European Union', *Public Administration*, 76: 601–28.

Burch, M., and Holliday, I. (1996), *The British Cabinet System* (London: Prentice Hall/Harvester Wheatsheaf).

Butler, M. (1986), *Europe: More than a Continent* (London: Heinemann).

Campbell, C., and Wilson, G. K. (1995), *The End of Whitehall. Death of a Paradigm?* (Oxford: Blackwell).

Christoph, J. B. (1993), 'The Effect of Britons in Brussels: The European Community and the Culture of Whitehall', *Governance*, 6/4: 518–37.

Denman, R. (1996), *Missed Chances* (London: Indigo).

Dowding, K. (1995), *The Civil Service* (London: Routledge).

Dunleavy, P., and Rhodes, R. A. W. (1990), 'Core Executive Studies in Britain', *Public Administration*, 68: 3–28.

Edwards, G. (1992), 'Central Government', in S. George (ed.), *Britain and the European Community: The Politics of Semi-Detachment* (Oxford: Clarendon Press).

Forder, J., and Menon, A. (1997), *The European Union and National Macroeconomic Policy* (London: Routledge).

Forster, A. (1998), 'Britain and the Negotiation of the Maastricht Treaty: A Critique of Liberal Intergovernmentalism', *Journal of Common Market Studies*, 36/3 (Sept.).

George, S. (ed.) (1992), *Britain and the European Community: The Politics of Semi-Detachment* (Oxford: Clarendon Press).

—— (1994), *An Awkward Partner: Britain in the European Community* (Oxford: Oxford University Press).

Guyomarch, A. (1993), 'The European Effect: Improving French Policy Co-ordination', *Staatswissenschaften und Staatspraxis*, 4/3: 455–78.

Harmsen, R. (1999), 'The Europeanization of National Administrations: A Comparative Study of France and the Netherlands', *Governance*, 12/2. 81–113.

Hayes-Renshaw, F., and Wallace, H. (1997), *The Council of Ministers* (London: Macmillan).

Hennessy, P. (1986), *Cabinet* (Oxford: Blackwell).

Howe, G. (1994), *Conflict of Loyalty* (Basingstoke: Pan).

Hull, R. (1993), 'Lobbying Brussels: A View from within', in S. Mazey and J. J. Richardson (eds.), *Lobbying in the European Community* (Oxford: Oxford University Press), 82–92.

James, S. (1992), *British Cabinet Government.* (London: Routledge).

Kassim, H. (1996), 'Air Transport', in H. Kassim and A. Menon (eds.), *The European Union and National Industrial Policy* (London: Routledge).

Kassim, H. and Menon, A. (eds.) (1996), *The European Union and National Industrial Policy* (London: Routledge).

——and Wright, V. (1991), 'The Role of National Administrations in the Decision-Making Processes of the European Communities', *Revista trimestrale di diritto pubblico*, 3: 832–50.

Kerremans, B. (1996), 'Do Institutions Make a Difference? Non-institutionalism, Neo-institutionalism and the Logic of Common Decision Making in the European Union', *Governance*, 9/2: 216–40.

Lawson, N. (1992), *The View from No. 11: Memoirs of a Tory Radical* (London: Bantam Press).

Lee, M. (1990), 'The Ethos of the Cabinet Office: A Comment on the Testimony of Officials', *Public Administration*, 68: 235–42.

Leicester, G. (1997), *Westminster and Europe: Proposals for Change,* King-Hall Paper No. 4, European Policy Forum (London: Hansard Society).

Lequesne, C. (1993), *Paris–Bruxelles: comment se-fait la politique européenne de la France* (Paris: Presses de la Fondation Nationale des Sciences Politiques).

Lord, C. (1992), 'Sovereign or Confused? The "Great Debate" about British Entry to the European Community Twenty Years on', *Journal of Common Market Studies*, 30: 4.

March, J. G., and Olsen, J. P. (1984), 'The New Institutionalism: Organizational factors in Political Life', *American Political Science Review*, 77: 281–97.

——(1989), *Rediscovering Institutions: The Organizational Basis of Politics* (New York: Free Press).

Mazey, S., and Richardson, J. J. (1993), *Lobbying in the European Community* (Oxford: Oxford University Press).

Menon, A., and Wright, V. (1999), 'The Paradoxes of "Failure": British EU Policy Making in Comparative Perspective', *Public Policy and Administration*, 13/4: 46–66.

Metcalfe, L. (1994), 'International Policy Co-ordination and Public Management Reform', *International Review of Administrative Sciences*, 60: 271–90.

Moravscik, A. (1994), 'Why the European Community Strengthens the State: Domestic Politics and International Co-operation', Centre for European Studies Working Paper Series, Centre for European Studies, Harvard University.

Norton, P. (1996), 'The United Kingdom: Political Conflict, Parliamentary Scrutiny', in P. Norton (ed.), *National Parliaments and the European Union* (London: Frank Cass).

Olsen, J. P. (1997), 'European Challenges to the Nation State', in B. Steunenberg and V. van Vught (eds.), *Political Institutions and Pubic Policy: Perspectives on European Decision Making* (Dordrecht: Kluwer Academic Publishers).

Rometsch, D., and Wessels, W. (eds.) (1996), *The European Union and Member States* (Manchester: Manchester University Press).

Schmidt, V. A. (1996), *From State to Market? The Transformation of French Business and Government* (Cambridge: Cambridge University Press).

Seldon, A. (1990), 'The Cabinet Office and Co-ordination, 1979–87', *Public Administration*, 68: 103–21.

Spence, D. (1995), 'The Co-ordination of European Policy by Member States', in M. Westlake, *The Council of the European Union* (London: Cartermill).

Thatcher, M. (1993), *The Downing Street Years* (London: Harper Collins).

Wallace, H. (1996), 'Relations between the European Union and the British Administration', in Y. Mény, P. Muller, and J.-L. Quermonne (eds.), *Adjusting to Europe* (London: Routledge).

—— (1997). 'At Odds with Europe', *Political Studies*, 45: 677–88.

—— and Wallace, W. (1973), 'The Impact of Community Membership on the British Machinery of Government', *Journal of Common Market Studies*, 11/3: 243–62.

Wallace, W. (1973), *National Governments and the European Communities*, European Series No. 21 (London: Chatham House).

Wessels, W. (1997), 'An Ever Closer Fusion? A Macropolitical View on Integration Processes', *Journal of Common Market Studies*, 35/2: 267–99.

—— and Rometsch, D. (1996), 'Conclusion: European Union on National Institution', in D. Rometsch and W. Wessels (eds.), *The European Union and the Member States: Towards Institutional Fusion?* (Manchester: Manchester University Press).

Willetts, D. (1987), 'The Role of the Prime Minister's Policy Unit', *Public Administration*, 65: 443–54.

Wright, V. (1996), 'The National Co-ordination of European Policy-Making: Negotiating the Quagmire', in J. J. Richardson (ed.), *European Union: Power and Policy-Making* (London: Routledge).

Young, H. (1998), *This Blessed Plot: Britain and Europe from Churchill to Blair* (London: Macmillan).

2

Germany

Hans-Ulrich Derlien

Failing Successfully?

Policy co-ordination is not a problem that is exclusive either to Germany or to EU policy making. The co-ordination imperative is synonymous with organizational specialization and differentiation (Simon 1947). To the extent that the problem is addressed at all in the EU literature, assessments of the German situation reflect the state of affairs of the 1980s brought about by the qualitative leaps of the Single European Act (1986) and the Treaties of Maastricht (1992) and Amsterdam (1997). At the core of most assessments is the observation that Bonn never developed a centralizing structural solution for co-ordinating EU matters: neither a ministry of European affairs nor a general secretariat as in France nor a strong cabinet committee as in the UK. The only deviation from most domestic policy co-ordination is a civil servant-operated interdepartmental committee system. Second, and somewhat embarrassingly, intensive bilateral contacts between ministries and experts in Brussels are paramount (Regelsberger and Wessels 1984; Bulmer 1986; Wessels and Rometsch 1996) and appear as treacherous relationships bypassing the co-ordination committees (or even cabinet as the ultimate co-ordinator). According to this account, high politics did not play a role in Germany; chancellors after Adenauer were occupied with domestic affairs or transatlantic relations, with *Ostpolitik* or with the oil shock of 1973, and even Chancellor Kohl then appeared to pay only lip service to the idea of European integration; policy coherence and continuity were allegedly missing. The sectoralization or even fragmentation of policy making at a bureaucratic level struck observers all the more so since German governments were caught by the self-imposed image of *Musterknabe* or Primus, that is, obliged to advance European integration (Bulmer and Paterson 1987: 41 ff.). Of course, this view was not shared by German participants in EU policy making (as far as they cared about their image in textbooks at all).

Somehow, contrary to these assessments is the impressive development of the European Union since the 1980s: its further widening and deepening; and the introduction of a common European currency by 1999 could hardly have been expected. The predicted 'joint decision trap' (Scharpf 1988) had obviously not worked out: rather, the German government was supporting even further sacrifices of national sovereignty. Perhaps, the predominantly national perspective in analysing EU policy co-ordination, heavily influenced by intergovernmentalist EU philosophy, is anachronistic and EU policy making should more adequately be perceived from a system theoretical (truly European) perspective. Wessels (1997) argues that the very lack of co-ordination in Bonn was a prerequisite for advancing the European cause; the ensuing issue-specific incrementalism contributed to building a broad consensus in federal Germany. Thus, what in the 1980s from a French or British perspective appeared to be a deficiency might have turned out a precondition of success.

All the developments of the EU since 1986 were brought about and consolidated without major structural adaptations of the machinery of government in Bonn, in the same way that it did not change in response to German unification. Deepening of the EU and unification were, however, consequential for intergovernmental relations in Germany: the position of the *Länder* in EU policy making was once again strengthened when the federal constitution was revised in 1993.[1]

The apparent paradox of insufficient co-ordination but nevertheless successful moves towards further European integration raises the classical question: does organization matter? My answer is: Yes, it does, but not in all kinds of EU policy. Vincent Wright (1996), in reviewing co-ordination mechanisms in EU capitals, drew attention to the quality of the policies at stake. It is my contention that, in order to arrive at a more balanced picture of the efficiency of German EU policy co-ordination, one has to distinguish more carefully various aspects of the term 'Europa-Politik' than experts on the EU usually do. Leaving aside the implied sociology of knowledge questions about the normative and conceptual cognitive frames of contemporary commentators, this chapter will draw on the polity–policy–politics distinction and other policy classifications customary in the field of policy analysis in pursuit of four objectives.

First, the already well documented *structural arrangements* in Bonn, the *Länder*, and in Brussels for co-ordinating various policy types in the multi-level decision-making system will be analysed. The German co-ordination machinery is basically a two-track system: a diplomatic track is built around the Foreign Office and leads to the Council of Ministers (and the European

---

[1] Article 23 (new) enshrined *Land* participation rights; see below and Goetz (1995) for a brief account.

council); and a sectorized expert track, contingent on long-established German bureaucratic co-ordination practice, runs down to the *Länder* and up to the Commission in Brussels. This differentiation is, in principle, functional in reducing the complexity of the labyrinth for the various actors; the Platonic separation of the diplomatic process from policy substance, however, hardly as problematic as the external complexity of the maze (Wright 1996: 151), became internalized in the government departments by establishing liaison units, thus increasing departmental requisites by giving inputs into both of the two tracks.

Secondly, *substantive policy* interdependencies reflected and articulated within the departmental division of labour (as well as on the other two layers of the European decision-making system) will be explored as to their issue salience and their bearing on the politics dimension of *Europa-Politik*. Constitutional, i.e. *polity, matters* are separated from policy issues (regulative, distributive) of a more or less technical nature. Polity (including financial) issues are processed on the diplomatic, regulative issues on the specialist track.

Thirdly, the place of *politics* (and *politicians*) in the apparently dip-lomat- and bureaucrat-dominated, expert-driven German subsystem of the European political system will be considered more systematically. Polity issues, important personnel decisions, and conflictual policies do not escape the attention of the Chancellor's Office and the Chancellor himself; the manage-ment of sugar production in the EU, however, does not bother him. My con-tention is that the German pattern of *ex post* co-ordination, a policy style resembling management by exception, is ultimately superior to a practice of *ex ante* co-ordination of all policy matters regardless of their salience. Such a strategy is counter-productive, for it leaves little room for the recurrent, multi-issue bargaining process at the European level and the informal norm of reciprocity.

Finally, even if the French and the British co-ordination systems are less thorough than their image suggests, the emphasis on *ex ante* central co-ordination can be explained by the more defensive nature of the two governments towards European integration in the past and, in the case of Britain, by features of the Westminster system that allow more hierarchical interministerial relations than does a coalition government, and that in a federal system.

The Architecture of Complexity

The formal structure of the German co-ordination system for EU policy making has been adequately described by other students (Wallace 1973;

Regelsberger and Wessels 1984; Bulmer 1986; Wessels and Rometsch 1996; Streinz and Pechstein 1995). Hardly changed over the forty years of European policy, the co-ordination machinery in Berlin is characterized by a high degree of decentralization with a hierarchically arranged committee structure. After a brief survey of the basic characteristics (1), the inherent two-track system and its rationale will be defined (2) and it will be indicated how a falling apart of both tracks is prevented (3).

The formal structure

Traditionally, co-ordination is achieved by cabinet and the Chancellor's Office which serves both the Chancellor and cabinet. There are EU units in the foreign policy division and in the economics and finance division of the office; it is, not though, an active policy centre, except in preparing European or G7 summits (Regelsberger and Wessels 1984: 481; König 1993). As a formal decision-making body, cabinet as a whole enters the legislative process only after EU directives have been issued and must be submitted to Parliament for national legislation; as a consultative body, cabinet is regularly informed about important EU matters.

Secondly, bilateral horizontal co-ordination between departments is insti-tutionalized in the government manual, and is mandatory in all affairs. The ministry with the broadest jurisdiction or the most concerned serves as a *lead ministry* in charge of co-ordination; it is obliged to consult with all other min-istries possibly affected by a policy issue. In cases of conflict, cabinet ultimately decides.

Semi-centralization of EU affairs

From the early 1950s when the European Community on Steel and Coal was negotiated, there was a rivalry between the Foreign Office (Auswärtiges Amt; henceforth: FO) and the Ministry of Economics, which was also responsible for foreign trade. Apart from natural departmental rivalries the conflict mir-rored diverging philosophies: Economics was in favour of a free trade zone and advocated the functional approach to European integration; the FO emphasized the institutional approach. The semi-centralized compromise solution between the two departments (summarized by Hesse and Goetz 1992) was to predetermine the way EU matters are co-ordinated between the by now far greater number of departments concerned by EU affairs. Theoretically, there would have been *three structural solutions*: a Ministry for European Affairs or some other special institution (the options applied in France, Italy, and Greece). Second, centralization onto the Foreign Office; or, third, centralization around another of the traditional departments. All three of these pure models were discussed in Bonn. The FO concentration of Euro-

TABLE 2.1. *EU capacities of German federal ministries, 1998*

Department	Sections/ task forces	In divisions	Special liaison	Perm. Rep. staff
Chancellory	2	2		
Foreign Office	11	2	div. E	15
Economics	16	4	div. E	12
Finance	12	4	div. IX	9
Agriculture	5	3	subdiv. 32	5
Development	1	1	subdiv. 40	1
Interior	5	5	subdiv. VII	1
Transport	1	1		1
Justice	5	1		1
Labour	5	1	subdiv. VIIA	2
Science and Technology	6	4	subdiv. 12	3
Family etc.	2	2		3
Health	4	1	subdiv. Z2	
Urban Affairs	1	1		
Environment	2	1	subdiv. GII	1
Defence	2	1	EU military interest group repr.	
Total 16	80	34		54

Source: Organization charts.

pean affairs was not acceptable for Economics because, after all, in 1957 there was only an economic community (Koerfer 1988). Further, EU policy should not be regarded as something special but be treated as part of domestic policy. On the other hand, the FO objected to centralizing affairs around Economics, as the treaties are international law and the further development of the Community required intergovernmental negotiations; diplomatic channels would have to be employed also for running the EU embassy in Brussels. After months of negotiations between the two departments, a compromise was reached in 1958, which basically is still in existence: the FO is responsible for EU treaties and institutional questions of the EU, e.g. enlargement, association of other states, and political aspects in general (before 1990, also relations *vis-à-vis* the GDR). Economics became responsible for economic and domestic policy matters affected by the EU, however, with the right to give direct instructions to the EU 'embassy' and the German Permanent Representative (PR). Consequently, both ministries built up divisions for European affairs, and the fifty-four staff of German Permanent Representation (1998) are composed of diplomats and of officials from Economics as well as other ministries involved in frequent interaction with Brussels (Table 2.1).

The transfer of the EU division of Economics to the Finance Ministry under Chancellor Schröder in October 1998 will not affect the technical procedure of intragovernmental policy co-ordination. It might, though, indicate EU policy subordination to fiscal priorities.

Departmentalization

Beside this semi-centralized, dual arrangement, bilateral contacts between departments and Brussels emerged where policy areas were congruent with subcommittees of the Council or directorates general of the Commission, such as in agriculture for example. Today, departmentalized contacts at the official level between specialists in Bonn and Brussels are the rule, eroding somewhat the competences of the FO and Economics. This 'vertical brotherhood of experts' which has developed between Brussels and Bonn is similar to that which has evolved in domestic policy making between federal and *Länder* governments. This departmentalization may have grown during the last thirty years as joint policy making between experts in Bonn and Brussels, departments and general directorates has intensified. Legislation in Bonn often goes hand in glove with EU initiatives, or Bonn initiatives are communicated to the Brussels technocrats.[2] The short travelling distance between Bonn and Brussels (2.5 hours by car) encouraged informal procedures. Last but not least, the constitutionally strong position (Article 65 Basic Law) of ministers *vis-à-vis* chancellor and cabinet legitimizes a certain degree of departmental autonomy in running normal business—and that is what a large part of EU policy has increasingly become.

Horizontal self-co-ordination within and between departments is a core element of German administrative culture. Only completely new policy problems need consideration of departmental interdependencies and adaptation of the co-operation patterns, that is genuine co-ordination decisions. In most policy areas there is, though, a stock of programmes requiring only marginal adjustment, admittedly increasingly stimulated by EU activities. Therefore, the imperative for the lead section is: round up the usual suspects! Material policy interdependencies are mostly recognized, and interdepartmental conflicts are frequently minimized by bargaining, resulting in solutions at the lowest common denominator and in what Scharpf (1972) has termed 'negative co-ordination'. However, this does not mean that the ministerial sections, the smallest organizational units in possession of policy expertise, operate on 'auto-pilot' (Rose 1985). When Bulmer and Paterson observed that policy was formulated at a 'technical level' with limited involvement of ministers, they were only partly right, for they misjudged the internal departmental reporting system that keeps a minister informed on all matters of political

---

[2] During implementation of EU directives the pattern is more top-down (Siedentopf and Hauschild 1988: 77).

importance (Bulmer and Paterson 1987: 43). Policy proposals are elaborated in an iterative process between experts in the sections and the hierarchy; drafts are submitted to superiors, discussed, revised, submitted again, and moved onto the next echelon where the procedure may start again. Neither bottom-up nor top-down models of decision making depict the process adequately, rather a *dialogue model* (Mayntz and Scharpf 1975) applies. This iterative process is matched by the *political role understanding* of German higher civil servants (Mayntz and Derlien 1989; Putnam 1973), who anticipate the ministers' priorities and information needs. Therefore, limited time and attention of ministers does not imply that political aspects are neglected or that the bureaucrats are out of control. As in educating children, it is intensity, not frequency of interaction that matters.

Co-ordination by committees

In addition to semi-central co-ordination and horizontal self-co-ordination a three-level committee system developed.

A *Committee for Briefing the Embassy*, with up to thirty civil servants of the various departments including the FO and Economics, meets every Tuesday in order to prepare the Permanent Representation. Its secretariat was located in the EU division of Economics for forty years, but it has recently been moved to Finance. The committee acts as a postman, passing documents up and down and co-ordinating German representation in the numerous Brussels committees, in particular in COREPER, which assembles the suggestions produced in the 200 or so committees and working groups of the Council (Pag 1987). Ninety per cent of the business is settled at the civil service level in these weekly meetings of section heads or in monthly division head meetings.

A *Committee of State Secretaries* (StS) deals with unresolved problems passed on from below; in general the more political as opposed to technical aspects have been filtered out at the lower levels and dealt with at the StS level since 1963. Besides the 'four musketeers' from the FO, Economics, Agriculture, and Finance, and since 1969 the StS of the Chancellor's Office, the Permanent Representative takes part, too. The chairmanship is with the FO, whilst the technical bureau of the committee again resides in the European division of Economics, now Finance. Meetings take place at three- to five-week intervals, enabling a broad overview of all of the activities going on at the three tiers of the German EU policy-making system.

The *Cabinet Committee for European Affairs* is of no practical significance—much like the other six cabinet committees. It has met only twice since its creation in 1973 (Wessels 1997). The chancellor and the foreign, finance, economics, and agriculture ministers prefer to meet ad hoc. Furthermore, EU affairs are a regular topic in all cabinet meetings for reporting and discussion. The Chancellor's Office serves cabinet as an information base independent of the committee system. It is technically supported by a computerized infor-mation system in which all legislative issues and other projects reported by the departments are stored, so that at any given point in time there is precise information on what goes on when and in which arena.

Obviously, there is a clear *hierarchical element* in the interdepartmental co-ordination system. The layers of the committee system as well as the early reports to the Chancellor's Office and its role in preparing the cabinet meetings filter out the 'political' topics. The system abides by the 'power shift law' (Downs 1967) in ensuring that unresolved conflicts come to the atten-tion of politically more legitimate superiors and eventually the politicians themselves.

The two-track system of EU policy making

Clearly recognizable, there is a policy specialist track and a diplomatic track, running largely parallel but with junctions in the Bonn committee system, the Chancellor's Office, and the Permanent Representation in Brussels. From the outset, the German co-ordination system has involved the FO, first of all for intergovernmentally negotiating the treaties pre-dating the 1957 Treaty of Rome,[3] the communities for Coal and Steel, the (not realized) European Defence Community with its provision for European political co-operation (Article 38), and Euratom. In all matters concerning widening and deepening of the EU, the international law nature of the treaties requires diplomats; they are also indispensable because of their overview of foreign relations and their language skills (and table manners), as well as for the time-consuming nature of travelling and attending conferences. After all, they link with other foreign diplomatic services. Once such a system of mutual players in whatever policy area is established, it tends to perpetuate itself.

Second, substantive policies that are designed within the EU institutional framework were initially predominantly of an economic nature (including agricultural and fiscal issues). Gradually the policies covered by the EU increased in number and affected other ministries; rough indicators of the present scope of EU-related policies are the departments represented in EU council working groups and meetings of the Councils of Ministers themselves (Wessels and Rometsch 1996; see Tables 2.2 and 2.3).

At the preparatory stage of Commission proposals, contacts with Bonn run in the expert, specialist track. However, this is not fully reflected in the juris-dictions of the DGs in Brussels; there is, for instance, no matching partner for the Health Department, although health aspects are involved in many

---

[3] As early as 1953 there were attempts to establish a European Agricultural Union analogous to the Coal and Steel Union (see protocols of the 1953 German cabinet meetings).

TABLE 2.2. *Departmental (and* Länder*) representation in working groups of Council in 1994 (German presidency)*

Policy area	President	Speaker of delegation
Economics	23	49 (12 *Länder*)
Foreign Affairs	22	22—
Agriculture	42	51 (23)
Finance	2	30 (1)
Justice	20	22 (10)
Health	23	28 (7)
Interior	18	21 (13)
Permanent Representative	96	30 (1)
Others	18	44 (18)
Total	264	297 (85)

Source: Wessels and Rometsch 1996: 83.

TABLE 2.3. *Meetings of Council of Ministers by department, 1990*

Council	No. of meetings
Agriculture	16
General	13
Economics/Finance	10
International Market	7
Environment	5
Research	4
Industry	4
Transport	4
Development	4
Others	24
Total	91

Source: Wessels and Rometsch 1996: 78.

product-related regulations (pharmaceutical or cosmetic products); also consumer protection remains of secondary importance, as are the health aspects of the production process itself. Perhaps, this is one of the reasons why Health, although a tiny department, has an official with the German Permanent Representation.

Furthermore, in federal relations with the *Länder* ministries, the Foreign

TABLE 2.4. *EU proposals/drafts/bills in Bundestag*

	n
1957–61	13
1961–5	224
1965–9	745
1969–72	946
1972–6	1,759
1976–80	1,706
1980–3	1,355
1983–7	1,828
1987–90	2,413
1991–4	1,860

Source: Töller 1995: 67.

Office is non-existent and all domestic policy contacts are run between ministries in Bonn and their counterparts at the *Länder* level. Instead, at the *Land* level a 'foreign relations' system has developed. The *Länder* transferred EU contacts to their Bundesrat ministers, who already had 'embassies' in Bonn; their job is to co-ordinate *Länder* policies in the second chamber, in particular EU affairs, as well as monitoring the *Land* bureau in Brussels. Consequently, some state chancelleries, for instance in Bavaria (until 1998) and Saxony, keep domestic policy as well as EU policy divisions. Other *Länder* make a special minister responsible for federal and European affairs. Last but not least, since 1993 the *Länder* may not only be part of the German delegation to Council sessions, but the *Länder*, in certain instances (e.g. matters of education) may even represent the Federal Republic in the Council of Ministers, as indicated in Table 2.2.

Finally, the special minister meetings of the *Länder* and the committees of the Bundesrat correspond to the ministerial division of labour between the federal ministries. The Bundestag committee structure is even completely congruent with the federal ministerial structure. The growth of Bundestag involvement is shown in Table 2.4, and the policy areas and committees affected by EU legislation are reflected in Table 2.5 (Töller 1995). After all, the policy ministries are the target of national interest groups; together with the Bundestag committees they form the 'cosy triangle' (Beyme 1997: 148).

Nevertheless, Economics has remained the spider in this federal, parliamentary, and interdepartmental domestic web, one of its tasks being the distribution of all the papers coming in from Brussels to the Bundestag committees (and the second chamber). It also passes on papers to the depart-

TABLE 2.5. *EU-induced bills in Bundestag, 1983–1994*

Department	EU-induced	Total legislation
Agriculture	28	61
Health etc.	24	71
Justice	28	142
Finance	27	118
Economics	8	52
Labour	5	94
Traffic	10	37
Education	1	16
Environment	11	19
Interior	10	135
Post, Urban A.	4	32
Total	156	777

Source: Töller 1995: 48.

ments, which in turn keep their *Länder* colleagues up to date as far as these are not already briefed through their own independent channel leading to the *Land* embassy in Brussels. All the procedures involved refer to the co-ordinating function of Economics, and its division E acts as a secretariat for the interdepartmental committees. In contrast, the Foreign Office track is very short connecting Berlin, other capitals, and COREPER.

This two-track feature is replicated in the Chancellor's Office with the foreign affairs and economics divisions monitoring the respective departmental policies. Here though the concern is less with managing the decision process; rather the threads are pulled together with respect to policy interrelatedness and conflicts. The same duality of the Foreign Office and Economics is built into the state secretary committee as well as into the COREPER staff—an ideal condition for preparing for package deals at the Brussels stage.

Internalization of the foreign relations dimension

From an organization theory point of view, the two-track system corresponds to the model of *matrix organization*. This becomes even clearer when we look at the Finance Ministry in the same way as we regard Foreign Office functions: financial aspects have to be matched with sectoral policies, in particular the system of funds, or are at stake with all revenue questions of the EU. Thus, finance and foreign relations are policy dimensions running across sectoral agricultural, environmental, or health policies. Traditionally, the organization of federal government involves matrix relationships between functionally oriented and policy ministries.[4] Since the late 1970s, though, the line departments themselves have begun to establish special sections or sub-divisions for departmental EU relations, so-called 'mirror units'.[5] In part these units have to co-ordinate activities within the ministry concerned, partly they act as liaison officials in the interdepartmental co-ordination system, and partly they maintain contacts to the Brussels arena.[6] These *EU co-ordination sections* became part of a matrix arrangement within the ministries, with frequent contacts to Brussels. Some of the ministries had foreign relations specialists from their involvement in other international organizations such as WHO, ILO, or special United Nations policies such as developmental aid. Those ministries that have an official on the staff of the German Permanent Representation normally appoint him the EU co-ordinator for channelling all departmental contacts to, in, and from Brussels.[7] This is because Brussels is a terrain less transparent for departmental policy specialists than the German policy arenas and communities. Also, the DGs have a diverse administrative culture owing to the nationally heterogeneous personnel and to what, from a German point of view, are loose procedures. In such surroundings, the liaison officials of one's own department are valuable path-finders and interpreters. This internalization of diplomatic functions (without having diplomats) has bred a sort of *hybrid role* of communication specialists, who are more familiar with substantive policies of a particular ministry than the FO diplomats, the 'brandy balloons' as they are occasionally called.

With the deepening of the EU, the policy-making arena became ever more complicated for Bonn officials. Bureaucratic professionals and (amateur) politicians are playing on three tiers these days: in the second division with sixteen teams (*Länder*), in the first division with fourteen teams (Bonn departments), and in European Cup competitions with fourteen teams (Brussels), alternating between indoor and outdoor matches (interest groups, Bundestag, and European Parliament). Internalizing the variety of the playground increases the internal complexity of the ministries. The system may produce some redundancy and noise, but it seems to be suited to this multi-level game. It lends the actors an invisible hand through the decision maze by establishing sectoral paths running up and down between Bonn, Brussels, and, say,

---

[4] Other functional ministries are Interior (civil sevice matters, government organization) and Justice (checking legality of all government bills).

[5] The mirror principle (Spiegelbild) is most prominent in the Chancellor's Office where each department is shadowed by a section; mirror sections developed also for internalizing concerns of the Ministry of the Environment.

[6] In the most recent organization charts of the ministries I counted 79 sections concerned with EU affairs; 40 of these were located in the Foreign Office (11), Economics (16), Finance (12), and the Chancellery (2); see Table 2.1.

[7] German PR staff grew from 19 (1960) to 28 (1986) and 59 (1995); in 1995, it was the largest of all countries (Wessels and Rometsch 1996: 84).

Munich where colleagues with the same problem perception and professional training meet. This routine combines with repetitiveness: there are play-off rounds and new seasons every year in working groups of the council and in the relevant sector of the comitology. Relations within this *vertical brotherhood* follow standard operating procedures and are predictable. The diplomats, in contrast, do not play in the second division; they appear to play according to different rules anyway, maybe even a different game (Eton football in contrast to the Rugby football of the policy experts). They cultivate the COREPER and Council of Ministers arena. The liaison hybrids, meanwhile, move between the rougher and the more gentle game and in the upper divisions of the league.

From the point of view of organization theory, the installation of special liaison officials comes close to a *divisional structure* of government as a whole. The incorporation of this function- (as opposed to product-) oriented activity increases the autonomy of ministerial departments with respect to the Foreign Office's external relations monopoly. From organization theory one learns though that divisionalization is problematic when the products are sold in interdependent markets: complementary relationships and synergy effects are spoiled. The question thus is whether there is a common market for the various German EU policy products requiring concerted promotion.

Co-ordination capacities compared

After having failed to establish the priority of foreign over domestic policy,[8] the Platonic division of labour between form and substance, between diplomatic relations and specific policy issues might one day make the diplomats largely superfluous on the European turf. Repeated demands from Bavaria (1994, 1998) to take EU matters away from the Foreign Office and create a ministry for European affairs are, however, more misplaced today than they were in the 1951–7 battle over competences between the FO and Economics. On the one hand, diplomats have lost centre stage but are needed from time to time for negotiating international treaties of all kinds, not just the EC treaties; each ministry continues to be obliged to report sectoral foreign contacts to the FO for co-ordination. A ministry for European affairs, on the other hand, would only turn out to be a second diplomatic staff or would have to incorporate all of the federal bureaucracy affected nowadays by EU policy, thus turning the co-ordination requirement from an interdepartmental one into an intradepartmental problem of such an imaginary giant ministry.

As the Commission in Brussels is as fragmented as the federal government,

[8] The FO, in fact, had tried in the early 1950s to subjugate foreign trade policy.

it simply does not have the capacity to impose its views as a 'superbureau-cracy' on the national bureaucracies; this might be the deeper reason why a 'co-operative multi-level bureaucracy' has replaced the 'diplomatic monopoly' (Wessels 1996). Looking at it from the point of view of the contingency theory of organization, sectoralization both of the Commission and of various national governments is mutually reinforcing.[9]

However, if Brussels is not the enemy and interdepartmental and federal conflicts are settled satisfactorily in Berlin, the target of co-ordination might be the governments of other member states of the EU. Before this problem is examined later in the chapter, I should like to discuss briefly how much of a difference there is in structure and function of various national co-ordination capacities.

First, the functioning of the Chancellor's Office (personal office and cabinet Secretariat combined) is equivalent to the separate Prime Minister's and Cabinet Offices in Whitehall. In both cases (and in Paris, too), we observe the same two-track system at the apex of which Foreign Office personnel is involved (division 2 of the Chancellery; officials from Foreign and Common-wealth Office in the Cabinet Office Secretariat). Seldon's descriptions of the head of the European affairs Secretariat in the Cabinet Office could as well apply to the German Chancellery: '[he] attended and briefed the PM person-ally for every European Council, and virtually every meeting of the Council of Ministers and of Cabinet when it discussed EC affairs . . . often possessing an overview held by no other single Whitehall department, [he] would be in a position to recommend strategies and policy decisions' (1990: 109).

Second, to have a special minister head the co-ordination unit as in France or to assign chairmanship of the interdepartmental committee in Berlin to a minister of state in the FO would hardly make a difference from a technical point of view.

Third, in Paris as well as in London and in Berlin, the central co-ordinating agencies are dependent on the factual information available and provided by the government departments concerned. Wallace (1996) reports that the European secretariat of the Cabinet Office regularly surveys the departments. The French SGCI, in 1994, was not able effectively to co-ordinate despite a co-ordination order, because of bilateral departmental contacts with the Com-mission; Matignon decisions are the 'product of micro-level negotiations' elsewhere (Lequesne 1996: 114). In the UK, too, policies of low salience are dealt with outside the Cabinet Office system, bilaterally in Whitehall and with Brussels. However, in all capitals it might be equally difficult to differentiate between technical and political matters. Vincent Wright's contention that 'the effectiveness of a country's domestic EU co-ordinating capacity must be

---

[9] Not surprisingly, ministries for environmental affairs have popped up in many EU countries; see Weale et al. 1996.

judged according to the issue, the policy type, the policy requirements and the policy objectives. Merely to examine the machinery of co-ordination is to confuse the means and the outcomes' (1996: 165) is, therefore, fully substantiated.

The Political Content of Policies

Of course, even binding decisions which the Commission takes in implementing European competition law have political consequences (Schmidt 1997), although they would not be regarded as part of EU policy making and are not negotiated in the various policy arenas but are rather taken in secluded bureau.[10] But what exactly is meant when the EU expert literature talks of political matters, or what is the meaning of a *Politische Abteilung* in the Foreign Office as opposed to the *Europa-Abteilung*? In these cases, 'political' implies intergovernmental negotiations of treaties. More generally, it might be maintained that 'political' refers to conflicts and their resolution, i.e. politics. Politics is definitely a functional aspect that brings politicians into the game, as previously indicated by quoting the power shift law. In a further step one could consider various *policies* in respect to their politics implications. Here it might be helpful to refer to Theodor Lowi's distinction between regulatory, distributive, and polity decisions. EU policy is actually a *policy mix* of all three categories resulting in different levels of conflict.

Regulatory policy is commonly regarded as a particular feature of EU policy. In order to achieve the free movement of goods, people, and finances, the EU has applied a traditional harmonization approach, by setting basically product-related common standards (e.g. catalytic combustion, ingredients of beer, lorry driving hours). This harmonization policy is at the core of the second pillar of EU policy, the Economic Community. It is this rather technical area where most sectoralized vertical contacts are taking place, where national interest groups are concerned, and considerations of package deals come up. Deregulation of markets (negative integration) is an alternative strategy which Prime Minister Thatcher favoured (Wallace 1990); the revolutionary changes in the telecommunications and railway sectors are results of this approach. Scharpf convincingly argues that consensus needs are lower in negative integration policy than in positive integration through harmonization. For, tensions between economic and non-economic policy purposes that are settled in national policy making through interdepartmental co-

---

[10] For example, the interdiction by the Commission of an economic subsidy by the *Land* Saxony to Volkswagen for inducing investment in a factory in that part of de-industrialized eastern Germany.

ordination or in cabinet are not articulated at the EU level because economic purposes tend to override non-economic ones. This is so because deregulation can be brought about by the Commission alone and the European Court of Justice. Positive integration, however, requires transformation into national law[11] involving, in the German case, the national Parliament and the Bundesrat, in particular where *Länder* competences are affected (Scharpf 1996). The Council of Ministers is involved also through the diplomatic track. Independent of qualified majority voting since 1986, the ministers in matters of health, industrial safety, environment, or consumer protection serve as national watchdogs and try to achieve unanimous decisions (Golub 1997).

In general, conflict intensity depends on the degree of deviation from existing national regulations, which tended to be small in the German case. Also, conflicts are low in product-related regulations strengthening the common market, but high in regulation related to the production process like environmental, safety, and social standard setting; for these standards tend to increase the costs of production or, more generally, the adaptation costs at home (Scharpf 1996: 20). Germany, obsessed with safety and environmental protection anyway, and with the burden of social market economy, used to be in a defensive situation only if standards were to be lowered by harmonization or deregulation.[12] Package deals or side payments are apparently only possible within a specific policy field and in the arena of specific councils (Scharpf 1996: 19).

Distributive Policy is at stake in various shapes: setting prices and quotas for national production (steel, farming products) has been a routine operation for some forty years; they are partly negotiated in the particular agricultural management councils. French farmers occasionally going berserk are familiar images. More important in distributive perspective are the structural funds and the decisions on their financing (as on EU revenues in general); they have high public visibility and invite contemplation on international distributive justice. Here, the finance minister comes on stage as the paymaster general, accompanied by his colleagues from Economics (regional fund) and Agriculture.[13] Finance is officially present in virtually all council meetings (Wessels and Rometsch 1996: 84). The German position, owing to the cost of national unification and the precarious fiscal situation, has definitely turned more

---

[11] The qualitative difference between regulations (immediately binding) and directives (merely setting goals) is not relevant here. First of all, substantively both types of law are hardly distinguishable; secondly, upcoming regulations are normally anticipated in national legislation; for they have to fit the existing body of law, otherwise codification would become untransparent or contradictory.

[12] An interesting question is how often the 'special national interest clause' is invoked in these matters.

[13] Witness the row of German farmers in 1998 over the Agenda 2000 proposal.

defensive compared with former decades; the recent transfer of the EU competences to Finance in the Schröder government is meant to strengthen the German bargaining position. The arena for settling major distributive conflicts is often the European Council.

Constitutional policy or polity decisions are about widening (negotiating association and membership) and deepening (direct election to EP, majority rule, parliamentary rights, additional EU responsibilities) of the EU. In polity decisions of this kind, the diplomats are on centre stage, simply because the treaties are negotiated in intergovernmental relations and constitute international law. Nevertheless, during the process of preparing for the Euro the Chancellor's Office as well as Foreign Office, Finance, and Economics set up special sections to deal with that matter (as did the Bundesbank). The *Länder*, too, have a say in polity matters when their competences are affected, and they have leverage because the Bundesrat is needed for the ensuing ratification process. Pillar 3 co-operations (foreign and security policy, police and justice co-operation) can be regarded as part of constitutional policy, too. Since Maastricht the FO is no longer merely a diplomatic negotiator for polity matters but is substantively in charge of CFSP. The German position is normally pro-European in polity matters, and in a Europe of different speed and scope the German government is among the most speedy and broadest, having adopted the EURO, the Schengen agreement, and the social charter from the beginning.

Finally, there are *personnel decisions*, such as appointing the president of the Commission or of the European central bank, but also—a matter for the domestic arena—German commissioners. Apparently, the German government keeps a low profile in personnel decisions, trying to accommodate the French rather than pushing national interests.

Obviously, the conflict potential of these decision types varies considerably, both in the national as well as in the international arena—as does the political salience and, consequently, political interest and attention. Without needing to go into details, it is evident that polity, major financing (distributive) decisions, and possibly some personnel decisions are dealt with on track one, leading up from Foreign Office (occasionally from the *Länder*, or ending at the constitutional court), through the Chancellor's Office and cabinet to the Council of Foreign Ministers and ultimately the European Council. Regulatory policy (with many more issues treated simultaneously), however, is bargained on track two with Economics and the interdepartmental committee system at the core and a multiplicity of sectoral contacts stretching over a maximum of three levels of the decision system. Most research on EU policy co-ordination focuses probably on these sometimes very specific regulative policy matters or the regional policy of the cohesion fund (Benz 1998). Generalizations across policy types and from policy to polity questions are, therefore, problematic.

Bringing Politics back in

The image of EU policy dominated by bureaucrats (Bach 1992; Bulmer 1986) is highly questionable—both for the lack of differential treatment of policy matters as well as for methodological reasons.[14] In this section, I can only point at the role of politicians and politics in the context of varying policy substance without hope of being exhaustive.

Politicized issues

Clearly, the intelligence of the expert, sectoralized track is not the problem: it may even suffer from an information overload.[15] Nor can it be maintained that the formal co-ordination machinery does not process all the policy-related information and signals of conflict. It works smoothly in co-ordinating the two-level game in the domestic arena. Unresolved conflicts between experts in the line departments are moved upward till they reach cabinet level. Micro-management is the matter of civil servants. All politicized issues which the media report are, as a matter of course, discussed in national and subnational cabinets, be they questions relating to mad cows, the purity of Bavarian beer, or disputed subsidies to Saxonian industry. Sensitive issues iterating between the levels of the system or between branches of government are also likely to be reported in cabinet under the regular EU topic. To the extent that these cases concern regulative policy or are not highly politicized, the federal government tends to take a *reactive stance.*

With *polity decisions* the Chancellor is involved earlier and more regularly; for instance a special section in his office was set up for shepherding the EURO decision process. As polity matters are often discussed in the regular Franco-Allemand talks and will be decided by the European Council, these things do not evade the Chancellor. Some of the summits are prepared by the Chancellor's Office, anyway. Bordering on the idiosyncratic, the Schengen agreement was negotiated by the Chancellery's interior division, not by the Foreign Office or by Interior as the natural lead ministry. For Kohl had approached Mitterrand during one of their bilateral meetings, recalling his attempt as a young man to crash a toll-bar at the western border of Rhineland-Palatinate. As this was a personal project initiated together with the French President, Kohl wanted it to be kept under the Chancellery's roof. Furthermore, had the job

[14] This is not to maintain that the observations and case studies are not valuable in themselves, they merely cannot be generalized to the whole body of EU policy. Also, what you get from interviews depends on whom you talk to (Miles's second law).

[15] Since the Commission no longer sends the comitology protocols but publishes (*sic*) them on the Internet, attention to and distribution of information has reached a new, problematic quality.

been allocated to the Ministry of the Interior, the police and immigration specialists would have been caught up in technical details. The Foreign Office, on the other hand, lacked the substantive expertise and was involved only ('to keep them busy') in writing the treaty according to the art of treaty making. In Paris, Mitterrand had given the task to the Foreign Office but ultimately the Matignon also became involved.[16]

Intrasectoral vs. intersectoral negotiations

In polity matters, national governments ultimately are in a veto position in Brussels. Bargaining is, nevertheless, attempted even at a very late stage in the decision process; substantive compromises, postponements, sequential decisions, and package deals seem to occur even in the European Council (Weber and Wiesmeth 1991). Negotiation tactics are sorted out by various experts. Undoubtedly, the same occurs in the Councils of Ministers about specific policy issues. As the number of items on the agenda can be large, there is ample possibility for intrasectoral compromise. COREPER has a notable role in sorting out the conflicting points. As Bulmer has observed, 'irrespective of sales strategy to the public, vigorous defence of German national interests [is mounted] in the Council of Ministers' (1986: 16). These intrasectoral linkages do occur and are often tolerable because external costs remain in the same sector and losses to special domestic interests can be compensated by side-payments at home (Moravcsik 1993: 506). Nevertheless, the conflict propensity of ministers may be a problem, as they are not always willing to risk a conflict in Brussels by presenting a package, after the individual issues have marched up the expert track in lengthy consensual preparations. Ultimately, though, the EU gives legitimacy or serves as a scapegoat depending on whether national government supports or rejects a specific policy (Moravcsik 1993: 514).

Intersectoral log-rolling may be more difficult. First, the Councils of Ministers are specialized extensions of the expert track. It is hardly conceivable that one could negotiate in Brussels below or in the Council of Ministers if one arrives with a pre-packed intersectoral solution; otherwise, compromises would need renegotiation at home.[17] Second, it is difficult to synchronize conflicting matters that involve high stakes but have not reached the same stage in the decision process. Third, as most national governments are not able to carry their co-ordination attempts to perfection, sectorized approaches may even increase influence in Brussels (Groennegaard Christensen 1981). Elegant

[16] Personal communication by Klaus König, 21 Apr. 1998; see König 1993.
[17] This problem reminds us of the logical deficiency of imperative mandates in Marx's council system.

as centralized models of co-ordination may look in game theoretical, inter-governmental perspective, decentralized, even fragmented systems might have some advantages under conditions of imperfect information. Hundreds of arrows may be more effective than one shot from Big Bertha. In multiple issue games it does not necessarily matter when you are occasionally overruled in the Council as the Germans appear to be (Wessels 1997).

Wessels and Rometsch (1996: 97 f.) are ambivalent when assessing German co-ordination in the light of the positive UK and French examples; on the one hand, sectoralation would (by definition) impair the capacity for package deals across sectors but make available political capacity to mobilize support with sectoral interest groups and the *Länder*; the latter being important for easing the implementation of EU law. On the other hand, they judge German EU policy output as not bad. There might, however, be an exception to the latent positive function of unavoidable sectorization: if players are purely defensive and try to minimize national costs of policies, they are more likely to resort to non negotiable packages, to blocking policy or opting out of spe-cific European policies altogether. For it is always easier to decide what you do not want than to determine what your positive goals are. The strategy, again, might be contingent on the type of EU policy concerned; already Bulmer conceded even a 'German obstructionism at low profile catching up with the masters of the art—the French and the British' (1986: 16). In turn, too much flexibility can be detrimental in the long run; as numerous studies of the budgetary process demonstrated, modest strategies, steadiness, and reli-ability of a player are a valuable resource in the long run.

Dashes and marathon runs

Short-term maximization of benefits or minimization of costs may be detri-mental in the long run when optimization of multiple issues in sequential, recurrent deals is eventually counted. In criticizing Scharpf's decision trap theorem, Guy Peters countered that the static, single issue game theoretical approach the dynamics and simultaneity of EU routine decision making (as opposed to high politics) would not hold true for (Peters 1997). Even in high politics, i.e. with politicized policy items or polity decisions, one can imagine that there is some room for manœuvre, as these matters, once again, are dealt with in one arena and do not require across-the-board deals (Weber and Wiesmeth 1991) without excluding the possibility of compensations. As Peters (1992) has argued, you cannot always win, what matters is to stay in the game; 'playing the game becomes more important than winning all the time'. A sophisticated poker player should allow the beginner to win occasionally; otherwise he may lose a partner.

The social logic of policy communities

This *marathon strategy* is not merely advisable under the conditions of the complexity given; there is recent empirical evidence that national actors are not following the intergovernmentalist maximization logic, but that their behaviour in the Brussels arena is shaped by European institutional exigencies. As politicians, 'in the shadow of the vote' (Golub 1997), strive for consensus solutions irrespective of the formal decision rules, expert officials (to varying degrees) tend to hold cosmopolitan rather than local orientations; professional standards prevail over bureaucratic obedience, collegiality across borders and tiers prevails (Kerremans 1996: 231). Britons returning from secondment to Brussels appreciated running on the long leash, noting the socialization effects of that supra-national environment (Christoph 1993). Officials in the DGs, irrespective of their nationality, identify strongly with the DG's mission (Egeberg 1996; Hooghe 1997). Not surprisingly, in the Commission-controlled comitology, on the expert track, problem solving ruled by the mutual tactical goal of consensual solutions is the dominant style; Wessels (1998) observed 'business-like working based on technocratic expertise and camaraderie' where one would expect clashing interests. Lewis (1998, in a rare empirical study of COREPER, the domain of the diplomats), observed that there is a margin of manœuvre beyond or even against national instructions; the imperatives of minimizing confrontation and avoiding the Council are paramount. Therefore, due to his mediating the contradictory role as national representative and European integrationist, the German 'permanent *Vertreter*' is nicknamed 'permanent traitor'.

Conclusion

There are undoubtedly national differences in EU policy co-ordination. In the *Westminster system*, *ex ante* co-ordination may be easier to achieve than in coalition governments of parliamentary regimes with many more veto points. Equally, for the same reason federal systems are more complicated to co-ordinate than unitary states.

Second, *political culture* plays a role in explaining national differences. In Germany, one of the founder members of the EU, there is a broad elite and sectoral consensus on EU integration; four-fifths of all national legislation are uncontroversial anyway. There was a silent grand coalition in EU matters in Bonn, although some cracks in the front were visible over the Euro. German commissioners in the Brussels elephant cemetery are regularly paired: one from the government parties, the other belonging to the opposition. Only Bavaria, the traditional watchdog of federalism, with some Euroscepticism as reflection of the slightly nationalist regional party base of the ruling CSU, cultivates the Astérix image of the last unconquered village in the south in possession of a magic potion.

In the UK, throughout the 1980s there was no firm EU consensus in the ruling Conservative Party. Severe tensions arose in cabinet over polity matters, and Prime Minister Thatcher displayed a combative style in intergovernmental relations (Wallace 1996: 67). It was clear what she did not want: Schengen, harmonization of VAT, the social charter, and EMU/Euro. Further, she was in favour of deregulation of capital market and financial and transport services (Wallace 1990) instead of positive integration through harmonization. Seldon (1990: 108 f.) notes that the Thatcher reign was characterized by an unusual 'pro-active style' not found in other cabinet committees that extended to questions about the EU budget, the accession of Spain and Portugal, the SEA, and new environmental and research areas.

Finally, marvellous EU policy co-ordination may be an artefact produced or nurtured by politicians wishing to demonstrate their concern for the national interest to an anxious electorate. Symbolic reorganization of the machinery of government is one way to achieve this impression. *Ex ante* central co-ordination before arriving at the negotiating table in Brussels follows the *police image* of EU policy making. The *fire brigade* approach might be less spectacular but its reactive style and management by exception may be well suited to the kind of incremental decision making in a multi-level game. European conviction politicians probably resort to a broader strategy mix.

By separating polity issues from sectoralized regulative policies, we may be able to locate more precisely the role of politics in the otherwise bureaucrat-dominated EU game. Also, the paradox of successfully failing[18] dissolves: despite occasional backlashes in routine policy making, the German (and other member states') record in advancing the European polity has not been bad. Perhaps we should add a third EU policy approach that one could call, in order to stay in the picture, the *campanile* approach: watching out from on high to discern regular kitchen smoke from the smouldering of dangerous policy quarrels and occasionally ringing the bells to celebrate important events.

References

Bach, M. (1992), 'Eine leise Revolution durch Verwaltungsverfahren: Bürokratische Integrationsprozesse in der Europäischen Gemeinschaft', *Zeitschrift für Soziologie*, 21: 16–30.

[18] Derived from a title used by Seibel (1996).

Benz, A. (1998), 'Politikverflechtung ohne Politikverflechtungsfalle: Koordination und Strukturdynamik im europäischen Mehrebenensystem', *Politische Vierteljahresschrift*, 39: 558–89.

Beyme, K. von (1997), *Der Gesetzgeber: Der Bundestag als Entscheidungszentrum* (Opladen: Westdeutscher Verlag).

Bulmer, S. (1986), *The Domestic Structure of European Community Policy-Making in West Germany* (London: Garland Publishing (outstanding LSE theses)).

—— and Paterson, W. E. (1987), *The Federal Republic of Germany and the European Community* (London: Allen & Unwin).

Christoph, J. B. (1993), 'The Effect of Britons in Brussels: The European Community and the Culture of Whitehall', *Governance*, 6/4: 518–37.

Downs, A. (1967), *Inside Bureaucracy* (Boston: Little, Brown & Company).

Egeberg, M. (1996), 'Organization and Nationality in the European Commission Services', *Public Administration*, 74: 721–35.

Goetz, K. H. (1995), 'National Governance and European Integration: Intergovernmental Relations in Germany', *Journal of Common Market Studies*, 33: 91–115.

Golub, J. (1997), 'In the Shadow of the Vote? Decisionmaking Efficiency in the European Community 1974–1995', Cologne: Max-Planck-Institut für Gesellschaftsforschung, Discussion Paper 97/3.

Groennegard Christensen, J. (1981), 'Blurring the International–Domestic Politics Distinction: Danish Representation at EC Negotiation', *Scandinavian Political Studies*, 4: 191–208.

Hesse, J. J., and Goetz, K. H. (1992), 'Early Administrative Adjustment to the European Communities: The Case of the Federal Republic of Germany', *Yearbook of European Administrative History*, 4: 181–205.

Hooghe, L. (1997), 'Serving Europe: Political Orientations of Senior Commission Officials', *European Integration Online Papers*, vol. i, No. 008.

Kerremans, B. (1996), 'Do Institutions Make a Difference? Non-institutionalism, Neo-institutionalism, and the Logic of Common Decision-Making in the European Union', *Governance*, 9/2: 217–40.

Koerfer, D. (1988), 'Zankapfel Europapolitik: Der Kompetenzstreit zwischen Auswärtigem Amt und Bundeswirtschaftsministerium 1957/58', *Politische Vierteljahresschrift*, 29: 553–68.

König, K. (1993), 'Organization und Prozeß: Zur Internationalisierung des Regierens', in C. Böhret and G. Wewer (eds.), *Regieren im 21. Jahrhundert: Zwischen Globalisierung und Regionalisierung* (Opladen: Leske & Budrich).

Lequesne, C. (1996), 'French Central Government and the European Political System: Change and Adaptation since the Single Act', in Y. Mény, P. Muller, and J.-L. Quermonne (eds.), *Adjusting to Europe: The Impact of the European Union on National Institutions and Policies* (London: Routledge).

Lewis, J. (1998), 'The Institutional Problem-Solving Capacities of the Council: The Committee of Permanent Representatives and the Methods of Community, Cologne: Max-Planck-Institut für Gesellschaftsforschung, Discussion Paper 98/1.

Marks, G., et al. (1996), *Governance in the European Union* (London: Sage).

Mayntz, R., and Derlien, H.-U. (1989), 'Party Patronage and Politicization of the West German Administrative Elite 1970–1987: Towards Hybridization?', *Governance*, 2: 384–404.

——and Scharpf, F. W. (1975), *Policy-Making in the German Federal Bureaucracy* (Amsterdam: Elsevier).

Mény, Y., Muller, P., and Quermonne, J.-L. (eds.) (1996), *Adjusting to Europe: The Impact of the European Union on National Institutions and Policies* (London: Routledge).

Moravcsik, A. (1993), 'Preferences and Power in the European Community: A Liberal Intergovernmentalist Approach', *Journal of Common Market Studies*, 31/4: 473–524.

Pag, S. (1987), 'The Relations between the Commission and National Bureaucracies', in D. Berlin et al. (eds.), *The European Administration* (Brussels: IIAS).

Peters, B. G. (1992), 'Bureaucratic Politics in Institutions of the European Community', in A. Sbragia (ed.), *Euro-Politics: Institutions and Policy-Making in the 'New' European Community* (Washington: Brookings Institution).

——(1997), 'Escaping the Joint-Decision Trap: Repetition and Sectoral Politics in the European Union', *West European Politics*, 20: 22–36.

Putnam, R. D. (1973), 'The Political Attitudes of Senior Civil Servants in Western Europe', *British Journal of Political Science*, 3: 253–79.

Regelsberger, E., and Wessels, W. (1984), 'Entscheidungsprozesse Bonner Europa-Politik: Verwalten statt Gestalten?', in R. Hrbek and W. Wessels (eds.), *EG-Mitgliedschaft: Ein vitales Interesse der Bundesrepublik Deutschland?* (Bonn: EUV).

Rose, R. (1985), 'Steering the Ship of State', mimeo, 85/46.

Sbragia, A. M. (ed.) (1992), *Euro-Politics. Institutions and Policy-Making in the 'New' European Community* (Washington: Brookings Institution).

Scharpf, F. W. (1972), 'Komplexität als Schranke der politischen Planung', *Politische Vierteljahresschrift*, Special Issue 4: 168–92.

——(1988), 'The Joint-Decision Trap', *Public Administration*, 66: 239–78.

——(1996), 'Negative and Positive Integration in the Political Economy of European Welfare States', in G. Marks et al. (eds.), *Governance in the European Union* (London: Sage).

Schmidt, S. (1997), 'Behind the Council Agenda: The Commission's Impact on Decisions', Cologne: Max-Planck-Institut für Gesellschaftsforschung, Discussion Paper 97/4.

Seibel, W. (1996), 'Successful Failure: An Alternative View on Organisational Coping', *American Behavioral Scientist*, 39: 1011–24.

Seldon, A. (1990), 'The Cabinet Office and Coordination, 1979–87', *Public Administration*, 68: 103–21.

Siedentopf, H., and Hauschild, C. (1988), 'The Implementation of Community Legislation by the Member States: A Comparative Analysis', in H. Siedentopf and J. Ziller (eds.), *Making European Policies Work: The Implementation of Community Legislation in the Member States*, 2 vols. (London: Sage).

Simon, H. (1947), 'The Proverbs of Administration', *Public Administration Review*, 8: 32–49.

Streinz, R., and Pechstein, M. (1995), 'The Case of Germany', in Spyros Pappas (ed.), *National Administrative Procedures for the Preparation and Implementation of Community Decisions* (Maastricht: European Institute of Public Administration).

Töller, A. E. (1995), *Europapolitik im Bundestag: Eine empirische Untersuchung zur europapolitischen Willensbildung im EG-Ausschuß des 12. Deutschen Bundestages* (Frankfurt: Lang).

Wallace, H. (1990), 'Britain and Europe', in P. Dunleavy and A. Gamble (eds.), *Developments in British Politics 3* (Houndmills: Macmillan).

—— (1996), 'Relations between the European Union and the British Administration', in Y. Mény, P. Muller, and J.-L. Quermonne (eds.), *Adjusting to Europe: The Impact of European Union on National Institutions and Policies* (London: Routledge).

Wallace, W. (1973), *National Governments and the European Communities* (London: Chatham House).

Weale, A., et al. (1996), 'Comparative and International Administration. Environmental Administration in Six European States: Secular Convergence or National Distinctiveness?', *Public Administration*, 74: 255–74.

Weber, S., and Wiesmeth, H. (1991), 'Issue Linkage in the European Community', *Journal of Common Market Studies*, 29: 255–67.

Wessels, W. (1984), 'Community Bureaucracy in a Changing Environment: Criticism, Trends, Questions', in J. Jamar and W. Wessels (eds.), *The Community Bureaucracy at the Crossroads* (Bruges: Collège d'Europe).

—— (1996), 'Verwaltung im EG-Mehrebenensystem: Auf dem Weg zur Megabürokratie?', in M. Jachtenfuchs and B. Kohler-Koch (eds.), *Europäische Integration*. Opladen: Leske and Budrich, 165–92.

—— (1997), 'Das politische System der Europäischen Union', in W. Ismayr (ed.), *Die politischen Systeme Westeuropas* (Opladen: Leske & Budrich).

—— (1998), 'Comitology: Fusion in Action. Politico-administrative Trends in the EU System', Journal of European Public Policy, 5: 209–34.

—— and Rometsch, D. (1996), 'German Administrative Interaction and European Union: The Fusion of Public Policies', in Y. Mény, P. Muller, and J.-L. Quermonne (eds.), *Adjusting to Europe: The Impact of the European Union on National Institutions and Policies* (London: Routledge).

Wright, V. (1996), 'The National Co-ordination of European Policy-Making: Negotiating the Quagmire', in J. J. Richardson (ed.), *European Union: Power and Policy-Making* (London: Routledge).

3

France

Anand Menon

French objectives concerning the co-ordination of EU policy are ambitious to say the least. As a prime ministerial circular of 1994 put it:

French positions in all the institutions of the European Union must be expressed with clarity and the greatest possible coherence . . . the unity of French positions is a necessary condition of the efficiency of our action. . . . [The] requirement of coherence in the French positions imposes the need for a strict respect of the procedures for interministerial concertation. (Premier Ministre 1994: 3, 6)

Despite such stated aspirations, however, this chapter argues that a profound tension exists between declared ambitions and the intrinsic difficulties faced in achieving effective co-ordination. Would-be co-ordinators must confront several elements of fragmentation within the core executive itself, most notably:

- a bicephalous and sporadically politically divided executive;
- a strong sense of departmentalism, frequently associated with entrenched interests (*l'État dans l'État*) and manifested in interministerial squabbles;
- 'vertical' divisions between the political and administrative levels, often characterized by tensions between senior officials and political appointees in ministerial *cabinets*.

At one level, the system put into place in France has succeeded in resolving these problems and resulted in effective co-ordination. At another, co-ordinators in Paris face significant problems as they strive to ensure the 'coherence' of French policy positions in Brussels.

The author would like to express his appreciation to the editors, and to Vincent Wright in particular, for helpful comments on an earlier draft of this chapter.

'Routine' Policy

A formal, institutionalized system of co-ordination has been created in France to deal with day-to-day EC legislative matters. Broadly speaking, the process of dealing with EC legislation proceeds via several stages:

1. A Commission proposal for legislation is communicated to the SGCI, which circulates it to the ministries potentially affected by it.
2. A process of intraministerial co-ordination ensues, which finalizes the negotiating stance of these ministries.
3. The SGCI hosts a number of interministerial co-ordination meetings to arrive at an agreed French position.
4. Should the SGCI prove unable to accomplish its task, the matter is referred to the political level and dealt with either by political appointees in the ministerial *cabinets* or, rarely, by ministers themselves.
5. Once a position has been arrived at, the SGCI communicates it to the French Permanent Representation in Brussels as the basis for negotiations in the Council of Ministers.

Clearly not all issues are handled in precisely the same way. For one thing, the publication of Commission proposals does not necessarily mark the first stage of member state involvement in the EC legislative process. For example, initial discussions in Brussels concerning legislation to limit automobile exhaust emissions led to the creation of a *Groupe à Haut Niveau*, which was put into place early in 1985. This allowed for senior civil servants to discuss the *dossier*, and shape what was to become the formal Commission proposal. Thus, even prior to the publication of a Commission proposal, co-ordination was necessary. The *sous-Directeur de la Pollution de l'Air* in the Ministry of the Environment was responsible for maintaining direct links with the various individuals (from three ministries—environment, industry, and transport) engaged in drafting the Commission Directive in Brussels. Moreover, certain issues can, during the formulation of a national negotiating position, become highly politicized. This entails the involvement of political leaders, altering the nature of the co-ordination problems involved and the institutional venue within which co-ordination occurs. The exhaust emissions Directive became highly politicized, with the result that, at critical junctures, French policy was run from and co-ordinated by the *cabinet* of the prime minister.

Yet routine policy generally follows the course set out above. Consequently, the first venue for co-ordination activities is within the various ministries themselves.

Intraministerial co-ordination

Initial attempts to define ministerial positions on European questions are carried out at the administrative level. All French ministries, with the sole exception of the department which looks after war veterans, have adapted their structures in order to cope with the need to define ministerial positions on EC policy (Lequesne 1993: 39–42; interviews, Paris, 1995, 1997).

The most widespread form of administrative adjustment within ministries has been the creation of a single, 'horizontal' unit intended to deal with all European issues. In general this has been achieved through the granting of increased autonomy to a section of the *Direction* in charge of international affairs. In 1990, eleven ministries were equipped with such units while by 1993 this number had dropped to nine (Lequesne 1993: 40: interviews, Paris, 1995). In some cases, the creation of such units has spawned bureaucratic resistance, and led to problems regarding competence, and hence clashes with other departments within the ministries involved (Potocki 1992: 465–6).

The other method commonly employed to ensure intraministerial co-ordination has been the creation of specialist units within the vertical *Directions* of ministries. All eleven Directions of the *Ministère du Finance, du Budget, et du Commerce Extérieure* possess *bureaux européens*. Bureau G3 (*Organismes Européens*), within the *Direction du Budget*, is charged with handling issues relating to the EC budget. A special unit within the *Direction du Trésor* is in charge of monetary policy in the context of the constraints imposed by the EMS. Finally, the Directeur of the *Direction des Relations Économiques Extérieures* is charged with representing France on the Article 113 Committee which prepares the work of ministers and assists the Commission in the conduct of external commercial negotiations (Lequesne 1993: 39).

A similar, though slightly different, model has been adopted by the Ministry of Agriculture, where European activity is concentrated in the *Service des Relations Internationales* (SRI), located within *Direction de la Production et des Échanges* (DPE). It is up to the SRI to 'bring about the synthesis of the positions expressed within the Ministry' (Ministère de l'Agriculture 1996: 2). Within the SRI is a *Sous-Direction des Affaires Européennes*, under which exist various bureaux: '*Union Européenne*', '*Relations Extérieures de l'Union Européenne*' and *Affaires Juridiques Européennes*.

Perhaps surprisingly, the Quai d'Orsay had, until 1993, no formal structures enabling it to deal with EU affairs. Previously, EC matters were handled within the *Service de la Coopération Économique* (SCE). In 1993, a new Secretary General was placed in charge of a *Direction de la Coopération Européenne*. The Foreign Ministry has traditionally enjoyed a special competence over matters relating to the foreign policy of the EU (Lequesne 1993: 83–90). Even this, however, has led to problems of intraministerial co-ordination. European Political Co-operation was entrusted to the *Sous-*

Direction d'Europe Occidentale in the *Direction des Affaires Politiques* and not to the SCE. From the 1980s the SCE and *Sous-Direction d'Europe Occidentale* adopted the practice of co-ordinating informally to assure the common management of shared dossiers. Yet even after the 1993 reforms and the incorporation of the Common Foreign and Security Policy into the European Union Treaty, separate units in different Directions dealt with Community affairs and the CFSP. This has increasingly caused problems, especially in cases where European Union foreign ministers have decided to impose embargoes. Whilst the Foreign Ministry alone is involved in taking the initial decision, implementation falls within the scope of Community business and is hence handled within the *Sous-Direction d'Europe Occidentale* and requires interministerial treatment via the SGCI (Arnould 1992: 461–3). Problems of effective co-ordination can arise as a consequence of the tensions between the different administrative cultures that characterize the *Direction des Affaires Politiques* and the *Direction de la Co-opération Européenne*: one senior official spoke of a 'choc des cultures' (interview, Paris, 1998).

The units charged with assuring intraministerial co-ordination attempt to foster the emergence of a common position on EU policy through discussions with the relevant departments. When co-ordination proves impossible to achieve, the *dossier* is passed to the ministerial *cabinet*, which attempts to use its influence and political weight to achieve a settlement within the ministry. The *cabinet* is a politically appointed group of advisers serving as a screen between ministers and the administration. Their role in the context of French EU policy is varied, but it includes sporadic consultation with interest groups about proposed EC legislation and the maintenance of contacts with the European Commission and in particular with the *cabinets* of the Commissioners (Lequesne 1993: 33).[1]

Dossiers concerning EU policy are usually entrusted to the *cabinet* member responsible for European affairs, but highly sensitive issues can, on occasion, be dealt with by the Directeur. Yet even *cabinet* intervention is not always successful in arriving at a co-ordinated ministerial position. Thus resentments were caused within the Ministry of Agriculture when the highly politicized issue of CAP reform within the GATT was handled by *cabinet* rather than in the Direction de la Production et des Échanges (Lequesne 1993: 38). One senior official within the SGCI recounted that, immediately prior to an SGCI co-ordination meeting, the *chef de cabinet* of a minister rang him to stress that what the *Directeur d'Administration* was about to say was not representative of the views of either the *cabinet* or the minister.

[1] Appointments within the Jospin government (elected in May 1997) illustrated the increasing importance of the EU to their work. Three members of the SGCI staff were appointed to positions in ministerial *cabinets*. Moreover, the Prime Minister's own adviser on European affairs was the third most senior member of his *cabinet*—outranking (unusually) the diplomatic.

Interministerial structures and co-ordination processes

The next stage of the co-ordination process entails the co-ordination of the positions of the various ministries with an interest in the *dossier*. At the administrative level, the task of ensuring such co-ordination falls to the *Comité Interministériel pour les Questions de Coopération Économique Européenne*, and more specifically, to its Secretariat General, the SGCI. Created in 1948 as a means of resolving the simmering dispute between the Ministries of Finance and Foreign Affairs as to which should be placed in charge of the administration of Marshall Aid, the SGCI is an administrative body with a staff of some 150, of whom 40 are of grade A. It is divided into 'sectors', certain of which—such as that dealing with industry, postal issues, telecommunications, the ECSC, and environmental questions—correspond to the work of several ministries.[2] Heading each sector is a *chef de secteur*, above whom are two *Secrétaires Généraux Adjoints* and a *Secrétaire Général*.

The precise position of the SGCI within the French politico-administrative system has varied over time. For most of its life it has been located within the office of the Prime Minister. Between 1981 and December 1984, however, it was placed under the authority of the Minister Delegate for European Affairs. It was placed back under prime ministerial authority as a result of its inability effectively to foster co-ordination when the link to the Matignon was severed. Indicative of this was the rise in the number of interministerial meetings called: 1,855 in 1982 as opposed to only 1,070 in 1980 (Lequesne 1993: 135). During these years, French positions in Brussels were also marked by an uncharacteristic inconsistency (Simonian 1985: 73).

The effectiveness of the SGCI has also varied as a function of the authority of its Secretary General. Generally, he or she has been a member of the *cabinet* of the Prime Minister and has hence enjoyed substantial political authority. The one exception to this was Élisabeth Guigou, named in November 1985 as both Secretary General and European adviser to the President of the Republic. This move was inspired by a desire to ensure close links between the SGCI and the president during the forthcoming *cohabitation* period, as the presidency enjoys no formal remit over the institution itself.[3]

Indicative of, and fundamental to, the SGCI's central role in EU policy

[2] To improve the links and facilitate co-ordination between the two organizations the sectoral responsibility of advisers in the French Permanent Representation are the same as those adopted in the SGCI.

[3] There is an interesting contrast here with the Secrétariat Général de la Défense Nationale (SGDN). Under the terms of a January 1978 decree, the latter was placed at the disposal of both the President and the Prime Minister. This reflected in part at least fears concerning the possible implications of *cohabitation* on the policy-making process in this sector. No equivalent arrangements have, however, been put into place for the SGCI, despite the fact that experience suggests that *cohabitation* prime ministers are more likely—and more able—to challenge presidential supremacy over European than military affairs.

making is its *de jure* control over contacts between Paris and Brussels. It enjoys a quasi-monopoly over the ability to send instructions to the French Permanent Representation in Brussels. Even when co-ordination is not necessary, that is to say, only one ministry is directly affected by proposed EC legislation, instructions to the Permanent Representation can only be sent via the SGCI, whose *Secrétaire Général* or one of his Adjoints must sign such instructions.[4] Moreover, all correspondence between French authorities and EC institutions is supposed to pass via the SGCI. Indeed, in theory at least, the SGCI exercises a right to control and monitor all meetings between members of the national administration and EC officials.

Routine policy co-ordination proceeds via a highly formalized process. The SGCI, upon receipt of a Commission proposal, circulates it to the ministries concerned, and convenes an interministerial meeting. Such meetings are initially attended by *chefs de Division*, and chaired by a *chef de secteur* from the SGCI. Pressures on the timetables of officials can sometimes mean that ministries send officials who lack either the seniority to take decisions or the technical knowledge to discuss a *dossier* (Boisdeffre et al. 1996: 763). The initial co-ordination meeting is usually held as the Commission proposal is being discussed in Council of Ministers working groups. The volume of Community legislation means that a virtually non-stop process of meetings takes place at the SGCI—around ten per day—each lasting around one to one and a half hours. In addition to this formal system, the SGCI is involved in a huge amount of informal contact with the *services* of relevant ministries by phone and fax.

Roughly one week before ministerial meetings of the Council, a meeting is held at the SGCI under the chairmanship of a *Secrétaire Général Adjoint* with representatives from the *services* of the relevant ministries with the purpose of thrashing out the final French negotiating position. The Ministries of Foreign Affairs and Finances are always present. On average, four or five ministries attend. The number of representatives each sends varies enormously— Finances often sends several, usually from its various European *bureaux*. Agriculture only sends one representative (the Chef du Bureau de l'Union Européenne). Interministerial conflicts generally take the form of Finances against spending ministries.

Should interministerial agreement prove elusive, the Secretary General of the SGCI can play an important role in fostering co-ordination, not least because of the influence derived from his or her position within the Prime Minister's *cabinet*. Guigou proved particularly successful in this regard when promoted, following the end of *cohabitation* in 1988, to the rank of *chargé de mission* in the President's *cabinet*. In contrast, under *cohabitation* the govern-

---

[4] The sole formal exception to this is the CFSP, for which the Coreu telegram system, based within the Quai d'Orsay, is utilized.

ment tried to limit direct contact with Guigou and communicated directly instead with the Assistant Secretaries General, and in particular with Pierre Sellal (Lequesne 1993: 107).

Since the ratification of the Maastricht Treaty, interministerial co-ordination has been extended to the second and third pillars of the EU. Thus, a circular from the Prime Minister dated 21 March 1994 specified that the Foreign Ministry must consult 'the competent ministries' when 'the implementation of a common action implies the adoption of national measures of a financial character'. When common actions call upon community instruments or policies, it is up to the SGCI to assure interministerial co-ordination. Furthermore, the security aspects of the CFSP imply the need for close co-operation with the Defence Ministry, which is officially associated with certain working groups (nuclear proliferation) and regularly consulted.

As far as Justice and Home Affairs is concerned, a co-ordinator of 'Internal Affairs and Justice' was, after the ratification of the TEU, attached to the Secretary General of the SGCI, allowing for interministerial treatment of those issues which require it. Because of the need for secrecy on certain delicate issues such as terrorism and drugs, a prime ministerial circular of 21 March 1994 stated that 'coopération opérationnelle' was excluded from SGCI's co-ordination remit. The Internal Affairs and Justice Co-ordinator was also placed in charge of the application of the Schengen agreements. He holds the title of *chargé de mission* so as to avoid overt rivalry with the Quai d'Orsay which had created its own structures to deal with Schengen, but is, in reality, a third Assistant Secretary General. He is a prefect who oversees five collaborators (from Justice, the Gendarmerie, the Police, Customs, and the Quai d'Orsay) and works closely with the two members of staff of the Permanent Representation who deal with the sector.

Recent years have thus witnessed the gradual extension of the highly formalized administrative co-ordination process. In general, the system has worked well, with interministerial agreement reached via the SGCI in over 90 per cent of cases. There is little question that France has suffered less from the appearance of contradictory national positions within the Council than have some of its partners (interviews, Brussels, 1997). For all this, however, certain failings of this system can be identified

First, those ministries that have the most frequent dealings with the EU have done the most to reinforce their autonomy from interministerial co-ordination procedures. The Ministry of Agriculture, for instance, possesses its own *Bureau des Affaires Juridiques Européennes*, freeing it from the dependence endured by other sectoral ministries on the *Direction des Affaires Juridiques* of the Foreign Ministry or the *Section Juridique* of the SGCI for expertise on European legal matters. Agriculture, moreover, is dealt with by a *Délégué pour les Affaires Agricoles* in the Permanent Representation, who is the sole French spokesman on the Special Committee for

Agriculture and who enjoys far greater autonomy than his colleagues (Lequesne 1993: 199).

The process by which the Ministry of Agriculture formulates its policies towards the EU, moreover, reduces the scope for prospective co-ordinators to question its decisions. On Thursday mornings, a video conference takes place between officials from the Ministry and the French representative on the SCA. At the SGCI meeting later that day which plans the French position for the Special Committee on Agriculture on Monday and Tuesday, Ministry of Agriculture officials have therefore discussed their preferences in detail and are armed with the necessary technical information to defend them. Other ministries often do not receive all the necessary information until the Wednesday evening, and are hence less able to impose their own view. Thus whilst the co-ordination process resembles those in other sectors in form, the information advantages enjoyed by what is effectively the lead ministry militate against effective co-ordination over the substance of policies.

Nor is it in the interest of those ministries who want to limit agricultural spending to appeal to the political level by blocking agreement in the SGCI. The high political salience of agricultural policy means that the ministry has little to fear from the politicization of the co-ordination process. Political leaders and their *cabinet* advisers are more preoccupied by the political consequences of decisions than by questions of financial efficiency, a fact particularly true of a right-wing government dependent on agricultural votes. Given this, the departmental interests of the Agriculture Ministry are likely to be furthered should co-ordination at the administrative level fail. Thus for all the strengths of the highly formalized routine co-ordination system, agriculture has managed to retain a good deal of autonomy and a disproportionate weight.

In contrast, for the Ministry of Finance effective interministerial co-ordination represents a useful means of preventing spending ministries from introducing ambitious, expensive proposals into EC debates. Members of the Ministry are keen to stress the central importance of the SGCI and to underline the importance of interministerial procedures. They also emphasize the necessity of the SGCI representative at the Permanent Representation closely monitoring French initiatives to ensure that co-ordination procedures have been respected. Such is the perceived importance the SGCI for Finances that, in marked contrast to the system employed by the Ministry of Agriculture, all contact with the *Agent Financière* in the French Permanent Representation in Brussels is conducted via the SGCI on the video conferencing facilities of the latter.

Yet whilst the Ministry of Finance is keen to preach the value of co-ordination when this suits its own interests, it has refused to accept its necessity in cases where this might limit its own autonomy. Thus the *Directeur du Trésor* is charged with communicating French instructions to and representing France within the EC's monetary committee—a procedure which, uniquely, does not involve the SGCI, despite the obvious (and, in the context of EMU in particular, wide-ranging) interministerial implications of the decisions arrived at. The increasing centrality of EMU and financial matters in general on the Community agenda has resulted in a growth in the role of the finance ministries throughout Western Europe an a concomitant decrease in the influence of foreign ministries.

A second failing of co-ordination processes is a tendency of the SGCI system to arrive at somewhat formalistic resolutions of interministerial disputes. Because of its lack of political clout, the SGCI has a tendency to adopt the practice of 'splitting the difference' as a means of reconciling interministerial squabbles. Thus if a spending ministry requests approval for a proposal requiring a French contribution of x francs, and is faced by objections from Finance which wishes to limit spending to y francs, a frequently used ploy is to compromise at a figure of $(x + y)/2$. This tendency is linked to the inability of the SGCI to undertake strategic assessments of France's European Union policies and of the relative merits of various policy options. It also reflects the relative lack of contact between the individual *chefs de secteur*. Co-ordination thus occurs in the absence of any clear sense of which EC programmes should take priority over others.

Should co-ordination at the administrative level prove unsuccessful, the SGCI sends details of all continuing disagreements to the Prime Minister's Office. On receipt of these details, the member of the Prime Minister's *cabinet* charged with European questions asks the *Secrétariat Général du Gouvernement* to arrange an interministerial meeting. The SGG on occasion (though rarely) advises that ministries not originally invited to the SGCI discussions should be invited to the Matignon meetings. A member of the President's *cabinet* is also invited to attend. The *chefs de cabinet* decide who should attend. A member of the Minister's *cabinet* and a member of the *services* usually attend such meetings. On some occasions, when the matter under discussion is particularly sensitive, meetings can be limited to *cabinet* members only. The SGCI is also represented (by a Secrétaire Général Adjoint on those occasions when the Secretary General is acting in his capacity as a member of the Prime Minster's *cabinet*). The Matignon meeting reopens the whole *dossier*, rather than taking up where the SGCI process had left off. Indeed these meetings are never held in the SGCI precisely to underline the separation between the political and administrative processes. Consequently it can be the case that previously agreed-upon ministerial positions may shift significantly, with or without the *ex ante* express approval of the Direction concerned.

Several meetings are often necessary before an interministerial position can be arrived at. When this is achieved, a selective *compte rendu* (detailing the agreements reached) then becomes a *Note Bleu du Matignon* (*bleu*) which is binding on all ministries. On those occasions when agreement proves elusive even at the *cabinet* level, the matter can be referred to the ministerial level, in which case the *Secrétaire Général du Gouvernement* himself takes over the *dossier*. A ministerial meeting was needed to decide on the French position relative to the EC budget for both 1997 and 1998. Even when inter-ministerial positions are adopted following political intervention, formal instructions to the Permanent Representation are still sent by the SGCI to the Permanent Representation in Brussels and to all French ambassadors in EU member states.

The presidency usually has no direct role in even politicized co-ordination of routine policy, though it is represented by a member of the President's *cabinet* who will, on occasion, make the preferences of the Élysée clear. Sporadically, however, presidential involvement can be more direct. On the exhaust emissions *dossier*, pressure from the Élysée on the government was intense. Mitterrand, having been briefed by Kohl earlier that year as to the importance of the issue for the Federal Republic, was anxious, despite the reservations of sectoral ministries, that the issue should not be allowed to sour bilateral relations with Bonn. Individual ministers who, dissatisfied with the process of co-ordination, appeal directly to the Élysée can also bring the presidency directly into the co-ordination process. Close personal links with the President constitute an important resource for ministers on such occasions.

Under the first *cohabitation* of 1986–8, co-ordination procedures were somewhat different. Because of the tense relations between the Prime Minister and the Secretary General of the SGCI, the Prime Minister's *cabinet*, directed by Maurice Lurich, intervened more frequently than had previously been the case, thereby exacerbating the *décalage* between political and admin-istrative co-ordination. Between March and December 1986, Yves Thibault de Silguy (European adviser in Chirac's *cabinet*) presided over ninety-one infor-mal interministerial meetings. Informality averted the need either to issue formal invitations (notably to the Secretary General of the SGCI) or to produce *comptes rendu*, allowing the government to marginalize the presi-dency. On other occasions, the Prime Minister himself chaired meetings of *comités restreints* with ministers and *Directeurs de cabinet* to which Guigou was not always invited. For all this, Guigou was necessarily informed of the outcome of such meetings via the circulation of a *bleu* to SGCI (Lequesne 1993: 157–8).

Despite the unique position of the SGCI during the first *cohabitation*, co-ordination still occurred between the President and Prime Minister over issues where agreement could not be reached at the administrative level. This was achieved through the development of an informal network of officials con-sisting of Pierre de Boissieu, head of the Foreign Ministry's SCE, Guigou, François Scheer, Yves de Silguy, and Emmanuel Rodocanachi from Chirac's staff, Claude Villain of Balladur's cabinet, and a senior official from the

Ministry of Agriculture. The SCE provided a neutral venue for such informal meetings, the SGCI being clearly unsuitable (Guyomarch 1993: 476).

EU policy of course includes far more than the positions adopted by France within the Council of Ministers. Bilateral meetings between ministers and their foreign equivalents can have an impact on community business. In some cases, given that ministers do not always see fit to consult with the SGCI, the outcomes of such bilateral meetings are seen to conflict with French positions in EC or to raise doubts on the part of other ministries. When this occurs, a Secrétaire Général Adjoint initiates a process of *ex post facto* co-ordination. Matignon is informed and a retrospective, fire-fighting process of interministerial meetings is started.

A final element of co-ordination at the political level is the Foreign Ministry. The European Affairs Minister, usually placed under the Foreign Minister, plays a co-ordination role in pointing out possible contradictions between positions adopted via the SGCI and other elements of European policy such as ministerial initiatives or bilateral relations. The argument used by his *cabinet* is that his *vision globale* of European policy allows him to perform this task (interviews, Paris, 1997). The influence of this Minister varies according to his formal position—whether a *Ministre Délégué*, Minister of State, or full ministerial appointment. André Chandernagor was given the task of simply following (through delegation by the Foreign Minister) questions related to the application of the EC Treaties (Lequesne 1993: 62). In contrast, his successor Roland Dumas, like Edith Cresson in 1988, was given the status of a full minister, and hence not subordinated to the Foreign Minister. Cresson took the symbolic step of moving her offices from the Quai d'Orsay to emphasize the point. A European Affairs Minister who enjoys close links with the Élysée may well also enjoy additional weight (as was arguably the case with Guigou after 1990). This can also lead to tensions with the Foreign Minister as happened between Michel Barnier and Hervé de Charette (interviews, Paris, 1997, and Brussels, 1997).

Whilst again the evidence seems to suggest that co-ordination at the political level functions relatively well in the sense that agreement is ultimately reached, the system is not without its drawbacks. For one thing, certain officials have complained that (as intimated above in the discussion of agriculture) co-ordination at the political level is too often based on short term political considerations rather than the need to promote French interests within, or strategy towards, the EU (interviews, Paris, 1997). Still others have bemoaned the fact that officials tend to resort too quickly to political intervention when administrative co-ordination proves difficult to achieve. Moreover, the role of ministerial *cabinets* remains somewhat ambiguous. Their interventions often takes the form of telephone consultations between *cabinet* members, leading to tensions with officials who have worked on particular *dossiers* for some considerable time. Such tensions can be exacerbated by the fact that the *cabinets* on occasion act in the manner of officials rather than political appointees, intervening on points of technical detail rather than providing an overall strategic direction (Arnould 1992: 462–4).

The role of Parliament

The National Assembly and the Senate play only a very limited role in the formulation of French positions on EC legislation.[5] In 1979, Parliamentary Delegations for the European Communities were created in both houses. These, however, were entrusted only with the limited role of following European legislation and keeping Parliament informed about developments. Therefore, they did not enjoy the kind of influence wielded by the permanent parliamentary commissions limited in number by the constitution to six.[6] Each delegation is composed of eighteen members, with membership initially forbidden for MEPs holding a dual mandate. Although these arrangements were modified in 1990, the increased activity of the delegations in terms of their regular production of reports and the lifted restrictions on MEP participation did not imply a greater role in deciding on French European policy (Guyomarch 1993: 469).

Partly as a response to calls by the EUT for greater parliamentary involvement in European affairs, a constitutional amendment of 25 June 1992 (Article 88-4 of the new title XIV of the constitution) attempted to enhance parliamentary control over proposed EU legislation. It stipulated that Commission proposals should be sent to the Conseil d'État, which would decide if these had legislative implications. Should this be the case, the Assembly and Senate were to be automatically informed.[7] Parliament was empowered to vote resolutions on such proposed legislation. For all this, however a prime ministerial circular of 19 July 1994 stated that whilst the government would wait for a parliamentary vote prior to voting in the Council of Ministers, it would not be bound by it. French representatives in Brussels could participate in Council of Ministers debates before Parliament delivered its verdict. More-

---

[5] '[t]he Fifth Republic has made of Europe another step on the pedestal which elevates presidential and governmental authority, and a way of further diminishing assemblies already resigned to their humiliation. The will of the Élysée dominates entirely, behind a smoke-screen of words about democratic legitimacy and respect for the rights of Parliament. The more power is exercised in Brussels . . . the less it is in the Palais Bourbon and the Palais du Luxembourg' (see Petot 1993).

[6] Interestingly, the debates in Parliament about the creation of these delegations revealed widely different conceptions as to their proper role. The Gaullists and Communists had insisted on the need for powerful committees able to scrutinize all proposals for European legislation (see Guyomarch 1993: 469).

[7] The text of the Avis of the Conseil d'État, hence the justification for the decision made, is not, however, transmitted to Parliament (see Lequesne 1993: 111).

over, the relative rapidity of some EC negotiations means that Parliament often simply does not enjoy the time to consider proposed legislation in detail. Thus, in 1993 and 1994, 100 proposals for Community legislation were submitted to Parliament. In 13 cases, Parliament had less than a fortnight between receipt of the proposal and its adoption as law by the EC. In 24 cases, transmission of Commission proposals to the National Assembly occurred either after EC adoption or on the same day (Boisdeffre et al. 1996: 766). Finally, even these relatively weak powers do not apply either to the second and third pillars, to interinstitutional agreements, or to EMU.

Non-routine Co-ordination

Whilst the bulk of 'EU policy' consists of routine matters in the various sectoral councils, it also comprises more set-piece decision making involving routine and substantial involvement on the part of political leaders. Such issues are not confined solely to what Derlien (this volume) refers to as polity-building measures (or IGCs), but also include the preparation of and participation in European councils, the organization of the French presidency of the Council of Ministers

Given the position of the President of the Republic at the summit of the French political system (a position rendered somewhat ambiguous in times of *cohabitation*), elements of French EU policy are handled by the Élysée alone, without reference to, let alone co-ordination with, other elements of the core executive. De Gaulle's European initiatives, such as his brusque rejection of the first British application for membership, often shocked his (previously uninformed) government. Pompidou's Prime Minister heard about the President's agreement to lift the veto on British entry on the television.[8] Prime Minister Chirac claimed only to have heard about the decision to introduce direct elections to the European Parliament at the same time as his ministerial colleagues (Wright 1990: 57–8). Yet for all this, even in those areas of EU policy making where the executive enjoys clear predominance, procedures—often informal—have been put into place to ensure effective co-ordination between the various actors who have come to be involved.

European councils

Co-ordination procedures for European councils represent something of a hybrid of procedures for routine and non-routine issues. Thus, the role of the

---

[8] Indeed, Jean-Louis Gergorin, a Foreign Ministry official, stated simply that under Pompidou, 'all European matters were judged at the Élysée' (see Simonian 1985: 72).

SGCI in preparing for European councils is very similar to that for the normal work of the Council of Ministers, in that *dossiers* are discussed at interministerial co-ordination meetings. Unlike the process for routine matters, however, a meeting at the Élysée, which is attended by, amongst others, the French Permanent Representative, precedes European councils. The Secrétaire Général of the SGCI attends European Councils and either he or a member of the Permanent Representation takes handwritten notes. These, as well as the formal conclusions of a summit are transferred back to the SGCI and circulated amongst the relevant ministries by the Secrétaires Généraux Adjoints.

Unlike routine policy, European Councils involve the direct participation of the leaders of the political executive. This can cause problems of co-ordination between political leaders and technical ministers, especially when technical issues on which agreement cannot be reached in the Council of Ministers are 'referred upstairs' for discussion at the heads of state and government level. At the European Council meeting at London in November 1991, agriculture was one such subject. Mitterrand finally arrived at a broad agreement with Schmidt whereby France compromised on cereal prices, the Federal Republic on soya. The President confided to Edith Cresson, then Agriculture Minister, the task of hammering out the details that night. By the next morning, the whole package deal had fallen through as Cresson, defending her sectoral interests, refused to grant the concessions to which her President had earlier agreed. As one close observer put it: 'The lesson will be remembered: never take technical Ministers to a European summit' (Attali 1993: 203–4).

The French presidency

On those occasions when France holds the presidency of the Council of Ministers, this also produces slightly different forms of co-ordination from those associated with routine policy. It is the Élysée which defines the overall priorities of a French presidency. However, the President and his advisers rely heavily on the SGCI to carry out the administrative work involved. It is up to the SGCI, together with a senior official from the Quai d'Orsay, to set the calendar for forthcoming Councils of Ministers, to draw up a list of working groups that could be convoked and to select officials who could preside over such group (Lequesne 1993: 114–16). Presidencies thus represent perhaps the only occasion on which the French administrative and political authorities undertake in unison a sustained phase of strategic planning concerning France's European policy objectives (Boisdeffre et al. 1996: 760).

Yet Lequesne paints a picture of increasing presidential domination over the process of defining priorities for French presidencies. For the 1979 presidency, the SGCI was the forum within which initial priorities were thrashed out, via interministerial meetings. In 1984 and especially 1989, Mitterrand's entourage steadily increased its influence over this process. Indeed, in August 1988, Guigou simply informed the assistant Secretaries General and *chefs de secteur* as to what French priorities were. The SGCI was left with the task of informing the various ministries and preparing the detailed arrangements for the next sixth months.

Intergovernmental conferences

Finally, we turn to polity building *strictu sensu*. The recent spate of Inter-governmental Conferences (IGCs)—of 1985, 1991, and 1996—has witnessed the emergence of novel forms of co-ordination in France, as the core executive takes charge of French negotiations regarding the EC's constitutional future. On matters pertaining to IGCs, the President comes to the fore as the ultimate decision maker and, if need be, co-ordinator. However, the President and his staff do engage in co-ordination, if only with the Prime Minister and the Foreign Ministry.

During the Maastricht negotiations, only a small number of actors were involved. At the political level, these were Mitterrand, Dumas (Foreign Minister), Bérégovoy (Minister of Finance), and Guigou (Minister for European Affairs). At the administrative level, certain officials of the rank of Directeur d'Administration participated. Notable amongst these were: Pierre de Boisseau (personal representative of Dumas during negotiations), Jean-Claude Trichet (Directeur du Trésor and personnel representative of Bérégovoy during the IGC on EMU), Bernard Vial, Secretary General of the SGCI, and Jean Vidal, Permanent Representative in Brussels. In addition, high-ranking *cabinet* members were also involved, notably: Hubert Vedrine (Secretary General of the Élysée), Pierre Morel (Conseiller Diplomatique at the Élysée), Caroline de Margerie (European adviser in Mitterrand's *cabinet*), Jean-Michel Casa (of Dumas's *cabinet*), and Pierre Vimont (of Guigou's *cabinet*) (Lequesne 1993: 179–80).

Caroline de Margerie was instrumental in organizing the negotiations. She organized fortnightly meetings of these officials at the Élysée, drew up notes for the President, and prepared *conseils restreints* to keep key ministers up to date with the state of negotiations. In addition, she prepared notes for the President on the two heads of state and government summits that took place during the negotiations. These were also attended by Dumas at Luxembourg, and Dumas and Bérégovoy at Maastricht, where finance ministers were, exceptionally, allowed to participate in the discussion over EMU (Lequesne 1993: 180–1). Details concerning France's stance on institutional questions were drawn up in the Foreign Ministry's SCE, under directives issued by Pierre de

Boisseau, Directeur des Affaires Économiques et Financières (Lequesne 1993: 181–2).

During the Maastricht II IGC, many aspects of the French position were again drawn up in the Foreign Ministry. During the work of the reflection group, the Élysée was only minimally involved, though the President was kept informed of progress. Michel Barnier, Minister for European Affairs, represented France during these preliminary negotiations. Once the President intervened more directly, he did not do so in isolation. Chirac's position paper of December 1995 was prepared in the Quai d'Orsay and involved careful consultation on a personal, informal level, between the Minister of European Affairs, the Foreign Minister, the Matignon, and the Élysée. The system of co-ordination involved frequent informal consultations between the highly limited number of actors involved in the process. The Matignon, Élysée, and Quai d'Orsay kept in regular contact by telephone about matters related to the IGC (interviews, Paris, 1995, 1997).

Another striking feature about the Maastricht II IGC was the fact that those directly involved had substantial experience of European affairs and had worked together in the past, either in the SGCI, the Quai, or the Permanent Representation in Brussels. Indeed, one reason why the French negotiating stance remained as consistent as it did even after the election of the Jospin government was that the new Prime Minister's adviser on European questions was a member of this tightly knit group. Indeed, the Socialists had maintained informal contact with those in the administration working on European affairs prior to the election.

Unlike in the cases of the SEA and TEU Maastricht II involved more formalized co-ordination, such as the regular meetings chaired by Michel Barnier and involving advisers to the Prime Minister and President during the work of the Reflection Group. Once the actual negotiations had started, these meetings were co-chaired by Barnier and de Charette. In addition, ministries were invited to meetings at *cabinet* or ministerial level, to discuss French proposals (on Fridays), but these tended to be largely 'rubber stamping affairs',[9] rather than an arena for real policy formulation, held simply as a way of informing ministers about initiatives that were planned. Be this as it may, this in itself marked an increase in co-ordination activity from what was the case under Mitterrand, when sectoral ministries were effectively shut out of the negotiations.

Initially, the SGCI played virtually no role in the co-ordination of policy for the 1996 IGC. Its role was limited to being asked by the Matignon or sectoral ministries to carry out studies on various aspects of European policy related to the negotiations. Thus in the spring of 1996 Juppé asked his adviser on European questions, Jean Cadet, who was also Secretary General of the

---

[9] The phrase is that of a member of Barnier's *cabinet*. Interview, Paris, June 1997.

SGCI, to prepare a paper on currency fluctuations and the impact of competitive devaluations. Cadet entrusted this task to the SGCI, whose report was circulated amongst all the member states.

Problems of co-ordination become apparent, however, in attempts to separate institutional and policy questions. The SGCI repeatedly complained that institutional matters such as QMV entailed significant implications for policy and therefore should not be treated independently of interministerial co-ordination mechanisms. The system of keeping the SGCI out of the process also came under pressure as the agenda of the IGC shifted. The French initially wanted to limit negotiations to purely institutional questions. However, pressure from the other states led to increasing incorporation of discussions on policy areas such as social policy and environmental questions.

The SGCI became more involved in the IGC from around March 1996. At this time, it was invited to attend (in the person of a Secrétaire Général Adjoint) the weekly Friday meeting at the Matignon involving the Foreign Minister, European Affairs Minister, the Prime Minister's adviser on European affairs, and on occasion his counterpart from the Élysée. The *bleus* that emerged from these meetings increasingly came to refer to the positions adopted by the SGCI. In addition, the SGCI hosted regular meetings of members of the *services* of ministries to discuss IGC-related issues. These sometimes occurred as often as twice a week. Evidence of the rivalry that can exist for prominence in co-ordinating policy was provided by the Foreign Ministry which initially practised, in the words of one SGCI official, a 'politique de la chaise vide' at these meetings.[10] The SGCI still, however, had no input into major presidential initiatives such as the document circulated by Chirac in December 1995. When an Assistant Secretary General pointed out that the paper raised certain problems in terms of possible implications for sectoral ministries, he was brusquely informed that he had no role in discussions of presidential initiatives (interviews, SGCI, 1997).

One of the striking features of the IGC was thus the *décalage* between the organs of technical co-ordination and political initiatives. Although, the technical nature of some of the issues discussed at IGCs can require detailed, technical cross-sectoral knowledge of the kind that the SGCI can supply, the latter enjoys no formalized role as a strategic thinker in the context of IGCs. As a consequence, political initiatives can on occasion be nonsensical. A case in point was a French proposal during the IGC for the introduction of QMV on Justice and Home Affairs, which would remain a separate pillar. The French faced the humiliation of having it explained to them that this could not happen unless the policy area were subject to the checks and balances

---

[10] Foreign Ministry staff, when interviewed, tried, virtually without exception, to play down the role of the SGCI. One member of the European Minister's *cabinet* stated that the SGCI had no role as far as 'real policy' was concerned.

imposed by the Court and Parliament within the first pillar. Whilst such thinking is mere speculation, it is reasonable to suppose that a more systematic inclusion of those officials who deal with the EC on a day-to-day basis in the preparation of such French initiatives could prevent such humiliating occurrences.

A final interesting aspect of the Amsterdam IGC was the light it threw on the problems that can arise as a result of personal difficulties. Barnier and de Charette competed openly for influence during the negotiations, souring relations to the point where even the two *cabinets* failed to communicate satisfactorily. Barnier enjoyed close relations with the President, which gave him the ability to compete with his ministerial senior. The situation was further complicated not only by the tendency of the Élysée to come out with unilateral initiatives without prior consultation, but also by the decision to remove the Head of the European Affairs section of the Foreign Ministry, Pierre Sellal, only months prior to the Amsterdam summit. As a result of such difficulties, informed observers in Brussels pointed to the incoherence of much of the French negotiating strategy and to the absence of effective co-ordination.

Conclusions

The response of the French politico-administrative system to the demands of European integration has been far-reaching. Virtually all aspects of this system have had to adapt as a result of French participation in the EC/EU. Adaptation, moreover, is a continuous process, with institutional tinkering and prime ministerial circulars forming an almost routine part of France's administrative response. France enjoys several clear advantages over some of its EC partners in terms of its ability effectively to co-ordinate its policies. It is a relatively centralized state, facing none of the problems with subnational governments that confront the Belgian central authorities (Kerremans, this volume). Core executive freedom of manoeuvre is further enhanced by the relative weakness of Parliament on matters of EC policy and by the existence of a broad political consensus on Europe, sparing the government the need continually to canvass political opinion when formulating policy. Perhaps unsurprisingly, therefore, the French co-ordination system in general has worked fairly well. France possesses in the SGCI a small, highly efficient centre of expertise on EC affairs that is the envy of many other member states. It has succeeded in imposing a degree of consistency on French positions in the Council. It is no coincidence that Paris has consistently been one of the prime shapers of the integration process.

For all this, however, there is evidence that at least two of the potential hurdles to co-ordination mentioned in the introduction have limited the effectiveness of the co-ordination system. For one thing, the relative autonomy enjoyed by certain powerful ministries undermines the ability of organs such as the SGCI to bring about effective (as opposed to apparent) co-ordination. Both the Ministry of Agriculture and the Ministry of Finance have retained significant autonomy and manage to avoid being subjected to meaningful interministerial co-ordination.

Second, French EU policy-making process is characterized by a significant *décalage* between the administrative and political levels. This is particularly apparent in so far as non-routine policy is concerned. The SGCI has only recently taken an active part in the preparation of France's positions for IGCs, and even then this role has been distinctly (and explicitly) limited. Vertical separation also applies, however, to more routine matters of policy. Several officials complained in interviews about the ambiguity of the role of *cabinets*, which often interfere on purely technical issues, whilst claiming to act with political weight.

One potentially damaging consequence of this is that France's efforts to define clear and coherent positions for the forthcoming reform of Community institutions and policies prefigured in the Commissions Agenda 2000 document will be limited. Whilst the co-ordination system in place ensures co-ordination over individual Commission proposals quite effectively, it lacks the ability to combine political bargaining with technical expertise, to arrive at package deals across numerous sectors, and to control the influence of powerful Ministries with long traditions of dealing with Brussels. In the face of such challenges, the French system for co-ordinating EU policy may well need to be adapted yet again.

References

Arnould, C. F. (1992), 'L'Interpénétration des affaires communautaires et des domaines de la coopération politique', *Revue française d'administration publique*, 63: 461–4.

Attali, J. (1993), *Verbatim 1: Chronique des années 1981–1986. Première Partie* (Paris: Fayard).

Boisdeffre, M. de, et al. (1996), 'Le Travail gouvernemental et l'Europe', in D. Laurent and M. Sanson (eds.), *Le Travail gouvernemental* (Paris: La Documentation Française).

Guyomarch, A. (1993), 'The European Effect: Improving French Policy Co-ordination', *Staatswissenschaften und Staatspraxis*, 43: 455–78.

Lequesne, C. (1993), *Paris–Bruxelles: Comment se fait la politique européenne de la France* (Paris: Presses de la Fondation Nationale des Sciences Politiques).

Ministère de l'Agriculture (1996), 'L'Élaboration de la position française en matière de la PAC', internal document.

Petot, Jean (1993), 'L'Europe, la France et son Président', *Revue du droit public* (Mar.–Apr.), 325–96.

Potocki, A. (1992), 'La Mise en place du service des affaires européennes au Ministère de la Justice', *Revue française d'administration publique*, 63: 464–7.

Premier Ministre (1994), *Circulaire du 21 mars 1994 relative aux relations entre les administrations françaises et les institutions de L'Union Européenne* (Paris: Premier Ministre).

Simonian, H. (1985), *The Privileged Partnership: Franco-German Relations in the European Community 1969–1984* (Oxford: Oxford University Press).

Wright, V. (1990), *The Government and Politics of France* (London: Unwin Hyman).

4

Italy

*Giacinto della Cananea**

Introduction

The frequent failures of Italian policies concerning the European Union (EU) have become, in some cases, a European problem, giving rise to debate about the necessary remedies. Although other member states frequently face similar problems, there is a twofold difference between Italy and the other countries: first, of scale, and second of the nature of the interests concerned, since many of the complaints about Italy concern EU policies which provide Italy with financial benefits. A double contradiction thus arises between the interests of the EU (as happens also in the case of regulatory policies limiting national autonomy) and national interests (as stressed by Cassese 1985).

These problems raise some interesting questions: for instance, are the policy failures a consequence of treating European integration as a relatively minor issue in spite of the diffuse pro-integration attitude constantly shown by public opinion? Or are they the result of the lack of co-ordination tools and processes, so well defined elsewhere and so often requested or promised at the institutional and political level in Italy? A careful consideration of these questions can also shed some light on the broader issue of co-ordination of public policies in a fragmented polity.

The Failures of EU Policy Making in Italy

Let us start by identifying and measuring the phenomenon. For this purpose, three general indicators may prove useful: Italy's record in the transposition and implementation of EC directives, violations of EC law, and the use of EC funds.

* The author wishes to thank Professor Sabino Cassese for his useful comments on an earlier draft of this chapter.

The most recent data available on implementing directives cover the years 1993–7 (EC 1998). They show, first, that Italy has the most cases (8 out of 32 in 1993 and still 11 out of 104 in 1997) in which internal measures are in contravention of EC directives. Italy has also led in inadequate implementation (16 out of 121 in 1993 and 24 out of 211 in 1997; France then took the 'lead', with 44 cases). This, of course, is but a quantitative element, which needs a more accurate evaluation. Attention should also be paid to the relative gravity of the infractions. Two examples are illuminating. First, the European Court of Justice (ECJ), besides affirming the doctrine of direct applicability of directives (whose term of transposition has expired), holds that public administrations are obliged not to implement national legislation contradicting such directives (*Fratelli Costanzo* judgment of 1988). Second, in 1991, the inadequate transposition by Italy of the directive on the protection of workers induced the ECJ to adopt the much discussed *Francovich* judgment, affirming state liability for failure to fulfil the duties stemming from the EC directives.[1]

What is even more evident is the poor performance which emerges when the more general problem of violations of EC law is considered. In this respect, Italy is almost alone in the number of actions begun by the Commission, which are the first step of the procedure (102 cases in 1994, when Portugal and Greece had 96 actions, France and Germany 90, and the UK only 73). There were 75 cases in 1996, when only Finland and Austria, who had just joined the EC, performed worse. In addition, Italy received by far the highest number of reasoned opinions (49 in 1993, when Greece had 40 and France 40; 36 in 1995, when Greece had 26 and Portugal 22; 71 the following year, when the other two states had, respectively, 51 and 49). Last but not least, there are a high number of actions brought against Italy before the ECJ (12 out of 89 in 1994, second only to the 17 of Greece, but 17 out of 72 in 1995, when Greece had 12 and Germany 10, and 20 out of 121 in 1997, when Germany had 19 and Belgium 18). This means that, if the distinct phases are considered as a whole, the high number of open procedures often results not only in reasoned opinions, but also in actions before the ECJ, where, it ought to be added, Italy has had poor outcomes (in 1993, the Commission won on 6 occasions out of 6 and these actions were one-fifth of the whole; in 1994, in 12 out of 13, almost half the cases; in 195, in 2 out of 3). Therefore, often, if not always, conflict proceeded without sound argument.

Italy's use of structural funds, and Community money in general, presents an even worse picture. First, for the period 1994–9, the expenditure used amounted to only 15 per cent in 1996 and 38 per cent in 1997—that effectively paid was even less—and the Commission declared that it was ready to divert these finds to member states such as Ireland or Spain which would use

[1] The judgment was delivered on 19 Nov. 1992, in the joined cases C-6/90 and 9/90. See, on this point, Caranta 1995 and Harlow 1996.

them more efficiently. The target for 1998 was 55 per cent. Second, in spite of wide-scale investigations, fraud against the EC budget is still high (Italy, in 1997, was second for both the number of frauds and their amount).

These data are not unrepresentative, or surprising. Indeed, in 1991 an official document produced by the Senate, as a result of a parliamentary inquiry, illustrated an impressive number of difficulties in Italian EU policy, ranging from conflicts of power to lack of coherence of action carried out and to dissipation of financial resources. These conclusions were confirmed two years later by another document, this time published by the Dipartimento della Funzione Pubblica (a branch of the Presidency of the Council of Ministers) where, for the first time, the serious problems concerning EC policy making (included those of personnel) were considered from the broader perspective of administrative reforms (Senato 1991; Presidenza 1993).

At the dawn of the millennium, these problems are considered to be so serious that they are deemed to require not simply administrative changes, but a reform of Italy's Constitution. However, the efforts of a parliamentary commission charged with formulating proposals for amending the Constitution, which declared an intention to introduce provisions into the constitution creating a foundation for Italy's EU membership, ended in failure just as its predecessors had done in 1983 and 1993.[2]

The Importance of the EU in Law and Policy Making in Italy

Disagreement over how these problems should be remedied leads to a broader issue, namely the importance of EU law and policies. Such failings could in principle be due to a lack of importance attached to EU membership or opposition to it, but neither is true of Italy. Not only is there widespread awareness of the importance of the EU and strong popular support for deepening integration, but Italy is rare among the member states for the scope and intensity of both. This can be illustrated by consideration of the legal implications of EC law, and the policies produced on that basis.

Curiously, the implications of EC law have often been overlooked by the extensive literature on European integration. Indeed, legal studies have focused on the connections, and conflicts, between the European and Italian legal sources. By concentrating on formal features, they have lost sight, until recently, of the content of EC law and its implications. Moreover, lawyers have paid greater attention to the rules applicable to EC institutions than to those which they themselves have created (Cassese 1995). At the same time,

---

[2] For a discussion of these proposals see Faro 1997.

political scientists have overlooked not only the binding effects of EC law on domestic policies, but also, more generally, administrative action (their analysis being limited to Parliament and political parties). The fundamental importance played by European integration is more likely to be properly appreciated if considered from both a political and a legal perspective. Membership of the ECSC, for example, was a highly political decision with far-reaching legal consequences.

The decision was highly political because it was taken quickly (as Alcide De Gasperi requested) by the executive with little or no attention to economic and other technical aspects. The aim was to strengthen Italy's place among the Western European countries, as opposed to the growing Eastern bloc (the same applies for NATO and the Council of Europe). This decision was characterized, on the one hand, by the strong influence exerted by the teleology of supranationality (the EC being seen as a means for 'an ever closer Union', capable of eliminating conflicts among European peoples),[3] and on the other hand by not being a bipartisan choice. Indeed, both right- and left-wing oppositions voted (for purely ideological reasons) against ratification of that treaty and the same thing happened when the Treaty of Rome was ratified. Even in 1979, when Italy's entry into the European Monetary System was debated, the strong Communist Party (PCI) voted against it, while the Socialist Party abstained from voting.

The legal consequences of involvement with Europe also were serious. On a formal level, accepting the ECSC implied accepting a clear transfer of sovereign powers (as provided by Article 11 of the Constitution, on which the entire process of integration has rested since 1952) (De Vergottini 1967; Cassese 1992; Greco 1998). On a substantial level, this also meant accepting both the market economy and its rules. To make this point clearer, it is necessary to explain that the Italian Constitution, adopted fifty years earlier (1948), is not based on market principles (strongly opposed, in fact, by the prevailing political forces, inspired by Catholic and collectivist theories). Rather, it recognizes the private sector's right to carry out economic activities, as long as it does not harm social utility. Moreover, the Constitution says nothing about free competition; there are no rules against monopolies or dominant positions. Indeed, the Constitution is so concerned with market failures as to provide that a good therapy for the negative effects of private monopolies may be replacing them with public monopolies (Amato 1991; Irti 1998). Accordingly, the economic policies adopted since have been based on

---

[3] This emerges clearly in Alcide de Gasperi's speech to the Senate on the ratification of the ECSC (8 Aug. 1951; doc. n.182 in *Le leggi*, 1952: 1587). See also the documents relating to the ratification of the EEC and Euratom Treaties in *Le leggi*, 1957: 1516 and Santoro (1989), Einaudi's essay (1988) on a future European federation and Spinelli's memoirs (1990–1) offer instructive insights on this position. Among the more recent literature on the subject, see Romano (1997).

a steady extension of direct public action (as opposed to regulation of private activities). As Giuliano Amato has pointed out, until the 1980s, those policies were based on state planning, nationalization (in areas such as energy, railways, and posts), state-owned companies, and state aid to private companies (Amato 1997: 158). All this, however, does not necessarily mean that EC legal rules and policies have failed. Quite the contrary, some of the most influential Italian politicians, like Andreotti and La Malfa, and *grands commis*, like Guido Carli, believed that only European commitments could impose those rigorous measures that the country would otherwise have refused. Guido Carli has put forward this argument forcefully in his memoirs, where he contends that membership of the Community enabled the market economy to survive in Italy in the face of persistent calls for protectionism from certain domestic constituencies and compelled politicians to practise principles of sound public finance which they would not otherwise have been able to do (1994: 266, 406; Cassese 1992: 889; Manzella 1992: 1491).

The EC has thus served as the external source of legitimization of pro-market policies. A statute aimed to protect competition, which included provisions for an antitrust authority, was established as late as 1990. Directed at restricting anti-market practices that impede the circulation of goods, it is an important internal market measure. In Italy, however, it did not prevent ministers from continuing to support public service monopolies and hindering the implementation of EC directives through administrative delays or litigation. A good example pattern is the case of mobile phones, where it is only due to the pressure exerted by the Commission that Italy has had a second, and now a third, provider of this service, in addition to the incumbent (i.e. the previous public monopolist).

More recently, public finance also has become subject to the forced virtue imposed by external rules and policies. A bipartisan agreement was reached about the modification of both budgetary legislation and the internal rules of Parliament concerning budgetary procedures at the end of the 1980s. It was, however, only when the financial crisis of the state and the risk of Italy's exclusion from the Economic and Monetary Union became a real possibility that the government led by Giuliano Amato and Carlo Azeglio Ciampi were able to adopt the extraordinary measures which allowed Italy to be a member of EMU from the beginning (della Cananea 1996, 1997).

It would be a mistake, however, to identify EC policies only as a source of limits to the action on national institutions. EC funds have been extremely useful at a time of severe pressure an financial resources. Moreover, they have tended to go directly into public investment rather than finding their way to families or companies as occurred during the 1970s.

In sum, the EU has acted as a shield against anti-market tendencies that had long prevailed in Italy. Its importance, which has grown in the 1990s and looks set to continue to increase further, confirms that any failings there may have been in Italy's European policy are not the result of a lack of interest.

Inadequate Co-ordination as the Source of the Italy's 'Failures' in Europe?

If the EU has been of such importance in acting as an external link to the more market-oriented countries of Europe, what exactly are the sources of Italy's shortcomings? This raises other questions such as whether Italy has been effective in protecting and promoting Italy's interests in the EU, and whether explanations that give Italy a secondary role in building Europe are sustainable. Usually, these failings have been attributed to governmental instability and inefficient administration.

Reconsideration of this widely held view is necessary, because, if true, it would imply that nothing has been achieved, when in fact this is not the case. The impact of instability and administrative inefficiency can be overstated. Both older and more recent studies have shown that, though coalition governments came and went, there was significant continuity or overlap in personnel. In particular, foreign policy remained in the hands of the same party, the Christian Democrats, until the late 1980s (Cassese 1985: 128; 1998). Moreover, the personnel responsible for EU policy did not change significantly. In other words, political instability has disguised bureaucratic continuity and with that a degree of continuity in policy terms. In addition, bureaucratic inefficiency is not only an Italian peculiarity.

Furthermore, the argument that administrative obstructionism resulted in a diminished ability to protect Italy's interests demands very close scrutiny. Delays in implementing EC directives are—to put it crudely—a weapon that can be used to protect strategic or vulnerable interests. It does, of course, carry risks. When used with respect to distributive polices, it may lead the EC to freeze payments, as, for example, in the procedure known as the *apurement des comptes*. Here again, an administrative procedure often turns into a judicial process where legal alternatives have not been already defined. In the case of regulatory policies, delays can enable public firms to strengthen their commercial positions against new entrants by buying time. This was, for example, the case with mobile phones. The need to renegotiate EC decisions or policy guidelines may also result in net gains. In other words, in this context, 'inefficiency' does not necessarily mean 'ineffectiveness'.

There is strong evidence that Italy has successfully pressed and promoted strategic national objectives in the case of the former. In the initial stages of post-war co-operation in Western Europe when the Schumann Plan was put forward Italy's two ambitions were to become a full member of the European Coal and Steel Community and to obtain derogations to allow some sectors time to catch up. Both goals were achieved. The creation of the Social Fund was, moreover, the result of a successful italian initiative. The key role subsequently played by Italy at Messina in relaunching the European project after the failure of the EDC—a personal triumph of Gaetano Martino, Minister of Foreign Affairs—is well known. Also, in negotiating the merger of the executives of the three communities in 1964–5 Italian officials from the diplomatic service contributed to achieving a compromise which was more than acceptable to Italy in view of its commitment to strengthen the power of the Commission—the same policy, incidentally, which was defended in the common declaration delivered by Italy, France, and Belgium after the Amsterdam IGC. In the early 1980s and 1990s, Italian presidencies have had a number of notable successes, including the decision to hold an IGC to write the internal market into the EEC Treaty in Milan in 1985 and the initiatin of negotiations on European Union in Rome in 1990 (Noël 1989: 87).

However, the most important strategic success achieved by Italy in the EU has been the accession to the third stage of the EMU. Guido Carli, who negotiated this point on behalf of the Italian delegation at Maastricht, claimed that the emphasis placed by the protocol (an annex to the Treaty of Maastricht) on progress towards a more virtuous GNP/debt ratio was mainly the result of joint pressure exerted by the Italian delegation and the Commission. This achievement inspired successful action on the part of several Italian governments after 1992. In particular, the dramatic reduction of the public deficit and public expenditure engineered by Carlo Azeglio Ciampi (using the EU as a means to avoid public blame), as Minister of the Treasury, 1996–8,[4] and the reduction of the inflation rate achieved by the Bank of Italy have created the necessary conditions for EMU membership which in 1996 appeared impossible.

A different situation emerges when considering 'low' politics. The most important—at least in terms of both budgetary resources and number of rules—common policy, namely agriculture, offers several examples of poor negotiation. When, for instance, the first common prices for grain and olive oil were adopted, in the early 1960s, the limited attention paid to concrete details resulted both in Italy being a net payer into the Common Agricultural Policy (CAP), and in its subsequent need to negotiate revised rules, thus being obliged to concede other gains to partners in complex packages, for example, quotas in milk production.

Although history is not meant to repeat itself, twenty years later, when milk quotas were being negotiated in the Agricultural Council, the Italian

---

[4] The government originally proposed to adopt a budget of 250,000 milliards billion lira in June, but five months later, when fears grew about Italy's possible exclusion from EMU, it fell to 60,000 billion (della Cananea 1998; Ross 1997).

delegation had not the vaguest idea of how much milk Italy produced, since this information had not been received from its national administration. As a consequence, not only were wrong quotas adopted, but the subsequent wide-spread violations were regarded by the Commission (and the British and Dutch delegations) as breaches of EC law. Those violations had the further consequence that, in order to obtain a reduction of the penalties to be paid, the Italian government (in 1994) withheld its approval from the new post-Maastricht financial perspectives (thus contradicting its request for more resources for the structural funds) and some years earlier had to accept a senses of compromises on unfavourable terms for other agricultural products (Saccomandi 1978: 146).

These examples drawn from agriculture are not unrepresentative. As an official report produced by the Chamber of Deputies recognized in 1982, Italian delegations have too often accepted proposals in the Council that it would have been better to oppose there and then than to have found it diffi-cult to implement later (*Camera dei deputati* 1982). Moreover, negotiation of policies of a technical nature without good technicians results in adopting rules and policies whose application is likely to be problematic. This in turn may lead to frequent delays in the transposition of directives and even their infringement of EU law.

A possible explanation is that the distinction between 'high' and 'low' politics roughly corresponds to another distinction in the nature of policies in Italian government. On the one hand are policies either backed by a strong political commitment and subject to hierarchical control or to one single, highly professional bureaucracy (the Ministry of Foreign Affairs with respect to the negotiation of new treaties; the Treasury and the Bank of Italy for finan-cial and monetary issues). On the other hand are policies prepared and carried out by 'ordinary' bureaucracies (from agriculture to transport). To put it more clearly, at the root of the strength and weaknesses of EU policy making in Italy lies the problem of co-ordination.

Before moving on to an examination of the co-ordination mechanisms, some warnings are necessary. First, failures are not always due to inappropri-ate goal setting or to incoherent action by the bureaucracies involved. Indeed, they may depend either on an inadequate building of alliances or on a 'cultural' cleavage. Both, for instance, affected the controversy surrounding Malpensa airport in Milan. The Italian government had succeeded in obtain-ing EU funds for enlarging the airport and making it a new 'hub' for north-ern Italy (with the effect, undesirable for foreign air companies, of not allowing travellers to pass through other 'hubs' in northern Europe to reach northern Italian cities). The decree, elaborated by the Minister of Transport together with the regional and the local authorities, mandated that all foreign companies (but not Alitalia, the Italian national company) follow the new pro-gramme, but this had not been cleared with the Commission. When adopted, the Commission challenged its legality on the basis of a negative opinion from an advisory group composed of national officials. The subsequent action brought before the ECJ by Italy appears unlikely to be accepted.[5] In sum, although co-ordination within the national system had worked well, it was not followed by an effective action of consensus building in Brussels (all national delegates sitting in the advisory committee were against the decree, except the Italian and Dutch representatives) and was further compromised by the confrontational style used against the EC Commissioner for transport. Insufficient care in ensuring that plans decided at home will work once presented in Brussels thus led to a serious failure.

Another point which deserves mentioning is that Italy lacks a serious policy towards staffing EC institutions. In the early years, a number of extremely competent EC senior officials came from Italy. However, when they retired no incentives were provided for young substitutes to go to Brussels (Cassese 1997).[6] Also high-level politicians refuse EC seats: the case of Malfatti who resigned as President of the EC Commission to run in a parliamentary election is a quintessential example. Also throughout the 1970s and 1980s Italian members of the Commission were, with few exceptions, politicians whose careers were nearing an end. Brussels was thus seen as a last step. The problem has become even more serious in recent years, when staffing EU institutions has become an important objective for other member states, such as Spain and the UK. It was only in 1994 that a committee was created with the task of diffusing knowledge about EU policies and opportunities within public administration.

European Policy Co-ordination: The Past

Let us now examine the instruments (bodies, procedures, and other tools) used for the co-ordination of EU policy making within the Italian political and administrative system. Since they have changed through the years, it is useful to consider their development. Two periods are readily distinguishable: the primacy of the government, especially the Ministry of Foreign Affairs (1952–80), and fragmentation (after 1980).

The earlier phase is characterized by three features (Olivetti 1969; della Cananea 1992; Ronzitti 1987: 210). The first was that EC policy making was considered an exclusive domain of the state. Accordingly, regions (established

---

[5] The faith in the ECJ appears curious for a minister who has declared himself not to be willing to enforce the Court's decision to consider as unlawful state aid to truck drivers.

[6] Staffing within the EU is so overlooked that there is no recent work or study such as that of W. de Marteau (1970).

by the Constitution in 1948 and set up in 1970) were used only as field administrations for EU matters. In other words, they are called upon to put into effect rules and policies which they had no part in negotiating and are, therefore, reluctant to expend their energies in implementing.

Second, EC policy making was a province of the executive, acting without any binding instructions from Parliament. Nor was the latter kept informed about EU developments. Parliament itself did not pay too much attention to EC affairs. Political debate, after the decision to join the ECSC and the EEC, was rare, if not entirely absent. Until the early 1970s the internal rules of procedure within the Italian Parliament were not adjusted in view of the increasing integration.

The third feature is the primacy of the Ministry of Foreign Affairs. When matters of high political profile were at stake, of course, the Prime Minister and sometimes the whole Council intervened. However, the daily management of EC affairs remained in the hands of that ministry. This ministry also directed the Permanent Representation (set up in 1958), which enjoyed a wider discretion compared with its counterparts elsewhere. Two coordination committees were established in 1960: one at the political, the other at the official level. The first was abolished in 1967 and its functions were transferred to the Comitato Interministeriale per la Programmazione Economica (CIPE). The second gradually lost its influence, thus contributing to the growing primacy of the Ministry of Foreign Affairs and especially Directorate-General for Economic Affairs. Each survived significant change in the 1980s, including deepening integration at the European level, a new political climate in Italy which saw the introduction of new rules and procedures in an attempt to cope with the pressure on public finances, and a growing awareness of the problems of existing mechanisms used for EU policy making (Cassese 1985; Franchini 1993).

The monopoly of the central state over external affairs (as EU affairs are considered) has remained stable, but the regions have demanded a greater role in the preparation of EC policies. They have also used their powers over implementation, where they have a constitutionally defined role, to press their case. As a consequence, implementation of EC directives can be delayed. This led to an increasing role for the regions, though limited to areas or relatively minor significance. A special body has been set up in the recent past to enable regions to participate in EU policy co-ordination, the Conferenza Stato-Regioni, and since 1995 regions have been permitted to establish *bureaux de liaison* in Brussels. Therefore, the state-as-a-unit paradigm which has long influenced EU policy making (the state is a single body speaking with one voice, that of the Ministry of Foreign Affairs) has been abandoned (Sirianni 1997).

The political balance has also been reshaped. First, Parliament has developed new mechanisms. The transposition of EU directives must be made by a yearly statute (called 'legge comunitaria'), thus removing from the executive the power to decide if and when this should be done. In addition, the executive is obliged to produce a report twice each year on its EC policies. Finally, parliamentary committees have been strengthened in order to cope with EU matters (1988–90) (Giddins and Drewry 1996; Morisi 1992). However, in practice, Parliament seldom acts decisively. The yearly bill suffers serious delays (the 1991 bill was adopted on February 1992; the 1996 bill was adopted in April 1998) and ignores the increased flow of information (as it does with other reports, such as those produced by the Court of Auditors on the public finances).

Second, deciding the fundamental orientations of EU policy is the responsibility of the whole cabinet, and CIPE's role in ordering priorities has been strengthened. In practice, though, rather than laying down guidelines, it has become more of a management body.[7] In addition, the Prime Minister determines national policy in key areas, either personally or through the minister of European affairs, a post created in 1980.

Other reforms have been introduced at administrative level. The basic one is the increasing involvement of several ministries in the elaboration of national positions on EU policy. In contrast with the past, when the Ministry of Foreign Affairs dealt with all phases, assisted, if necessary, by senior officials from technical ministries, the expansion of EU competencies has resulted in a greater number of line ministries participating in co-ordination. As a further consequence, since 1980 a specific minister without portfolio—and without a ministry, since the new department was reviewed three years after the 1987 bill and a consultative committee of senior officials which was to assist him was never set up—has been responsible for co-ordinating EC policy and most ministries have created dedicated units to perform this task. Moreover, financial co-ordination has been introduced and entrusted to the Treasury, through a new financial instrument (*Fondo di rotazione per l'attuazione delle politiche comunitarie*).

These developments give rise to a number of considerations. First, as the Ministry of Foreign Affairs could no longer deal with wide-ranging technical dossiers and as EU affairs began to cut across institutional boundaries, co-ordination rather than hierarchy was called for. In a fragmented administrative system, however, the uncertain and unstable shape of co-ordination mechanisms undermines the effectiveness of more co-operative styles of policy making.

Second, they show that it is mistaken to assume that the Italian political and administrative system is rigid. Indeed, quite the opposite is true. Several solutions have been tried, but have proved inadequate. In other cases,

---

[7] A recent Court of Auditors' report noted that from 1995 to 1996 its deliberations increased by three-quarters. Moreover, 236 out of 321 meetings concerned the allocation of money and only 10% policy guidelines or orientations.

remedies were counter-productive, as in the case of financial co-ordination, which in practice has produced centralization. The *Fondo di rotazione* is not used by the Treasury as a mere financial tool. Rather, it serves, first, as a support for the leading role of the Treasury within CIPE and, if necessary, as a substitute for implementation in areas in which regions do not manage EU financial resources promptly. Although the regions accept this, so as not to lose this source of funding, it is clear that their autonomy is restricted and this moves power back to the centre.

This raises a further question: why is such a failure tolerated? A possible explanation lies in the absence, or low visibility, of sanctions at EU level; there appears to be little real reason to comply with EU directives. Other explanations are cultural. One is the lack of a serious culture of evaluation of the results achieved by new legislation: it is easier, paradoxically, to adopt a new bill than to make an old one work. Another explanation is that the failure of co-ordination tools does not imply that no co-ordination has taken place: it may result from 'personal co-ordination', deriving from networks of politicians and higher civil servants, who share more or less the same ideas about European integration.

There is still another explanation, based on the different approaches followed at the European and national levels. European integration, though not proceeding as far or as quickly as supporters had hoped, has followed the path envisioned by neo-functionalists such as Monnet and Hallstein: integration on low key policy issues will result in the need for integration elsewhere. This is the spill-over doctrine: apolitical and stressing the technical aspects of integration. The functionalist logic has had the consequence that the importance of the practical means of integration is emphasized at European level but neglected in Italy. The effects have been demonstrated recently, with the criticism (inspired by the idea of the primacy of the *politique politicienne*) of the 'accountant-like' attitude of the Commission's way of dealing with Italian budgetary data.

EU Policy Co-ordination: The Present

At the end of the 1990s, EU policy making is characterized by three, partly conflicting, trends. First, no change has occurred at the constitutional level, due to the failure of the third parliamentary commission entrusted with this task. Therefore, the discrepancy between the European and the Italian constitutions—the former preoccupied by both market failures and government failures and the latter focusing exclusively on market failures—is still pronounced. The question thus arises as to whether the correct and complete implementation of EU principles aiming at coping with government failures (for instance, as regards excessive public deficits) is possible without a constitutional amendment. The urgent nature of this question is demonstrated by the constitutional changes introduced by France, Germany, Spain, and Portugal in an effort to align their national constitutions with the principles established by the Treaty on European Union in matters such as EMU and European citizenship. Needless to say, such an adjustment could assist all activities aiming at preventing or attenuating the costs deriving from lack of compliance with EU rules, for instance with regard to the Stability Pact.

A second development is the creation of a new framework for administrative co-ordination, following a directive issued by the President of the Council of Ministers.[8] First, the role of the Permanent Representation has been reshaped: it must now send all available information about EU political and administrative processes not to the Ministry of Foreign Affairs, but to the department for the co-ordination of EC policies. Second, a procedure has been created for obtaining comments on EU proposals from all interested public institutions: they must be gathered by the department and sent to the Permanent Representation within thirty days. If further analysis is needed, the latter will ask for any decision by EU bodies to be suspended for one month. Third, the department will ensure that EU directives are transposed and implemented within an appropriate period. Fourth, the Permanent Representation must provide possible solutions for problems arising with respect to EU law. These measures demonstrate the awareness that administrative co-ordination matters and lies at the root of Italy's problems with EU law.

Doubt, however, arises whether a further act assigning functions to the department will achieve the goal which several statutes have failed to achieve in the past. What happens if a minority neglects its duties? Apart from political remedies, which are unlikely to be used, it seems unlikely that the department could act as a substitute. The directive not only reaffirms the choice in favour of semi-independent structure within the PM's Office for EU matters made in the early 1970s but also strengthens the presidency vis-à-vis the Ministry of Foreign Affairs. At the same time, however, the lead on EU matters is assigned to the Under-Secretary of State for Foreign Affairs, a choice which may well contradict the other one.

Finally, while there is an effort to replace the old centre (the Ministry of Foreign Affairs) with a new one (the department operating within the presidency), fragmentation is enhanced by recent decisions concerning the new independent authorities dealing with highly complex technical issues. Indeed, they are entrusted with the power to co-operate directly with EU institutions, as in the case of the antitrust authority established in 1990, but this power of co-operation was only formally recognized in 1996.

---

[8] The directive, adopted on 30 Mar. 1988, is published in the *Giornale di diritto amministrativo* (1998), 897–8, with a critical comment by C. Franchini.

Conclusion

The European Union is a central concern for any Italian government, and that centrality is widely recognized by politicians and by the public. Despite that centrality, Italy has been slow to create effective and efficient mechanisms for co-ordinating the formulation and implementation of EU law. This has, in turn, resulted in the loss of funds and legal sanctions. This chapter points to a number of administrative and political reasons that may explain the apparent failures of Italy in policy making with respect to the EU. There have been some advances, but fragmentation and duplication appear still to dominate. It may be that EU co-ordination in Italy itself requires some co-ordination.

References

Amato, G. (1991), 'Il mercato nella Costituzione', *Quaderni costituzionali*.
——(1997), 'The Impact of Europe on National Policies: Italian Anti-trust Policies', in Y. Mény, P. Muller, and J.-L. Quermonne (eds.), *Adjusting to Europe:The Impact of the European Union on National Institutions and Policies* (London: Routledge).
Camera dei Deputati (1982), *Direttive delle Comunità Europee: Elenco delle direttive e stato di attuazione (1959–1981)*, 13 (Rome: Servizio delle Relazioni Internazionali).
Caranta, R. (1995), 'Judicial Protection against Member States: A New Just Commune Takes Shape', *Common Market Law Review*: 703.
Carli, G. (1994), *Cinquant'anni di vita italiana* (Bari: Laterza).
Cassese, S. (1985), 'La regola e le deroghe: Il sistema politico amministrativo italiano e le direttive comunitarie', *Scritti in onore di Vezio Crisafulli* (Padua).
——(1992), 'La riforma costituzionale in Italia', *Rivista trimestrale di diritto pubblico*, 905–50.
——(1995), *Le basi del diritto amministrativo* (Milan: Garzanti).
——(ed.) (1997), *Funzione pubblica e integrazione europea* (Rome: Cedar).
——(1998), *Lo stato introvabile* (Rome: Donzelli).
della Cananea, G. (1992), 'L'Italia e l'Europa: La politica "comunitaria" nel periodo iniziale del processo di integrazione (1952–1967)', in E. V. Heyen (ed.), *Early European Community Administration*, in *European Yearbook of Public Administration*, 4: 207–28.
——(1996), 'Reforming the State: The Policy of Administrative Reform in Italy under the Ciampi Government', *West European Politics*, 19/2: 321–38.
——(1997), 'The Reforms of Finance and Administration in Italy: Contrasting Achievements', *West European Politics*, 20/1: 194–209.
——(1998), 'Riordino dei conti pubblici e "riforma" dello stato sociale', *Giornale di diritto ammministrativo*: 124–9.
de Marteau, W. (1970), *La presenza italiana nelle strutture delle Comunità Europee* (Rome).

de Vergottini, G. (1967), *Pianificazione statale e interventi comunitari* (Milan: Giuffrè).

EC (European Commission) (1998), *Fifteenth Yearly Report on the Supervision on the Implementation of Community Law-1997*, OJ C 250 (10 Aug.).

Einaudi, L. (1988), *La guerra e l'unità europea* (Bologna: Il Mulino).

Faro, S. (1997), 'Il tema della partecipazione dell'Italia all'Unione Europea nei lavori della Commissione Parlamentare per le riforme costituzionali', *Rivista italiana di diritto pubblico comunitario*, 1323–30.

Franchini, C. (1993), *Amministrazione italiana e amministrazione comunitaria* (Padua: Cedam).

Giddins, P., and Drewry, G. (eds.) (1996), *Westminster and Europe: The Impact of the European Union on the Westminster Parliament* (London: Macmillan).

Greco, G. (1998), 'Rapporti tra ordinamento comunitario e nazionale', in M. P. Chiti and G. Greco (eds.), *Trattato di diritto amministrativo europeo*, vol. i (Milan: Giuffre).

Harlow, C. (1996), 'Francovich and the Problem of the Disobedient State', *European Law Journal*: 199.

Irti, N. (1998), 'Iniziativa economica e concorrenza', in G. della Cananea and G. Napolitano (eds.), *Per una nuova costituzione economica* (Bologna: Il Mulino).

Manzella, A. (1992), 'Il "vincolo europeo" sul governo dell'economia', in *Studi in memoria di Franco Piga*, vol. 2 (Milan: Giuffrè).

Morisi, M. (1992), *L'attuazione delle direttive CE in Italia: La 'legge comunitaria' in Parlamento* (Milan: Giuffrè).

Noël, F. (1989), 'Italia: Vizi e virtù di un membro fondatore', *Relazioni internazionali*, 22.

Olivetti, M. (1969), 'La Préparation de la décision communautaire au niveau national italien', in P. Gerbet and D. Pepy (eds.), *La Décision dans les Communautés Européennes* (Brussels: Presses Universitaires de Bruxelles).

Presidenza del Consiglio del Ministri—Dipartimento della Funzione Pubblica (1993), *Rapporto sulle condizioni delle pubbliche amministrazioni* (Rome).

Romano, S. (1997), 'L'integrazione europea: bilancio e prospettive', *Rivista di studi politici internazionali*: 323–50.

Ronzitti, N. (1987), 'European Policy Formulation in the Italian Administrative System', *International Spectator*, 22.

Ross, F. (1997), 'Cutting Public Expenditure in Advanced Industrial Democracies: The Importance of Avoiding Blame', *Governance*, 10: 175–200.

Saccomandi, V. (1978), *Politica agraria comune e integrazione europea* (Bologna: Il Mulino).

Santoro, C. (1989), 'Politica estera italiana: Come nacque la scelta europea', *Relazioni internazionali*, 22: 91.

Senato della Repubblica (1991), *Partecipazione dell'Italia alle fasi formativa ed applicativa del diritto comunitario* (Rome).

Sirianni, G. (1997), *La partecipazione delle regioni alle scelte comunitarie* (Milan: Giuffrè).

Spinelli, A. (1990–1), *Diari*, 3 vols. (Bologna: Il Mulino).

5

Spain

Ignacio Molina

Introduction: The Spanish Policy Process and the Challenges of EU

The impact of European integration on the domestic politics and administration of the member states is contested. One perspective suggests that
domestic processes have been substantially altered and that a pattern of convergence among member states has emerged (Rometsch and Wessels 1996).
Other authors contend that EU membership leads to similar policy outputs,
but that it has not substantially diminished, still less eliminated, administrative variation among the EU-15. According to this view, national differences
not only remain (Bulmer and Burch 1998; Harmsen 1999), but they may even
have been reinforced (Goetz 1995).

The purpose of this chapter is to examine the co-ordination of EU policy
in Spain. This concern inevitably raises three questions of a more general
nature. The first is the extent to which the co-ordination of EU policy differs
from domestic policy processes. The second relates to whether, and, if so, to
what extent, mechanisms for dealing with EU matters have affected domestic
processes by adjusting institutional relationships within the state. The third
concerns the degree to which there exists evidence of convergence among the
member states.

The most striking feature of the Spanish political system is the centralization of power and the dominance of the executive (Heywood 1998; Gunther
1996). Though segmented at the official level, at the political level the core
executive is monolithic. The government is neither subject to the constraints

This chapter draws upon four non-attributable interviews with senior officials involved in
Spain's system of EU policy making that were conducted between Dec. 1997 and June 1998.
It has also benefited from the assistance of Tanya Börzel, Rachel Jones, and Albino Santos.
Any shortcomings, however, remain the responsibility of the author.

of neo-corporatist decision making, nor does it depend on Parliament, parties, or interest groups to establish political priorities. Its power has, though, been increasingly circumscribed by the devolution of power to regional Autonomous Communities, so that the central executive now confronts two constraints: first, the aggregated pressure exerted by the seventeen regional governments; and second, the demands of nationalist Catalan and Basques, who on ethno-territorial grounds have called for privileged status within the quasi-federal political structure.

With the completion of a consociational transition to democracy, and despite the fact that the style of policy making has changed according to the size of the governing majority, a rather majoritarian and conflictual policy style at the decision stage and at the political level has developed in Spain. The combination of characteristic features of Spain's political and administrative and political opportunity structures, such as the weakness of civil society and of political parties, an adversarial party system, a legalist administrative tradition, and specific features of Spain's quasi-presidential executive, have been contribution factors. However, the policy style is more consensual in the initiation and implementation phases, even in sectors where bureaucratic fragmentation or particularist pressures are present. In these areas where policy networks have emerged, statism is replaced by the capture of institutions by actors who uphold their interests and exploit their relative power, though the imposition of vetoes, clientelism, and personal ties. When co-ordination is necessary because the problems affect different departments, each one with its own policy community and bureaucratic corps, meetings at the official level—usually, informal contacts between officials and more rarely interministerial committees—are organized. Strategic issues, or those which have become politicized, are handled by the core executive which consists of horizontal ministries[1] and the Presidencia del Gobierno in the Moncloa Palace, where the Prime Minister, the deputy PM, and the Prime Minister's Office are located. This very narrow set of actors and their aides are able to control formal (the Council of Ministers) and informal arenas of interministerial relations through the party-government that they dominate.

Spain's preoccupation with the need to consolidate democracy rather than concern for its economic position marked the first years of Community membership. However, since the late 1980s, Spain has been more assertive in the defence of the national interest, and identifying this with progress towards further integration (Closa 1995*b*). This strategy has been based upon Spain's interest in maximizing available EU funds and support for EMU in order to facilitate liberalization and competitiveness of the economy in the Internal

---

[1] The main horizontal ministries are Economy and Finance, Justice (Legal Service), Public Administration (responsible for the civil service and relations with regional and local government), and Foreign Affairs.

Market. Despite some initial fears about its short-term costs, particularly regarding the deregulation of monopolies and the prohibition of state aids, the implementation of the single market programme has ultimately been accepted as beneficial. However, at the same time, Spain supports the principle of sufficiency of resources in order to guarantee the affordability of any further supranational advance, particularly in the areas of environmental and social policy (Gil 1992: 110–11).

Spain has also pursued political goals. Though in some respects it is a small country within the Union (Morata 1998), action has been taken to try to prevent any institutional reform that threatens to undermine its position as one of the five larger member states, as well as to ensure that Latin America and the Mediterranean figure in the EU's external relations. To achieve these objectives, co-ordination, which in the Spanish tradition means to speak with a single voice and is ultimately imposed from above (Section 98.2 of the Constitution), has become a priority.

The aim of this brief analysis is not to survey the entire national EU co-ordination process but rather to concentrate on the internal dimension, the prior stage to the final articulation of the Spanish position in Brussels. Though, of course, this distinction is useful for analytical purposes, as Wright (1996: 149) reminds us, the domestic and the European levels are, in practice, strongly intertwined and continuously interacting. This chapter concentrates on the processes that take place in Madrid (see the central and right-hand side of Fig. 5.1). Using a threefold categorization, it examines the mechanisms used by central government in its dealings with the other main actors involved in the process. The first set of relationships are horizontal, and relate to non-governmental actors, including the Parliament, political parties, and interest groups. The second are vertical, or more precisely intergovernmental, and concern relations between the centre and the periphery under the surveillance of the Constitutional Court. The third are internal, and relate to intragovernmental co-ordination within the central administration and the core executive. This overview, though brief, makes it possible to assess which domestic groups emerge as winners and which losers from EU processes, and to examine the extent to which the central government has been strengthened or weakened, or become more or less autonomous *vis-à-vis* other actors, including firms, trade unions, regions, parties, or line departments that are linked into transnational, multi-level networks.

This chapter argues that Spain's politico-constitutional uniqueness has been retained, and even reinforced. This would seem to imply that, though affected by EU membership, integration has not led to administrative convergence and that the governing structures of the member states remain diverse. The way in which domestic actors respond to external constraints and the apparatus that is established in each country to handle co-ordination varies significantly between member states. In addition, the Spanish case appears to challenge the

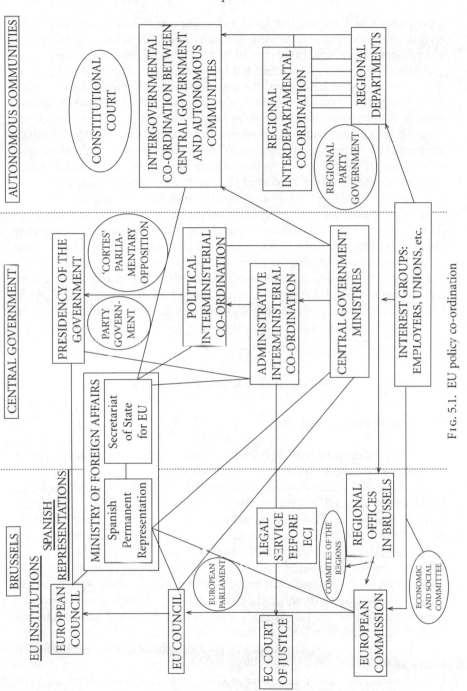

FIG. 5.1. EU policy co-ordination

assumption that Europeanization is hollowing out the state (Heywood and Wright 1997: 93). Indeed, the Spanish state, here identified with its central government (Moravscik 1994), has been strengthened since accession.

It might have been anticipated that the conditions in Spain during accession negotiations, which allowed the centre to dominate the decision-making process, would not continue once Spain became a member. After accession, when policy decisions had to be agreed in the domestic arena and when the involvement of key domestic actors was required to ensure effective policy implementation, the government would necessarily become dependent on a wide range of domestic actors, particularly since regional authorities and other key domestic actors developed their capacity to make an input into the policy process (Jones 1998). But in fact EU membership may actually have increased the autonomy of the Spanish executive in the domestic arena since the accession in 1986. Yet, and not as paradoxical as it seems, membership may also have reduced the scope of government intervention, especially where such action is incompatible with the rules and regulations of the internal market. The opposite is true domestically where the simultaneous processes of democratization and decentralization have contributed to the expansion of public spending and the size of the state, but at the same time have limited the central government's control of the policy process.

Beyond the Core Executive

The role of Parliament

The transfer of decision making from the domestic to the European level, given the executive nature of Union decision making and the few links that EU institutions have with national parliaments, has been to the detriment of the latter. In the sectors affected by Union action, Parliament's role has been reduced to formally transposing EU directives and the control of the executive on a strictly reactive basis. This trend is certainly apparent in Spain where the intervention of the Cortes is not a key stage of the co-ordination process. However, the marginal input of national parliaments into EU policy making is accentuated in the Spanish case by the majoritarian features of its political system and the irrelevance of the territorial chamber, the Senate, as an arena for intergovernmental bargaining. Moreover, the Spanish Parliament's already limited role has become little more than symbolic due to its limited experience in EU matters, as well as the positive consensus among political parties to EU membership. It is also worth recalling, as Closa (1995*a*: 137) has argued, that Spain's 'democratic parliamentary tradition, interrupted for forty years, has been restored and redeveloped in parallel with European Community (EC) membership'.

Within the bicameral Cortes, a Joint Committee of the Congress and the Senate for the EU was established in 1986. Composed of forty or so members from both houses, in proportion to party strength, the Committee plays a minor role in the system, despite the improvement of its functions and resources in 1988 and 1994. It has no legislative capacity, neither does it debate wider Spanish ambitions within the EU. Its main task is to monitor EU policy making and implementation, using information from hearings and other sources. Scrutiny of EU developments is also carried out by other parliamentary committees, in particular those dealing with Agriculture and Fisheries, Budgeting, Public Administrations—which handles intergovernmental relations—and Foreign Affairs.

Control of a political nature takes place when the junior minister for EU matters appears before the Committee or when the Prime Minister reports to plenary sessions of the Lower Chamber after European Councils. These reports and responses to the questions addressed by the opposition parties have somewhat reinforced the political role of the Cortes (Closa 1995a: 149). In fact, since 1993, due to the controversy surrounding Maastricht and coinciding with the end of parliamentary majorities, a more critical perception of the cost of EU membership has emerged. The increased powers of the opposition and the Committee,[2] which is not chaired by a party government deputy, have recently led to agreements and resolutions aiming to influence Spanish policy making on EU affairs. Subcommittees, usually of about ten members, have sometimes been created to deal with issues that are particularly important for Spain, such as IGCs, the completion of the single market, EMU, and the Structural Funds.

Despite the fact that the Senate has not become an effective chamber of territorial representation, the growing importance of the regional Autonomous Communities (discussed below) has affected the level of parliamentary influence. Regional parties that support the government (Basque, Catalan, and Canary Nationalists) and the regional branches of national parties have set up a special committee in the Senate to report on regional participation in Europe. In addition, the Joint Committee approved a recommendation for including regional representatives in the Spanish delegation to the EU Council. In spite of these advances, which remain largely theoretical as long as deputies and senators do not generally have direct access to Brussels (Morata 1996: 142), the central government still retains a large margin of autonomy in deciding Spain's position. The government takes little account of the Committee's activities and, generally, the actual impact of the Cortes is minimal.

[2] From 1986 to 1993, the Joint Committee was chaired by members of the governing party. Since then, the major opposition group has appointed the chair. The EU experience of its incumbents, notably Marcelino Oreja, during the last years of PSOE's government, and Pedro Solbes from 1996 to 1999, has enhanced the standing of the Committee.

Non-institutional actors

As noted above, the partisan dimension does not affect executive co-ordination. This is also the case with European integration issues where no important decision has ever been taken during party meetings. In fact, one of the most interesting achievements of the two Prime Ministers that Spain has had since 1982 has been their ability to silence backbench dissent and to end the factionalization which characterized the UCD government of the transition. Both Felipe González and José María Aznar have managed their party and parliamentary groups from the Moncloa, controlling internal discipline and imposing their views on controversial issues concerning Spain's European identity, like NATO membership (Marks 1997: 43–75).

In spite of Spain's usual categorization as a corporatist regime, interest groups and opposition parties in Spain are relatively weak and unable to overcome the majoritarian style of governance and the autonomy of state actors in the policy process. A sense that collective responsibility and accountability is restricted to general elections has led Spain to drop the consociational practices which were a feature of the democratic transition. As a result of Spain's *dirigiste* past, the failure of the Cortes as decision-making body, the lack of interest of catch-all parties to articulate private actors, and the limited institutionalization of civil society, pressure groups lack permanent channels of consultation with the state.

In fact, the involvement of private interests in politics has traditionally been considered in the dominant administrative legalistic culture to be detrimental to the 'general interest' (Morata 1996: 150). Of course, that is not to say that unions, employers, or sectoral groups do not have any impact an policy outcomes. In fact, as Gunther (1996: 44) emphasizes, a great deal of particularistic lobbying continues to be focused on individual ministers, reflecting the extent of departmental autonomy. However, interest groups do not exert systematic influence on the government—the core executive, the interministerial co-ordination arenas or party government—as a whole. In relation to EU matters, these features of the political opportunity structure, combined with a consensus about Europe, have minimized the input of opposition parties. Social forces participate only in the domestic EU decision-making process through sectoral policy networks, which are often linked to regional governments.

Neither the hubs of EU policy co-ordination in Madrid nor the Spanish Permanent Representation in Brussels receives inputs from the private sector. Consequently, domestic unions (UGT, CCOO), employers' federations (CEOE), agricultural organizations (COAG), environmentalists, and a broader array of minor groups intervene in European affairs through their regular lines of communications with the vertical ministries. Furthermore, consultation is channelled through informal and occasional contacts, since formal procedures of private involvement are inefficient. Any contacts have more to do with an interest in facilitating later implementation than with the formulation of the Spanish position. Indeed, in contrast with the *statist*, and usually confrontational, style of the government in the decision-making phase, the co-ordination of the final stage of the policy process is consensual and interest groups make use of various access points that enable them to influence policy output.

Only occasionally, when controversy does erupt, do sectoral associations assume a national profile. Action has included including mass mobilization, common in protests against CAP, CFP, or industrial adjustment as a result of European Competition rules, political pressure through regional governments when territorial interests are involved, or alliances with the European Commission, such as when the government's failure to comply with the EU Treaty in areas such as telecommunications, consumers, or environment policies has been invoked.

The Intergovernmental Dimension

The insertion of regional authorities in the domestic EU policy-making process and the impact of European integration on decentralization are key issues in member states where the central government is not the only player in the game (see Derlien, and especially Kerremans, in this volume). Although supranational integration clearly affects functions that have traditionally been performed by the regions (agriculture, environment, infrastructure), they were not mentioned explicitly in the treaties before the TEU. Central governments in some decentralized countries were able to take advantage of the situation by treating the EU as foreign policy and, therefore, the exclusive responsibility of the centre. The challenge to regional jurisdiction can indeed lead to a transformation of the existing territorial balance, but it is also true that EU membership has provided an opportunity for some regions, particularly the most activist, to bypass national governments in some areas. The direct relation between the European Commission and subnational governments is resulting in *multi-level governance*, which is transforming the traditional European polities of nation states or static decentralized models into much more dynamic and complex systems.

The tension between re-centralization and regional reaction is important in Spain, where the gradual formalization of participation by the regions in the domestic system of EU policy co-ordination clearly shows 'how Europeanization may affect the domestic institutions of the [decentralized] member states . . . in order to compensate for the progressive transfer of regional competencies to the European level' (Börzel 1998). However, the

Spanish case is of particular interest, because of its unique form of decentralization, which is neither federal, in the German style, nor purely administrative. Indeed, the way in which the subnational authorities have become actors in the national system of EU policy co-ordination underlines the extent to which 'Europeanization' is 'institution dependent' and, therefore, country specific, and why the overall pattern is one of national differentiation rather than institutional convergence (Kassim, this volume; Harmsen 1999). In Spain, since the late 1980s, the Autonomous Communities (ACs) have become concerned about their loss of input into Europeanized policy fields in which they had jurisdiction before accession. But the peculiar nature of the Spanish model of decentralization, which is characterized by selective devolution to some ACs and so by an asymmetrical pattern of self-government, has put obstacles in the way of establishing intergovernmental procedures for EU issues. Thus, the perpetual difficulties of attaining co-ordination in any policy area where competence is shared by central and regional governments have been extended to the EU field and raised to a higher power, since nationalist governments in the Basque country and Catalonia rejected a multilateral system, other regions show no interest in European affairs, and the central executive has shown disloyalty (Burgorgue-Larsen 1995). During the first decade, a few partial agreements were made and a pact drafted which was never signed. These small advances did not, though, reduce the pressure on the central government to encourage regional participation in the definition of the Spanish position to be defended in the EU Council. Regardless of the effects that EU membership may have exerted on delaying or triggering further advances towards a more decentralized Spanish state, central government has increasingly been obliged to take regional interests into account. This was a necessary consequence of the growing role played by the seventeen ACs in many areas.[3] Coinciding with the Socialists' loss of their majority in 1993, new mechanisms were established which have strengthened the role of the regions in the formulation of Spain's EU policy.

The current framework, which was strengthened in 1997, should, however, be regarded as a starting point rather than the final destination. The institutionalized arena for co-ordination is not the second chamber, as in Germany, but a special Committee (Conferencia para Asuntos Relacionados con las Comunidades Europeas) where top officials at the centre and representatives of the regional co-ordination organs for EU (created in all seventeen ACs) meet. This forum, informally established in 1988 and institutionalized six

[3] The Constitutional Court, a key actor with regard to the definition of intergovernmental relations in Spain, had already declared in 1988 that regions were competent for the implementation of EC law according to the standard internal distribution of functions (Alonso García, García de Enterria, and Piner 1991: 185–92). In 1994, the Court recognized the right of the ACs to set up offices in Brussels to represent their specific interests.

years later, discusses horizontal issues relating to the first pillar of the EU. To deal with vertical issues, the Committee on EC Affairs is linked to the general system of the so-called 'conferencias sectoriales'. At these meetings, sectoral ministries and regional departments fight to determine how responsibility should be divided between central and subnational government in areas where competence is shared. As shown in Fig. 5.2, Spain's system of intergovernmental co-ordination is loosely articulated, even if the horizontal Conferencia is supported by a co-ordinating committee of senior civil servants and assures, through working groups, the functioning of the system.

According to the agreement of 1994, matters of shared and exclusive regional competence are treated differently. In the case of the former, the central government must try to agree with the ACs the national strategy to pursue at the European level, though it retains the final say. With respect to the latter, if the regional authorities can reach a common position, this must be defended in Brussels, whatever the centre thinks. Some authors have praised this pragmatic approach, which promotes co-operation, on the one side, amongst the seventeen ACs and, on the other, between the periphery and the central authorities (Ortuzar et al. 1995). This framework has served to advance regional involvement in Brussels in other areas too, including the participation of the ACs in fifty-five committees of the European Commission (Pérez Tremps, Cabellos, and Roig 1999: 303) and the presence of a regional counsellor, appointed by the central government, at the Permanent Representation. It is also the case that, after an unsuccessful strategy of cost-shifting by the ACs which led to constitutional conflict and circumvention of the state to prevent further loses of power, the more co-operative approach adopted by the regions has redressed the balance of power (Börzel 1998). However, it remains unclear whether these gains in power in relation to the central state are the consequence of the new method of co-ordination, since the new system has failed to connect the Committee on EC Affairs with the sectoral committees and has not been able to produce a common regional position in the first five years of its existence (Pérez Tremps, Cabellos, and Roig 1999: 290).

The regions with the strongest political will or organizational capacities have been disillusioned with the multilateral system and, occasionally, with the obstructionism of central government. Some regions have exploited new opportunities for dealing with EU affairs, but though this encouraged some of the developments mentioned above, it has also delayed the emergence of genuine multilateral co-operation or intergovernmental co-ordination. The difficulty of reaching a common position between the seventeen regions remains the biggest obstacle to making an effective input into EU policy making at home.

It is worth underlining that this is not a new feature brought about by Europeanization, but the result of pre-existing features of the Spanish political

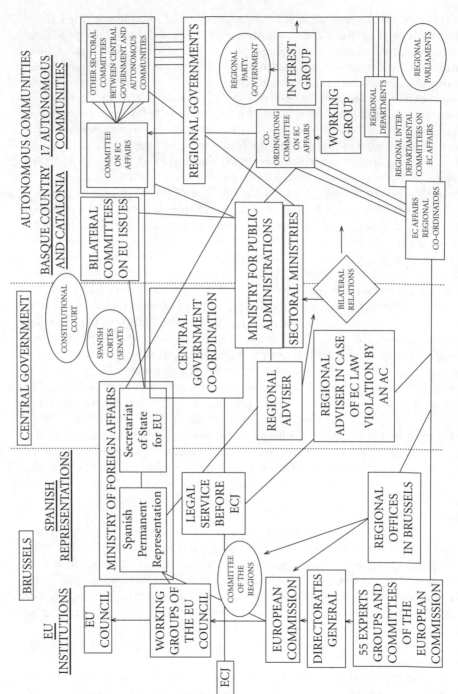

FIG. 5.2. Spain's system of intergovernmental co-ordination

system, such as the heterogeneity of interests and power among the ACs, and the prevalence of bilateralism over multilateralism in relations between the centre and the regions. Once more, an existing trend has been exacerbated by EU membership. Commission intervention combined with the varying competencies of the ACs has led to the development of stronger relations with some regions than with others, making the asymmetries of the system even more apparent. The main controversies involve the nationalist regions—particularly the Basque Country, but also Catalonia and, to a lesser extent, the Canaries. Their governments, supported by non-state-wide parties (CiU, PNV) with a frequently unilateralist discourse, reject symmetrical co-ordination and a common multilateral framework for the seventeen regions that may weaken the high level of political power and enhanced bargaining leverage.[4] The Basque government has traditionally been very assertive in its quest for special status in EU policy. It finally achieved its ambition in 1996 with the creation of a bilateral committee—a feat followed two years later by Catalonia.

Other ACs, with a similar, though less well-developed level of self-government, also see themselves as relatively distant, geographically or politically, from the centre. However, and inversely to the Catalan or Basque cases, the regional governments of Andalusia, the Valencian Community, or Galicia (which constitute, with the Balearics, Aragon, and Navarre, the second group of the Spanish periphery) have always been controlled by the PSOE or the PP. As a consequence, and though they also represent a challenge to the government's central position in the system, they are more willing to embrace a co-operative strategy. Their interests are ultimately national rather than regional and they have thus preferred to promote a multilateral approach in which they can exert more influence based on their socio-economic and demographic importance. Finally, the remaining ACs of central Spain, and, to a lesser extent,

---

[4] Since accession, these regions have tried to establish their own channels, at national and European level, to ensure the effective representation of their interests. Their initial demands (see Ortuzar et al. 1995) were rejected by Socialist governments in Madrid. However, once the era where single parties enjoyed an absolute majority came to an end after 1993, governments led by the PSOE and then the PP were dependent on the support of the regionalist parties in Parliament. Even if this appeared to increase the leverage that these regions could exert, under the prevailing conditions of competitive regionalism (Bulmer and Burch 1998: 623), other regions contested the granting of selective privileges. Any advantages bestowed first only on a few regions were later extended to all ACs. Insisting on individual channels of representing their interests on EU policy making, both at national and European levels, has been evident since accession. The early involvement of Spanish regional authorities in general policy making is illustrated by the existence of sectoral meetings which sought to maximize regional involvement in specific policy areas. These meetings, including the forum for discussing horizontal issues related to the EU, were formalized during membership. However, even if their development has been encouraged by the European context, it must be noted that sectoral meetings already existed prior to Spain's EU membership.

Asturias or Extremadura, lack the political, demographic, and economic resources to articulate a clear own-interest identity. Although they too may have pursued federal interests, like the second group, any additional competencies that they have gained have generally been the result of advances made by the other regions rather than the outcome of their own demands for greater autonomy.

To sum up, it would appear that the Europeanization of the Spanish model of centre–periphery relations should not be overstated. On the one hand, the strengthening of regional competencies has occurred in both highly Europeanized sectors and those on which the EU has had minimal impact. On the other hand, it is not even clear that the overall impact of supranational integration works towards further decentralization. Although the ACs are increasingly gaining influence in European policy making, the EU can also be considered to have had a negative impact because the Spanish regions have lost significant power as well. In any case, a number of strong regions have been able to counterbalance the increased level of autonomy enjoyed by the central government during the first years of EU membership. What seems clear is that the European context has led to an enhanced level of heterogeneity in intergovernmental relations. This conclusion is valid for Spain because growing asymmetry is congruent with the pre-existing structure and functioning of relations between the centre and the regions, but it does not imply, still less entail, that other member states are destined to experience a similar trend.

The Intragovernmental Dimension

This section has two aims: the first is to describe the actors in the Spanish executive that co-ordinate EU policy; and the second is to examine how membership has affected the functioning of the executive. It will be argued with respect to the latter that the impact of the EU on the Spanish executive has been limited and that the convergence thesis mentioned above is not substantiated in the Spanish case.

The Secretariat of State for the European Union (SSEU)

In spite of their great importance in the Spanish political system, neither the Department of the Premiership (*Moncloa*) nor the Ministry of Economy and Finance has been entrusted with responsibility for the co-ordination of EU policy. For historical (see Bassols 1995) and institutional reasons (see Bulmer and Burch 1998: 606), the task was given instead to the Ministry of Foreign

Affairs. This Ministry is responsible for the Permanent Representation in Brussels and, at the national level, the Secretariat of State for the European Union (SSEU). The SSEU has a formal monopoly, externally, with the Permanent Representation and EU institutions, and, internally, with the ministries and regions. The SSEU is connected to all ministries at the departmental level through the Technical General Secretariats, since no specialized unit exist in the various sectoral ministries to deal with EU business (Salas and Betancor 1991: 509; MAP 1997: 162).

The SSEU was merged in 1996 with the former general secretariat of foreign policy and its current designation is the Secretariat of State of Foreign Policy and for the European Union. However, given that the two departments of this division of the Ministry of Foreign Affairs are distinct and their physical location separate, the SSEU can be regarded as free-standing, as it was for the first ten years of Spanish EU membership. The following discussion is limited to the first pillar of the EU, though it is worth noting that all three EU pillars are co-ordinated by the Ministry of Foreign Affairs. The EC and CFSP is the responsibility of the Secretariat of State of Foreign Policy and for the EU, while JHA is handled by the Under-Secretariat of the Ministry.

The SSEU has its origins in the Ministry (and, later Secretariat of State) for Relations with the European Communities. The Secretariat of State, directed by a junior minister and a General Secretary (both with a private office), has a number of roles:

- overseeing sectoral policies, which is performed by two Directorates General: the DG for the co-ordination of EU General and Technical Affairs, which is in charge of Customs and Trade Affairs, and Economic and Finance Affairs; and the DG for the co-ordination of Internal Market and other EC policies, responsible for Agriculture and Fisheries, Education, Culture, Social, Health, and Consumer Affairs, and Industrial, Energy, Transport, Communication, and Environment Affairs;
- maintaining relations with the Permanent Representation in Brussels and with the ministries in Madrid;
- monitoring institutional policy making, legal affairs, and co-ordination of sectoral information (e.g. preparation for the General Affairs Council), as well as horizontal tasks;
- taking the lead in formal arenas of intragovernmental and intergovernmental co-ordination. The Secretary of State participates in both the interministerial committees and the Sectoral Committee, which brings together central government and the Autonomous Communities.

Although the SSEU is generally regarded as very capable, it is also over-burdened (Ordóñez 1994: 378), suffering from limited personnel and scarce resources. This was particularly marked during the first years of membership (see MAE 1987, 1988, 1989) when the SSEU lost the coherence that it had

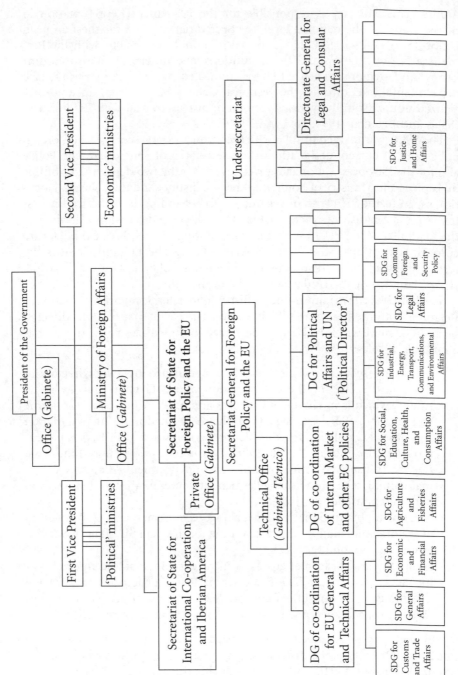

FIG. 5.3. The structure of the Ministry for Foreign Affairs

built up during accession negotiations (Zapico 1995). Locating the unit in the Prime Minister's office (MAP 1997) has been proposed as a way of addressing this problem, but the Moncloa is not keen to become involved in routine matters. A further constraint is imposed by the preference of the line ministries and the ACs for an SSEU that is not politically powerful. As Salas and Betancor (1991: 513) observe, absolute and formalized control of the system by the SSEU is not desirable. Indeed, Spain's relatively loose system of co-ordination is regarded as efficient by foreign observers (Metcalfe 1994).[5]

Interministerial co-ordination

The SSEU and the Ministry for Foreign Affairs are at the centre of the national system of EU policy co-ordination, as illustrated in Fig. 5.1. Other horizontal ministries—Economy, Public Administration, and Justice—as well as sectoral departments have important parts to play in the process (Burgorgue-Larsen 1995: 108). Formally, the SSEU and the ministries maintain contact and co-ordinate by means of an Interministerial Committee in which information is exchanged information by each ministry that is negotiating in Brussels. In practice, this Committee is not an arena within which decisions are taken (Dastis 1995: 325) nor the locus for strategic planning (Ordóñez 1994: 378). It meets at a more junior rank than was originally intended (i.e. assistant director level) and has been largely downgraded (Dastis 1995: 348; MAP 1997: 168). The committee has been even more ineffective since 1995, when it was enlarged. However, some specialized working groups, which are subordinate to it, such as state aids, do carry out important functions (Rivero and Heredia 1994).

The body to which the Interministerial Committee reports is the Delegated Committee of the Government for Economic Affairs. The junior minister for the European Union sits on both, and the secretary of the Delegated Committee is also the first deputy chairperson of the Interministerial Committee. However, co-ordination does not take place in the Delegated Committee, nor does it occur in the Council of Ministers, which is very formalized. It is, though, important to note that on the few occasions where these bodies become active, the representatives of the SSEU—the junior minister for the EU or the Minister of Foreign Affairs—are final, but not very powerful, gatekeepers (Zapico 1995: 55). The Prime Minister can impose decisions, but intervenes only in exceptional cases. For example, though a representative of

[5] For discussion, see Wright (1996) and Carnelutti (1989). The initially poor record of Spain in transposing EC directives (Alonso García, García de Enterria, and Piner 1991) has been substantially improved. Spain now stands in fifth place and is, moreover, subject to a relatively low number of appeals to the European Court of Justice (see Rometsch and Wessels 1996: 355–6).

- Chair: Junior Minister for the EU and Foreign Policy
- First Deputy Chair: Secretary of the Delegated Committee for Economic Affairs (Secretary of State of Economy)
- Second Deputy Chair: Secretary General for the EU and Foreign Policy
- Secretary: Director General for EU Technical Affairs

Members:
- Director of the Prime Minister's Office
- Under-secretary of Economy and Finance (Trade included)
- Under-secretary of Employment and Social Affairs
- Under-secretary of Industry and Energy
- Under-secretary of Justice
- Under-secretary of Home Affairs
- Under-secretary of Promotion (Public Works and Transports)
- Under-secretary of Health and Consumers Affairs
- Under-secretary of Education and Culture
- Under-secretary of Public Administrations
- Under-secretary of Environment
- Under-secretary of Agriculture, Fisheries, and Food
- Secretary General of Sea Fisheries

FIG. 5.4. Interministerial Committee for EU Affairs

the Moncloa is formally expected to be present in the various arenas of inter-ministerial co-ordination, this is not always the case. Since the SSEU lacks the authority to direct other departments, co-ordination is informal, operating through networks that link members of the SSEU through its subdivisions—composed of secondees from the line ministries—with officials in other ministries and personal ties that connect them to the various *corps* (Dastis 1995: 331). In the absence of these linkages or the political will to impose a solution, the lead ministry makes its own decisions on how to negotiate, leading to a fragmentation that the Ministry for Foreign Affairs cannot always overcome.

The importance of these informal contacts—and the continuation in office of experienced personalities since the 1980s—means that formal institutional channels may be circomvented. However, the existence of this network of personal contacts is an advantage because it suggests that the spoils system, characteristic of the most senior levels of the Spanish administration, is not a feature of EU policy making. There is a continual circulation of technical experts between Madrid—through the SSEU and the line ministries—and Brussels—through the Spanish Permanent Representation and EU institutions.

The Interministerial Committee for Proceedings before the European Court of Justice relating to Spain

This committee also has a significant role to play. Chaired by the junior minister for the EU, with a secretary from the division of the SSEU responsible for EU legal affairs, its members include a solicitor from the State Legal Service, and Technical General Secretaries of the Prime Minister's Office, the Ministry of Economy and Finance, and the Ministry for Public Administrations (when the regions are involved). Representatives of the same rank from other interested ministries may also attend. In theory, the Committee studies all actions brought against Spain, as well as those which might affect Spanish interests, including preliminary rulings applied by Spanish courts. In practice, however, it is a venue for the exchange of information rather than an effective arena for co-ordination. Strategy is actually decided by informal contacts where particular ministries and regional governments participate. In fact, co-ordination tends to be weak due to the inter-corps rivalries between, on the one hand, the Legal Service of the State, the equivalent of the Treasury Solicitor's Office in the UK, which is accountable to the Ministry of Justice, and, on the other, the *Subdirección General* of EU Legal Affairs within the SSEU (Dastis 1995: 330). The monopoly of state legal defence by the bureaucratic *corpa*, the *Abogados del Estadv*, creates problems and tensions with generalist diplomats or civil administrators who will have negotiated with the Commission right up to the pre-litigation phase, only to be sidelined when the case finally reaches Court.

Is there a pattern of convergence?

Given that national administrations have responded to similar pressures (see Kassim, Peters, and Wright, this volume), some authors contend that there is evidence of a growing convergence. Even though no blueprint has been laid down in Brussels,[6] the trend, it is argued, has been an indirect consequence of integration—the result of frequent meetings between national officials in Brussels (Burnham and Maor 1995: 191) and of the multinational character of the European institutions, including detached national experts—which promotes administrative interaction that leads to convergence (Wessels 1990: 229; Harmsen 1999; Derlien and Kassim, this volume). The European Commission also maintains constant contact with national administrations through information channels, the training of civil servants on short courses,

[6] EU institutions have not developed a standard administrative procedure for the application of European legislation. In fact, the very different ways of putting EU decisions into practice in each member state are one source of the 'implementation deficit' (Olsen 1997).

  • Chair: junior minister for the EU and Foreign Policy
  • Secretary: official from the SDG for EU Legal Affairs within the SSEU

Members:
  • Technical General Secretary of the Ministry of Presidency
  • Technical General Secretary of the Ministry of Justice
  • Technical General Secretary of the Ministry of Economy and Finance
  • Technical General Secretary of the Ministry for Public Administrations (when regions are involved)
  • Technical General Secretary from any other interested ministry
  • Solicitor from DG of Legal Service of the State

FIG. 5.5. Follow-up and Co-ordinating Interministerial Committee for Affairs Related to the EC Court of Justice

and the exchange of officials responsible for the implementation of Internal Market legislation. Convergence is also evident at a political level, since similar pressures tend to strengthen the same actors—the Prime Minister, as well as the ministers of strongly Europeanized issues such as Economy and Finance, Agriculture, or Foreign Affairs—within the core executive (Kassim, this volume).

This view is contested by other interpretations that either highlight the impact of private sector models (new public management) as the main factor behind administrative change or deny that there is any evidence of the emergence of an general European model of executive organization (Page and Wouters 1995). The latter view confronts the 'isomorphy hypothesis' with the 'autonomy hypothesis' (Olsen 1997: 161): 'all institutions develop robustness towards changes in their functional and normative environments, as well as towards reform attempts.' Administrative and governmental convergence, including the autonomy of the central banks, the creation of new departments, the deregulation of monopolies, and the privatization of public firms, may be encouraged, but not explicitly so: 'the suggestion is that a variety of processes of autonomous or mutual adaptation and harmonization may be more important' (Olsen 1997: 174). The administrative response to these common stimuli will depend, in each country, on the relative position of the executive within the national political system. The strengthening of a core executive in Great Britain (already majoritarian and autonomous) is not the same as in consociational Belgium, corporatist Sweden, or bicephalous France. And the effects of sectorization (enhanced by the EU) will be very different in those countries with political capacity and/or culture of co-ordination from those in which fragmentation (Germany), weakness (Italy), or bureaucratic division into corps is the rule. Therefore, an assessment of the growing coherence and autonomy of national governments or, otherwise, their capture by sectoral policy networks as a result of EU membership will differ according to the original resources of the executive in each member state.

The Spanish central government has responded to the demands of membership in a number of ways. Apart from the creation of the system of co-ordination described above, ministries have been Europeanized,[7] and, coincident with accession, a programme of modernization was launched to improve the functioning of the executive which had been historically inefficient in Spain. It is true that these measures were intended to create a public administration similar to those in the rest of Europe, but it would be misleading to claim that EU membership provided the main impetus. Other factors, such as democratization and decentralization, gave rise during the same period to a series of innovations which brought Spain closer to its neighbours. Moreover, Spain implemented reforms inspired by the *new public management* in order to cope with the challenges common to all West European countries in the 1980s: economic austerity, new issues, and technological development. Even if the EU has been a factor that has contributed to the modernization of the Spanish administration, it has not been the only influence, nor even the most important.

Furthermore, it is crucial, following the distinction made by Nystrom and Starbuck (quoted in Olsen 1997: 176) between the way in which institutions match their changing environments and the way in which they attempt to manipulate those environments, not only to consider what changes where introduced by Spain to deal with EU membership, but to examine how the executive in Spain took advantage of accession to the EC to strengthen itself. The first democratic governments faced an extremely austere, *dirigiste*, and poorly co-ordinated administrative apparatus, and when in 1982 the socialists came to power, they were committed to four ideas: that 'markets were to be reinforced, the public sector was to be reformed, direct state intervention was to be reduced, and a greater international integration of the domestic economies was to be promoted' (Maravall 1992).

---

[7] Although no specialized units for EU affairs were created within sectoral ministries, organizational adaptations to the European integration took place in the Department of Agriculture, Fisheries, and Food (affected by the CAP), Public Works and Transports (which merged in 1991 to place infrastructures policy under a single authority given the big importance of European funds in these issues), Industry and Energy (eliminating the division into sectoral directorates that followed an interventionist orientation), and, above all, Environment (created as a response to the need to implement EU environmental policy). The Europeanization of the Ministry of Economy and Finance led to the independence of the central bank and the creation of the independent Servicio de Defensa de la Competencia, to enforce competition policy. The agency for promotion of external trade was altered by requirements of the Treaty of Rome and, finally, the priority given to European regional policy led to the organization special units to track the EU budget and manage structural or cohesion funds (Zapico 1995: 59–62).

To succeed in the 'Spanish social democratic model of transforming society through welfarism, while increasing international competitiveness of industry and services conforming to the dictates of the market' (Webb and Sheldrake 1993: 16), centralized, effectively co-ordinated policy making was essential. Otherwise, the traditional fragmentation of the Spanish administration where each department was dominated by its own corps of specialized bureaucrats might reinforce sectoral policy networks with interests antagonistic to those of the core executive. Given this general ambition, Europeanization constituted both a risk and an opportunity. On the one hand, the so-called multi-bureaucratic policy-making process (Burnham and Maor 1995: 191) which characterizes the EU could exacerbate the sectorization that might threaten the implementation of radical reforms (deregulation, liberalization, and increases in taxation). On the other, membership helped the strategy, not only because many of national objectives coincided with EU goals, but also because the challenge itself encouraged and legitimized the concentration of political authority in the narrower core executive that had designed the overall reform.

Sectorization at the administrative level

The complex and differentiated process of EU policy making in Brussels makes it difficult to define a national position and has encouraged the development of multi-level policy networks.[8] The traditional autonomy of individual ministries has certainly led to problems of policy co-ordination in Spain, as illustrated by the contradictions between instructions from the SSEU, and influential ministries, such as Industry or Agriculture. The non-ministerial status of the SSEU in Spain has reinforced the position of vertical ministries. However, the support of the Prime Minister, and the technical, relatively neutral nature of decision making within the SSEU, have worked in its favour, even if not sufficient to tip the balance permanently. Co-ordination of EU policy depends on the effectiveness and capacity of the Spanish government to aggregate its internal interests and to formulate a common position, which is problematic when each ministry tends to establish direct contact with its interlocutor in Brussels. In short, the traditionally strong fragmentation of the Spanish policy making has been exacerbated by EU membership, which, again, seems to be a factor that reinforces previous patterns.

However, even if dependence on policy networks, empowerment of middle-echelon bureaucrats, and departmentalization may have increased as a con-

---

[8] That is to say, each area of EU activity has its particular system of governance in which actors, both private (business, unions, social organizations) and public (Commission DGs, vertical departments of the central government, regions), meet and make decisions, according to their sectoral interests and the powers at their disposal.

sequence of Europeanization, strong sectorization has remained limited to 'low politics'. In the same way as the Spanish executive is fragmented at the administrative level, it is uniform and homogeneous at the political level. This has enabled actors within the core executive to achieve a high level of co-ordination with respect to the most important issues. In key areas, some of them crucial for the reform of the Spanish capitalist model, the government has asserted a majoritarian style in establishing and implementing policy priorities. As a result of this, governmental autonomy *vis-à-vis* policy networks has been significantly enhanced.

Political co-ordination

The political opportunity structure in Spain with its quasi-presidential executive structure, majoritarian party system, the weak institutionalization of interest intermediation, and the supportive consensus among the public on Europe allowed, at least until 1993, the strengthening of the state executive. Moreover, the power of the core executive has been personalized and hierarchical, as illustrated by the fact that key policy areas remain the preserve of the Prime Minister and a few other actors.[9] Although the Prime Minister does not play a part in the routine co-ordination of EU affairs, Felipe Gonzáles and his successor as Prime Minister do take responsibility for matters of strategic importance and take charge of issues that become controversial. EU policies have given the core executive an opportunity to strengthen its position and increase its autonomy in the domestic policy process, and the central actors have certainly profited.

Even if sectoral networks in specific sectors can exert a significant influence on central government, the internal power of the core executive has ultimately been redistributed in favour of the Prime Minister and the generalist ministries, thus creating the conditions for putting a coherent set of demands to the EU and for achieving the implementation of general priorities at the national level. In the case of Spain, the strengthening of central co-ordination has made it possible both to speak with a single voice in Brussels and to promote a radical transformation of the capitalist model in Spain, which up to 1975 had linked extreme fiscal austerity with protectionism and *dirigisme*. Without the help of the EU, which provided specific schedules for deregulation, blame avoidance (Moravscik 1994), and financial resources, mainly from the structural funds, to support infrastructural development, it is a distinct

---

[9] Personalization is illustrated by the minister of Economy and Finance and an elite of senior officials (Elorza, Westendorp, or Matutes to name a few) which have remained relatively constant since the accession negotiations. High-level policy decisions are taken largely within this small group, whose members have similar views about Spain's priorities in Europe.

possibility that the sectoral interests of strong policy communities opposed to deregulation and privatization would have been able to defeat the core executive's strategy.[10] Moreover, the government's autonomy in horizontal and high-level political issues has benefited from low politicization, creating the conditions for a co-ordination process characterized by limited transparency and parliamentary scrutiny, even in respect of extremely salient issues. Both here, and with respect to EU presidencies (Ruíz Tartas 1995) and IGCs, a coherent statist co-ordination has been at work. This can be contrasted with the strong pressures of policy networks in both low politics and sectoral economic issues, such as state aids and agriculture, in which regions are also present.

Conclusion

Although EU membership has had a far-reaching effect on the Spanish polity and has obliged Spain to adapt its institutional frameworks and decision-making procedures to a new environment, it has also tended to reinforce previously existing trends. The system for EU co-ordination is little different from arrangements in other areas within the wider polity. In spite of some evidence of growing similarities between European administrations, significant differences remain. The vigour of distinctive policy-making traditions is corroborated in the case of the Spanish central government since the impact of EU, rather than altering previous patterns, has actually reinforced the segmented functioning in which a very integrated political level of government coexists with a fragmented administrative structure. Moreover, the Spanish executive has been able to take advantage of the challenge posed by membership. The risk of sectorization, which would jeopardize the unity of the state, has been counterbalanced by the establishment of central co-ordinating mechanisms. Evidence can be seen in the ability of the central executive to achieve important changes that had been opposed by sectoral interest, such as increasing taxation, reducing the budgetary deficit in order to expand public spending, and pushing ahead with market liberalization. Ironically, the loss of autonomy *vis-*

---

[10] The concept of blame avoidance refers to the mechanism used by national governments as a means of legitimizing and securing agreement at home on controversial decisions. *Blaming* Brussels enables central policy makers to escape the demands of sectoral networks that include not only private groups that benefited from protection (some firms or unions) but also some public actors (certain officials, regional authorities, and sectoral departments such as Industry). Moreover, as the cohesion funds were adjusted in line with the Maastricht criteria for EMU, these actors (the Ministry of Economy in this case) were able to use this *external discipline* to achieve previously unknown levels of budgetary rectitude (Kassim, Peters, and Wright 1998: 5).

à-vis the neighbouring countries has resulted in greater autonomy *vis-à-vis* sectoral interests and at home. Confirming the interpretation put forward by Metcalfe (1994: 271), Europeanization has meant more national government rather than less.

At first sight, the core executive's self-sufficiency would seem to be preferable to weakness or the dependence on selfish interests. However, it should be noted that the trend towards centralized decision making in the core executive is not necessarily in Spain's interests. First, the definition of the general interest is defined by a small number of actors that are only weakly accountable, not to the Parliament, but to the electorate every four years. Second, 'pressures to co-ordinate may remove some of the capacity of individual departments to achieve their own goals [while] playing multiple games and having multiple points of access may lead to better solutions' (Kassim, Peters, and Wright 1998: 5). Finally, the imposition of priorities by central authorities may help short-term resolution of conflicts with sectoral departments and social actors, but a bargaining process with more participants involved could turn out to be, although difficult, more enduring and less liable to miscalculations.

In any case, the capacity of the Spanish core executive to assert its goals should not be exaggerated. As in all member states, the Spanish system of EU policy making is sometimes loosely coupled. Hierarchies and formal co-ordination procedures are often circumvented or ignored. Jones (1998) has demonstrated that a range of domestic actors from business organizations to environmentalists are increasingly involved in EU decision-making. In a number of sectors, including banking and finance, energy and telecommunications, the extraordinary concentration of private interests has produced strong policy communities that have captured the parts of the state responsible for their regulation. At the same time, vertical ministries and middle-ranking public managers are able to escape from political direct control in some routinized issues, thus provoking certain empowerment of bureaucracy and relative fragmentation.[11] However, advances made by the most active Autonomous Communities in establishing a role for themselves in EU policy making constitute the main challenge to the ability of the central government to pursue a coherent and consistent strategy.

The general conclusion to be drawn from the Spanish case is that the impact of the EU on the institutional framework has had an impact on the balance between government, Parliament, regional governments, and other key

---

[11] However, often the logic is precisely the opposite since sectoral departments use politicization to promote their interests and those of network to which they belong, even against the generalist core executive. For example, the Ministry of Agriculture may use farmers' organizations and public opinion sympathetic to peasants to defend some aspects of the CAP, or the Ministry of Industry might assist ailing public firms and protection with the help of unions, parties, and regional governments.

domestic actors. However, Europeanization of the institutions themselves is not so immediately evident. The structure and functions of central and regional governments in Spain have largely developed independently of the *European* factor, even if the EU has exacerbated existing trends. The notion of convergence is most in evidence in particularly Europeanized sectors where very similar pressures have been applied in all member states for adaptation to the new European context, as illustrated by the areas of monetary, competition, and environment policy. However, the key importance of the core executive, the weakness of the Parliament, and the growing influence of the Autonomous Communities, particularly of the more active regions, are evident in both Europeanized and non-Europeanized policy areas.

In conclusion, EU policy making in Spain is characterized by the dominant role of an autonomous core executive which, however, faces a double challenge. The first derives from administrative fragmentation, and produces an apparent contradiction between centralization and sectoralization. The second is the result of the emergence of powerful peripheries which negotiate, at the same time, multilaterally and bilaterally with the central government, but which also bypass Madrid, and deal directly with the EU institutions.

References

Alonso García, R., García de Enterria, E., and Piner, J. L. (1991), 'Spain', in J. Schwarze, U. Becker, and C. Pollak (eds.), *The 1992 Challenge at National Level* (Baden-Baden: Nomos Verlagsgessellschaft).

Bassols, R. (1995), *España en Europa: Historia de la adhesión a la CE 1957–85* (Madrid: Política Exterior).

Börzel, T. (1998), 'The Domestic Impact of Europe: Institutional Adaptation in Germany and Spain' (Ph.D. thesis, EUI, Florence).

Bulmer, S., and Burch, M. (1998), 'Organizing for Europe: Whitehall, the British State and European Union', *Public Administration*, 76: 601–28.

Burgorgue-Larsen, L. (1995), *L'Espagne et la Communauté Européenne: L'État des Autonomies et le processus d'intégration européenne* (Brussels: Éditions de l'Université de Bruxelles).

Burnham, J., and Maor, M.(1995), 'Converging Administrative Systems: Recruitment and Training in EU Member States', *Journal of European Public Policy*, 2: 185–204.

Carnelutti, A. (1989), 'La Formation des agents de l'État aux affaires européennes', *Revue française d'administration publique*, 51: 510.

Closa, C. (1995a), 'Spain: The Cortes and the EU—a Growing Together', in P. Norton (ed.), *National Parliaments and the European Union* (London: Frank Cass).

—— (1995b), 'National Interest and Convergence of Preferences: A Changing Role for Spain in the EU?', in C. Rhodes and S. Mazey (eds.), *The State of the EU*, iii: *Building a European Polity?* (Boulder, Colo.: Lynne Rienner).

Dastis, A. (1995), 'La administración española ante la Unión Europea', *Revista de estudios políticos*, 90: 323–49.

Gil, A. (1992), 'Spain', in F. Laursen and S. Vanhoonacker (eds.), *The Intergovernmental Conference on Political Oman* (Maastricht: European Institute of Public Administration).

Goetz, K. H. (1995), 'National Governance and European Integration: Intergovernmental Relations in Germany', *Journal of Common Market Studies*, 33: 91–116.

Gunther, R. (1996), 'Spanish Public Policy: From Dictatorship to Democracy', Madrid: CEACS—Instituto Juan March de Estudios e Investigaciones, Series Working Papers, No. 84.

Harmsen, R. (1999), 'The Europeanization of National Administrations: A Comparative Study of France and the Netherlands', *Governance*, 12/1: 81–113.

Heywood, P. (1998), 'Power Diffusion or Concentration? In Search of the Spanish Policy Process', *West European Politics*, 21/4: 103–23.

——and Wright, V. (eds.) (1997), 'Executives, Bureaucracies and Decision-Making', in M. Rhodes, P. Heywood, and V. Wright (eds.), *Developments in West European Politics* (London: Macmillan).

Jones, R. (1998), 'Beyond the Spanish State? Relations between the EU, Central Government and Domestic Actors in Spain' (Ph.D. thesis. Loughborough University).

Kassim, H., Peters, G., and Wright, V. (1998), 'National Policy Co-ordination and EU Policy making', Oxford: Nuffield College, unpublished manuscript.

Lequesne, C. (1996), 'French Central Government and the European Political Stystem: Change and Adaptation since the Single Act' in Y. Mény, P. Muller, and J.-L. Quermonne (eds.), *Adjusting to Europe* (London: Routledge).

MAE (1987, 1988, 1989), *España en la CE* (Madrid: Secretariá de Estado para las Comunidades Europeas—Oficina Información Diplomática).

MAP (1997), 'La necesaria y continua adaptación de la administración española al proceso de integración europea', in *Contribución al análisis de la Administración General del Estado: Ideas para un Plan Estratégico* (Madrid: Ministerio para las Administraciones Públicas).

Maravall, J. M. (1992), 'What is Left? Social Democratic Policies in Southern Europe', Madrid: Centro de Estudios Avanzados en Ciencias Sociales del Instituto Juan March, Estudio/Working Paper No. 36.

Marks, M. P. (1997), *The Formation of European Policy in Post-Franco Spain: The Role of Ideas, Interests and Knowledge* (Aldershot: Avebury).

Metcalfe, L. (1994), 'International Policy Co ordination and Public Management Reform', *International Review of Administrative Sciences*, 60: 271–90.

Morata, F. (1996), 'Spain', in D. Rometsch and W. Wessels (eds.), *The European Union and Member States: Towards Institutional Fusion?* (Manchester: Manchester University Press).

——(1998), 'Spain: Modernization through Integration', in K. Hanf and B. Soetendorp (eds.), *Adapting to European Integration: Small States and the European Union* (Harlow: Weslay & Longman).

Moravcsik, A. (1994), 'Why the European Community Strengthens the State: Domestic Politics and International Cooperation', Cambridge, Mass.: Center for European Studies—Harvard University, Working Paper No. 52.

Olsen, J. P. (1997), 'European Challenges to the Nation State', in B. Steunenberg and F. van Vught (eds.), *Political Institutions and Public Policy* (Dordrecht: Kluwer).

Ordóñez Solís, D. (1994), *La ejecución del Derecho Comunitario Europeo en España* (Madrid: Fundación Universidad Empresa/Cívitas).

Ortuzar, L., et al. (1995), *La participación de las Comunidades Autónomas en los asuntos comunitarios europeos* (Madrid: Ministerio para las Administraciones Públicas).

Page, E. C., and Wouters, L. (1995), 'The Europeanization of the National Bureaucracies?', in J. Pierre (ed.), *Bureaucracy in the Modern State* (Aldershot: Edward Elgar).

Pérez Tremps, P., Cabellos, M. A., and Roig, E. (1999), 'Informe general', in *La participación europea y la acción exterior de las Comunidades Autónomas* (Madrid: Marcial Pons/IEA).

Rivero, M., and Heredia, D. (1994), 'Le Cas de l'Espagne', in S. Pappas (ed.), *Procédures administratives nationales de préparation de mise en œuvre des décisions communautaires* (Maastricht: European Institute of Public Administration).

Rometsch, D., and Wessels, W. (eds.) (1996), *The European Union and Member States: Towards Institutional Fusion?* (Manchester: Manchester University Press).

Ruíz Tartas, C. (1995), 'La Présidence du Conseil de l'Union Européenne et la deuxième Présidence espagnole', Maastricht: European Institute of Public Administration-Eipascope, 3: 2–10.

Salas Hernández, J., and Betancor Rodríguez, A. (1991), 'La incidencia organizativa de la integración europea en la administración española', *Revista de administración pública*, 125: 495–538.

Webb, J., and Sheldrake, P. D. (1993), 'State and Market in Western Europe: Traditions and Themes', in J. Webb and P. D. Sheldrake (eds.), *State and Market: Aspects of Modern European Development* (Aldershot: Dartmouth).

Wessels, W. (1990), 'Administrative Interaction', in W. Wallace (ed.), *The Dynamics of European Integration* (London: Pinter).

Wright, V. (1996), 'The National Co-ordination of European Policy-Making: Negotiating the Quagmire', in J. J. Richardson (ed.), *European Union: Power and Policy-Making* (London: Routledge).

Zapico Goñi, E. (1995), 'La adaptación de la administración española a la Unión Europea: Un proceso de evolución y aprendizaje permanente', *Gestión y análisis de políticas públicas*, 4: 47–65.

6

Portugal

José M. Magone

Introduction: The Growing Importance of EU Policy Co-ordination

The experience of Portugal is instructive on three counts. First, it offers a clear illustration of how the institutionalization of a culture of co-ordination takes time. Before it put its system in place, there was a period of diplomatic, administrative, and political learning about how other more experienced countries dealt with the same phenomenon. Second, it shares with Spain and Greece a special feature. Like them, its accession to the European Community took place at the same time as the consolidation of democracy. The parallel process of democratization and Europeanization distinguishes the three countries from the other member states, which were already established democracies in the 1980s when Greece, Portugal, and Spain joined the EC. Europeanization has been an important factor in the democratization of administrative structures and culture in Portugal. Third, Portugal had to overcome the policies of the past, characterized by the Salazarist attitude, 'we are proudly alone'. Community membership necessitated continuous co-operation with other European states, a convergence of policy, and a similarity in administration. In this context, Portugal is not unique: the same experience is to be found among the other member states.

Two lessons were quickly learnt. The first was that the definition of the Portuguese position has to be appropriate for a medium-sized member state: realistic and pragmatic. The second was that the key to success is to have well-

I should like to thank Zélia Nunes Dias, Alzira Cabrita, Josefina Carvalho, Rui Marques, and Luis Inez Dias for insightful additional information on the process of national policy co-ordination. I am especially grateful to the librarians Maria Antonia Rosário and Maria Francisca Fontes for responding to all my queries in terms of documentation during my stay in the library of DGAC. A special thanks also to Vincent Wright and the other editors for the comments and improvements made to the text.

trained political, administrative, and diplomatic negotiators, who are able to defend the vital interests of Portugal (particularly the structural funds), but leaving the negotiating table when all the other partners appear to leave as winners as well. It is this twofold aspect of Portuguese EU policy co-ordination that makes the Portuguese case so interesting.

This chapter is divided into three parts. The first deals with the creation of the EU policy co-ordination machinery in Portugal. In the second, the structure and culture of the present EU policy co-ordination machinery is thoroughly examined. The last part focuses on the interaction of the EU policy co-ordination machinery and the political and administrative environment.

The Development of EU Policy Co-ordination

The post-revolutionary period since 1975: the making of democratic EU policy co-ordination

It was only after the adoption of the Constitution on 2 April 1976 that the relationship between Portugal and the EC was normalized. The application for membership was submitted by the first Socialist minority government under the leadership of Mario Soares on 28 March 1977. The positive opinion of the Commission forwarded to the Council of Ministers on 19 May 1978 established the conditions for starting negotiations of accession (Kommission 1978). Negotiations between Portugal and the European Community were officially opened in Luxembourg on 17 October 1978. It is in this period that co-ordination between the different ministries began to be important.

In August 1977, a Commission for European Integration (*Comissão para a Integração Européia*) was established within the presidency of the Council of Ministers. It maintained a close relationship and contact with the members of the mission to the EC. The positive opinion of the Commission and the negotiations with the EC led to the creation of the Council of Ministers for European Integration in July 1979, which met monthly. The whole administrative apparatus of policy co-ordination in relation to the negotiations with the EC began to grow and differentiate steadily. In the run-up to accession, policy co-ordination gained overwhelming importance during the negotiation process. The creation in 1979 of the Secretariat for European Integration (*Secretariado de Integração Européia*), a specialist administrative service dedicated to European affairs in 1979, which began functioning from 1981, became the stable element of the construction of the Portuguese system of EU

policy co-ordination before and after accession. During the accession negotiations, the Secretariat was partially integrated into the Prime Minister's Office
and the Finance Ministry, but in 1985 shortly before membership the Secretariat was transferred to the Ministry of Foreign Affairs. The main reason presented in the decree law no. 526/85 of 31 December 1985 was that 'looking at
the experience of the current member states in the conduct of EC affairs, they
clearly give the responsibility to the corresponding Ministry of Foreign Affairs
in co-ordinating internally and presenting externally the positions of the different sectoral interests of the state'. At the same time, its responsibility for co-
ordination gave the Secretariat administrative autonomy within the Ministry
of Foreign Affairs.

In spite of governmental instability and ideological conflicts between left
and right, neither EU membership nor Portugal's administrative structures
has been questioned by the various parties in power. Although there were
administrative discontinuities in the different ministries, the Secretariado was
able to extend and enhance its position, mainly due to the fact that the
accession negotiations, as well as membership, required a great effort of co-
ordination and specialist expertise.

Portugal in the European Community/European Union: the challenge for the Portuguese administration

After 1986, the administrative framework, policy co-ordination, and policy
processes became more stable and long-term planning a priority. This was
partly due to the fact that Prime Minister Anibal Cavaco Silva won three con-
secutive elections in 1985, 1987, and 1991. For a decade, the Portuguese
experienced strong stable government which had a positive impact on
administrative structures and the processes of policy formulation, policy
making, and implementation. A long-term approach was taken by the
Socialist government under António Guterres who was clearly determined to
emphasize the continuity of policy making in EU affairs. The Cavaco
Silva decade led to a stabilization and institutionalization of the former
Secretariat of European Integration which changed its name in 1994 to
the State Secretariat of Community Affairs (*Secretariado de Estado para Assuntos Comunitários*—SEAC) supported by the administrative unit General
Directorate for Community Affairs (*Direcção-Geral para Assuntos Comunitários*—DGAC).

The DGAC grew in size and dealt with a widening range of EU policies. It
took about four to six years to learn to co-ordinate the various ministries and
to create a culture of dialogue and consensus. Between 1986 and 1990, Portuguese administrators dealing with EU affairs had to cope with a substantial
workload. According to the first report on the membership of Portugal in the

European Community in 1985–6, the Portuguese government completely restructured the organization of its interaction with Brussels by creating the Interministerial Commission for the European Communities (*Comissão Interministerial para as Comunidades Européias*—CICE) to exist alongside the General Directorate for European Communities. At the same time, technical ministries with an interest in Community affairs established specialized agencies. Within the space of a year, Portugal had to appoint representatives for all the committees and working groups of the Council. Moreover, it had to guarantee Portuguese participation in the various structures of the Community, including about 250 committees and 500 expert groups, which work in the Commission. The report estimated that Portuguese administration, via the co-ordination of the State Secretariat of European Integration, was able to guarantee participation of Portuguese representatives in over 2,500 meetings. The Portuguese experience clearly shows that the structures of the EC/EU were a major factor in restructuring the administrative machinery, which had until 1985 been searching for its own identity within the new democratic structures. The effort of adjustment required not only a change of mentality, it also provided a new dynamism and orientation to the wider policy-making culture in Portugal. Indeed, one could say that after 1986 a postmodern culture emphasizing administrative learning through participation was steadily institutionalized.

The institutionalization of EU policy co-ordination: The 1992 presidency and the 1996 Intergovernmental Conference

Events such as holding the Council presidency or the Intergovernmental Conferences are taken very seriously by the Portuguese government. The main reason is that it is important to ensure that national prestige is not undermined by an ill-prepared Portuguese representation. Therefore, the Portuguese administration attempts to be extremely well prepared and up to date during such events. This was one of the reasons why Portugal decided to give up its first presidency, because its turn was due so soon after accession. Consequently, the first Portuguese presidency did not take place until the first half of 1992. This serious attitude has become a distinctive element of the behaviour of civil servants dealing with EU affairs. The main reason is that for a small country to represent the member states is a great honour.

The 1992 presidency of the European Communities: learning by doing

Preparations for the 1992 presidency started four years in advance. They began with a general assessment of what the presidency does and what functions it has to perform. For this purpose, a report of over a hundred pages was internally entitled 'Preparation for the First Portuguese Presidency of the Council of the European Communities' (no. 45/MNE/88). The report also included information on other presidencies, as well as the constraints and opportunities of the presidency. At the same time, it was decided to construct a new building which would be used by the presidency for the Council meetings—the Centro Cultural de Belem (Cultural Centre of Belem—CCB). A general assessment of the resources needed both in Lisbon, as well as in the representations in other member states, was undertaken. At the same time, contacts with, and missions in, other member states were intensified and the liaison with the General Secretary of the Council strengthened (Ministério dos Negócios 1989: 331–3).

During 1989, several civil servants dealing with EU affairs were prepared for the big event. The main institution undertaking this training was the National Institute of Administration (*Instituto Nacional de Administração*—INA) which created modules tailored to the needs of Portuguese civil servants. Moreover, several civil servants were sent to France, the United Kingdom, and the Netherlands for training courses. At the same time, working groups were constituted to study the Spanish presidency in the first half of 1989, the French in the second half, and contacts were intensified with those responsible for preparing the Dutch presidency and the British presidency which would take place before and after the Portuguese presidency respectively, in order to ensure continuity of policy making and formulation among the three presidencies (Ministério dos Negócios 1990: 351–3).

Final preparations took place throughout 1990 and 1991. The training of civil servants involved in the presidency was reinforced. Several courses on the presidency of the Council of the European Communities were organized in the European Institute of Public Administration in Maastricht, relating to techniques of negotiation. Language training was also enhanced, and several civil servants were sent to the United Kingdom and the Netherlands to reinforce the co-ordination of the three presidencies. The government also created the Council of Ministers for Community Affairs (*Conselho de Ministros para Assuntos Comunitários*—CMAC), a ministerial-level cabinet to deal with co-ordination issues related to European affairs. In terms of the final structure, it was decided to organize three working groups within the overall structure related to the co-ordination of EU affairs for the period before and during the presidency. These were:

- the Working Group on Organization and Logistics (*Grupo de Trabalho de Organização e Logística*—GTOL), presided over by the Secretary-General of the Ministry of Foreign Affairs, which was in charge of promoting, co-ordinating, and supervising the necessary actions in terms of organiza-

tion, logistics, and promotion of the preparation, organization, and exercise of the presidency;
- the Working Group of Community Affairs (*Grupo de Trabalho de Assuntos Comunitários*—GTAC), chaired by the General Director of the General Directorate for the European Communities which was in charge of co-ordinating the training programme for the civil servants; identifying the priorities and defining the strategic approach to the dossiers; and proposing decisions which permitted the functional operation of presidency;
- the Working Group of European Political Co-operation (*Grupo de Trabalho Cooperação Política*—GTCP), which was in charge of identifying and studying national priorities, proposing a calendar for various EPC meetings, and co-ordinating and liaising with the Secretariat of Political Co-operation and with the preceding and following presidencies of the Council of European Communities.

As well as these measures, the Ministry of the Interior established a working group on Security (*Grupo de Trabalho Segurança*) to deal with security problems during the presidency. A subcommittee of CICE, the interdepartmental commission, was established to support the preparation of the presidency. This subcommittee functioned as a supervisory body for the preparation of the presidency of the European Communities, and submitted quarterly progress reports to the CICE until June 1991 (Ministério dos Negócios 1991*a*: 381–6).

During 1991 the structure developed for the presidency intensified its work. The CMAC began to meet weekly rather than monthly, as did the Governmental Commission for Community Affairs (*Comissão Governamental para Assuntos Comunitários*—CGAC) which supported the CMAC. At the same time, both Prime Minister Cavaco Silva as well as the junior minister for European Integration, Vitor Martins, were provided with a small co-ordination staff with the task of keeping an overall oversight over the presidency. Each department appointed a delegate for affairs related to the presidency within the competences of the corresponding department. These delegates had the task primarily to provide support in dealing with the dossiers as well as to reinforce the logistics of the presidency.

Training programmes, the distribution of a *Guide for the Conduct of the Presidency* (*Guia para o exercício da presidência*), a work of 158 pages on how to deal with aspects of the presidency, and a document called 'Towards the European Union' (*Rumo a União Européia*) defined the main aims of the Portuguese presidency. These included the consolidation of the Maastricht Treaty, the preparation of the Delors II package, strengthening of ties with the international community, and the preparation for Nordic enlargement (Ministério dos Negócios 1991*b*).

The presidency of the European Communities was, despite unexpected events, well co-ordinated. If there was a lack of success in completing most of the dossiers, it was because of the extreme complexity and controversial nature of the issues the Portuguese presidency had to deal with. The ratification of the Maastricht Treaty by the member states was slowed by the negative first referendum in Denmark on 3 June 1992. Other countries such as the United Kingdom and France faced difficulties in ratifying the Treaty. Moreover, the decision on the Delors II package, which was important for the Portuguese government, had to be postponed until the British presidency. Some success was achieved in trying to end the reform of the Common Agricultural Policy (CAP) by the Agricultural Minister, Arlindo de Carvalho. A high point of the presidency was the representation of the European Communities by Prime Minister Anibal Cavaco Silva at the Rio de Janeiro Conference which required a very high degree of co-ordination to ensure that the European Community spoke with one voice (Magone 1997: 164–7; Martins 1993: pp. i–xi; Ministério dos Negócios 1992a). Preparations for the Portuguese presidency in the first half of 2000 were well under way in 1998.

Intergovernmental Conferences in the 1990s

Portugal has participated in two intergovernmental conferences. In the first, at Maastricht, the Portuguese delegation adopted a position close to that of the Spanish delegation, which was willing to support Economic and Monetary Union and the overall Treaty, if they could achieve an increase of structural funds for the adjustment of their economies to the SEM and the impact of Economic and Monetary Union. During the Edinburgh European Council in December 1992, Portugal and Spain were very keen to secure the doubling of structural funds as well as the creation of a new cohesion fund for all the countries which had an average GDP/per person of less than 80 per cent of the EC/EU average. In the end, they were successful. Indeed, after the end of the Portuguese presidency, the Portuguese government became more self-confident in defending its interests, searching for alliances with Spain and other countries (Martins 1993: pp. i–xi).

At the 1996 IGC, the Portuguese government took a more reserved position. According to the then Junior Minister for European Affairs (*Secretário de Estado de Assuntos Europeus*), the position of Portugal in the previous intergovernmental conference had been very defensive and unco-ordinated. The presidency clearly helped to change this defensive perspective. In 1996, the Portuguese administration was keen to improve the co-ordination of the Portuguese position, internally and externally. On the whole, one could argue that sporadic events such as the presidency of 1992 and the IGC in 1996 were important in making EU policy co-ordination more salient within the Portuguese institutional framework. Thus, in just over a decade, the Portuguese administration had defined its own style, characterized by an emphasis on a minimalist, flexible, but strong, permanent structure of policy co-ordination, which is complemented by temporary structures—such as working groups, subcommissions, temporary co-ordination staff allocation, and so on—for specific events (Seixas Costa 1997: 25–30).

The importance of the structural funds for Portugal

From the time of its accession, Portugal has been concerned with guaranteeing the continued flow of structural funds to the country, so that this became the most salient country-specific item on the agenda. This could be observed during the final negotiating stages on the Delors II package which led to the doubling of the structural funds for the period 1993–9. The final decision in the Edinburgh European Council was achieved in alliance with Spain, Greece, Ireland, and other countries interested in this issue. This was accomplished to the detriment of the still large agricultural sector, which even today is not regarded as a priority item for Portugal. Indeed, the declarations of the Junior Minister for European Affairs clearly indicated that Portugal prefers to see a considerable reduction of the financial support for the Common Agricultural Policy rather than of the funds allocated for the structural funds in the whole discussion of Agenda 2000 (Seixas Costa 1997: 21–3). According to the official in charge of the financial negotiations related to the structural funds, the European Commission originally planned to exclude the main region of Lisbon from receipt of structural funds, because it had a GDP/per capita higher than the EU average. However, the Portuguese government was able to persuade the Commission to grant Lisbon and Vale do Tejo the status of transitional region, thus ensuring the flow of structural funds which will enable it to sustain its development—crucial, since this area is the motor of the Portuguese economy. Most of the financial and economic transfers for the five NUTS II regions (Norte, Centro, Lisboa e Vale do Tejo, Alentejo, Algarve) are done through Lisbon, so that it is necessary to continue to include Lisbon and Vale do Tejo as a recipient of structural funds. Portugal is determined to keep this issue on the agenda. The referendum on the regionalization on 8 November 1998 proposed a split of the national territory into eight administrative regions (Entre-Douro e Minho, Trás-os Montes e Alto Douro, Beira Litoral, Beira Interior, Estremadura e Ribatejo, Lisboa e Setubal, Alentejo e Algarve) and was regarded as a further factor for looking at the Portuguese case, not only from a NUTS II perspective, but also at the lower NUTS III level.[1] The negative outcome of the referendum put an end to the DGAC's advocacy of this argument.

[1] Interview with Dr Alzira Cabrita, 24 Nov. 1998.

EU Policy Co-ordination in Portugal: Simplicity is the Name of the Game

The structure of EU policy co-ordination in Portugal

The structure of EU policy co-ordination in Portugal achieved its stability only after the signature of the treaty of accession on 12 June 1985. The transfer of the administrative structure from the Prime Minister's Office and the Ministry of Finance to the Ministry of Foreign Affairs took place during 1985. One of the main reasons, according to Luis Inez Fernandes, a senior official in the DGAC, was that it was more efficient to locate the administrative structure charged with EU policy co-ordination in the Ministry responsible for communication with the outside world, so that internally and externally Portuguese policy co-ordination could have a more efficient impact.[2] In so doing, the government elected to follow the approach taken by most other member states. Today the key position of the Ministry of Foreign Affairs in leading the EU policy co-ordination machinery is uncontested in Portuguese public administration. This fact provided stability and routinization to the whole process of EU affairs. In spite of the restructuring of the Ministry of Foreign Affairs after the democratic transition from the authoritarian regime, the administrative structure of EU policy co-ordination was characterized by continuity. These arrangements were maintained by the governments of Cavaco Silva and Guterres.

The main administrative unit in charge of EU policy co-ordination is the DGAC, which supports the work led by the Junior Minister for European Affairs (*Secretário de Estado de Assuntos Europeus*), a political appointee of the government. Although the Junior Minister is supported by a small staff in the State Secretariat, most of the research and co-ordination work is carried out by the officials of the DGAC. The DGAC is the filter between the EU co-ordinators of all other ministries and the Permanent Representation, as well as the European institutions. It disseminates the information coming from the Permanent Representation, as well as the institutions and organs of the Union, and assures the transmission of instructions and documents to the permanent mission. The DGAC also deals with the technical co-ordination of Community dossiers. Moreover, it is the supervisory body of the implementation of European law and the contentious issues that may emerge in this process (Direcção Geral 1998).

The DGAC is organized into ten departments (*direcções de serviço*—DS),

---

[2] Interview with Luis Inez Fernandes, Director of the Department for Legal Affairs, DGAC, 22 Sept. 1998.

each of which is responsible for a different aspect of the European Union. Each department is headed by a director (*director/a de serviço*) who co-ordinates the work within the department. This structure has been, with minor exceptions, quite stable since 1984 when the then government started to upgrade the State Secretariat for European Integration (*Secretariado de Estado para a Integração Européia*—SIE). For the ten departments and their functions see Fig. 6.1.

Department of Community Institutions (Direcção de Serviço das Instituições Comunitárias)

This department is probably the most important in terms of internal EU policy co-ordination. It is in charge of organizing the weekly meetings of the Interministerial Commission for Community Affairs (*Comissão Interministerial para Assuntos Comunitários*—CIAC) which includes representatives from all the other ministries, and it aims at resolving policy formulation problems, as well as competency disputes, between the different ministries. It is also the main addressee for the substantial preparation and conduct of the presidency of the Council of Ministers that Portugal may assume.

Department of Legal Affairs (Direcção de Serviços de Assuntos Jurídicos)

This is the main department dealing with the transposition of European law into Portuguese law. It is the main body responsible for legal issues. It advises both public and private actors on how to deal with issues before the European Court of Justice.

Department of Economic and Financial Questions (Direcção de Serviços das Questões Económicas e Financeiras)

This department has become quite important over the past ten years, due to the fact that it handles dossiers such as the allocation of structural funds to Portugal as well as adjustments in line with the requirements of Economic and Monetary Union. It has a mandate to oversee all economic, monetary, fiscal, budgetary, and financial policies and relate them to the economic and regional development of the country.[3]

Department of Questions Related to Agriculture and Fisheries (Direcção de Serviços das Questões da Agricultura e das Pescas)

This unit deals with issues relating to CAP and Common Fisheries policy. It works closely with other sectoral departments in other departments to co-

---

[3] Interview with Dr Alzira Cabrita, Director of Department on Financial and Economic Issues, DGAC, 29 Sept. 1998.

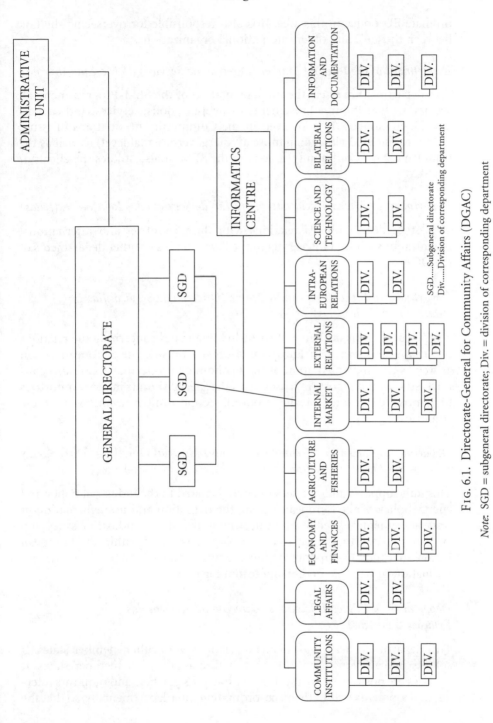

Fig. 6.1. Directorate-General for Community Affairs (DGAC)

Note: SGD = subgeneral directorate; Div. = division of corresponding department

ordinate EU policy in this area. It is also responsible for overseeing the link between the CAP and other international organizations.

Department of the Internal Market (Direcção de Serviços do Mercado Interno)

This department oversees the implementation of the SEM-Programme in all sectors, so that the free movements of people, goods, services, and capitals may be guaranteed. It is involved in the Community negotiations of issues related to the SEM (including those at intergovernmental level) as well as the complementary Community actions of the SEM. It also studies the effects of the SEM.

Department of External Relations (Direcção de Serviços das Relações Externas)

This office deals with EU relations with third countries and international organizations without interfering in the competences of other departments of the DGAC.

Department of Intra-European Relations (Direcção de Serviços das Relações Intra-Européias)

This department is in charge of co-ordinating issues concerning the relations of European Union with European countries outside the European Union as well as the implementation of the Economic European Space. It also conducts studies and reports in liaison with the specialist units in other ministries to apprise companies of the economic opportunities available in these countries.

Department of Scientific, Technological, and Industrial Questions (Direcção de Serviços das Questões Científicas, Tecnológicas e Industriais)

This unit supports and oversees the issues related to the industrial policy and energy policy of the European Union, the definition and implementation of trade agreements related to scientific, technological, and industrial issues, and all topics related to science and technology developed within the European Union in order to support national entities directly involved in the co-ordination of national bodies and technology policy.

Department of Bilateral Relations (Direcção de Serviços das Relações Bilaterais)

This department deals with bilateral relations with other member states. It collects information of an economic nature about other member states. It analyses the position of Portugal in relation to its partners and monitors internal developments within them, co-ordinating interdepartmentally, so that the administration can speak with one voice in its bilateral contacts. It also provides continuous information to the diplomatic missions about the latest developments in the European Union. Finally, it is in charge of monitoring agreements and treaties of an economic nature.

Department of Information, Training, and Documentation (Direcção de Serviços de Informação, Formação e Documentação)

This office provides a documentation and training service to other departments. It oversees developments in culture, education, information, health, and youth. It is also responsible for co-ordinating and organizing most of the training courses for civil servants and defining the training policy of administrators with a view to meeting the challenges of the European Union, particularly in advance of holding the Council presidency. In the early 1980s Portugal sent civil servants for short training periods to the European Commission, though in the run-up to accession a more professional course was offered. The National Institute of Administration (*Instituto Nacional de Administração*—INA) prepares tailored courses for civil servants.[4]

The DGAC is chaired by the Junior Minister for European Affairs, who works within the general policy guidelines laid down by the Minister of Foreign Affairs. The Junior Minister is also competent for questions related to the Council of Europe and the OECD, where other General Directorates within the Ministry of Foreign Affairs such as the Directorate General for Bilateral Relations and the Directorate General for Multilateral Affairs are responsible. The State Secretary has a small staff of assistants and advisers and is supported by a *chef de cabinet*. Both the former Junior Minister, Vitor Martins, as well as his successor, Francisco Seixas Costa, are experienced professionals who move between the worlds of diplomacy, administration, and politics. Such a mix of experiences equips them with the skills necessary to deal with the very difficult task of co-ordination.

The Interdepartmental Commission of Community Affairs (CIAC)

The senior body in EU policy co-ordination in Portugal is the CIAC. This interdepartmental commission is the main institution where conflicts between ministries, policy decisions, as well as administrative cohesion (thus preventing sectorialization), are discussed. The CIAC meets every Friday morning in the Palace Cova da Moura, the DGAC's HQ. It includes representatives from all ministries, the representatives of the governments of the

---

[4] Interview with Rui Marques, Department of Information, Training, and Documentation, DGAC, 23 Sept. 1998.

autonomous regions of Madeira and Azores, and the newly created national co-ordinator for the affairs related to the free movement of persons in the European 'space' (*coordenador nacional para os assuntos da livre circulação de pessoas no espaço europeu*). There are generally around twenty participants at each meeting. Formally, the CIAC is chaired by the Minister of Foreign Affairs and most representatives are at junior minister level. In practice, the meeting is chaired by the Junior Minister for European Affairs and most representatives are delegates of the officials who actually deal with EU affairs in the individual ministries. Rontine has, however, led the CIAC to become something of a pro forma meeting, a ceremony that must take place every Friday morning, and most of the major problems of EU policy co-ordination are resolved by informal telephone calls or personal bilateral meetings which help solve the most difficult problems. Nevertheless, the CIAC continues to play an important role when conflicts arise, when Portugal holds the presidency or in preparing for IGCs. It is a flexible body, which creates temporary subcommittees to prepare, discuss, or monitor certain aspects that are relevant for the position of Portugal in the European Union. The CIAC is the focal point for all departments of the DGAC to create specialized committees for certain issues such as the ongoing discussion about the allocation of the structural funds, the single European currency, or the implementation of EU legislation in Portugal.[5]

The relationship between the DGAC and the Permanent Representation in Brussels is excellent. Formally, members of the permanent mission receive instructions from the DGAC. In reality, they receive more detailed informal technical instructions or advice from the delegates dealing with European Union affairs in the individual ministries. As a result, before any meetings in Brussels, Portuguese members of the Permanent Representation may receive both formal general as well as informal technical instructions to speed up the information process. The DGAC aims to include other ministries where necessary in order to provide information channels between officials in the Permanent Representation and the national institutions. Members of the Permanent Representation are required to write reports after each meeting, which normally include additional comments or suggestions on how to deal with certain issues. This is greatly appreciated by the DGAC because it helps the decision-making process in Lisbon. The relationship between the DGAC and the permanent Representation in Brussels is one of partnership rather than of subordination to the decisions taken in Lisbon. If neither the CIAC nor the bilateral informal contacts can sort out a problem, the issue is discussed in the Portuguese Council of Ministers for European Union Affairs (*Conselho de Ministros para Assuntos da União Européia*), consisting of the Prime Minister and relevant ministers.

[5] Interviews with Josefina Carvalho, CIAC, 22 Sept. 1998; Luis Inez Fernandes, Department for Juridical Affairs, 21 Sept. 1998 and Alzira Cabrita, Department of Financial and Economic Questions, 24 Sept. 1998.

Political and Administrative Opportunity Structures

Political opportunity structure

As noted above, EU issues are extremely salient domestically. The EC/EU has been regarded, since the application for membership, as an important mechanism for consolidating and institutionalizing democracy. The flow of structural funds since 1986 has clearly strengthened this positive image of the European Union among all Portugal's political parties. Portugals main two parties, the Socialist Party (*Partido Socialista*—PS) and the Social Democratic Party (*Partido Socialdemocrata*—PSD), are strongly pro-Europe. The two smaller parties are sceptical in relation to certain aspects of the European Union. The Communist Party (*Partido Comunista Português*—PCP) is opposed to aspects of the European Union related to the liberal SEM programme and the single European currency, but is supportive of a 'Social Europe' which would protect stronger worker rights.

Portuguese political parties have been pragmatic in their support of EU policies in the interest of Portugal. On the right, in 1992 the populist-conservative Democratic Social Centre–People's Party (*Centro Democrático Social-Partido Popular*—CDS–PP) started a campaign against the Maastricht Treaty and in support of a *Europe de Patries*. It also opposed the Treaty of Amsterdam. Under the leadership of the former journalist Paulo Portas, the party has moderated its position on the European Union, even if he continues to be a Eurosceptic (Magone 1996*b* and 1998*b*).

The executive system is dominated by a Prime Minister who chairs the cabinet. The Prime Minister is accountable to the Portuguese Parliament, the Assembly of the Republic (*Assembléia da República*). The Prime Minister may be dismissed by a motion of censure which may be proposed by a parliamentary group or 25 per cent of MPs. The motion of censure is successful if an absolute majority of MPs vote for it. Since 1987, the Prime Minister has grown in strength and worked harmoniously with the Assembly of the Republic. Indeed, the flow of information between the government and parliament has increased in the past decade, particularly in relation to EU affairs. Anibal Cavaco Silva, Prime Minister between 1985 and 1995, contributed a great deal to increasing the status of the executive, and his successor, Antonio Guterres, continued this tradition (Magone 1997: 43–6; Bandeira 1996, 1998).

A good relationship exists between the DGAC and the Assembly of the Republic's Committee for European Affairs in terms of the dissemination of information, exchange of opinion, and ex-post monitoring of EU policy making, formulation, and implementation. A Committee of European Integration was established during the accession negotiations, but remained dormant and unimportant until 1992. Though it was granted responsibilities and powers under Law 29/87 of 29 June 1987 and Law 111/88 of 15

December 1988, it was only after the ratification of Treaty on the European Union that a real partnership between government and the Committee of European Affairs became possible. The presidency of 1992 led to a spill-over effect and revitalization of the already existing institutions. The Law of 15 June 1994 replaced the obsolete Law 111/88, and the former Finance Minister Jorge Braga de Macedo, who became chairman of the Committee in 1993, led to an awakening of Parliament in monitoring and controlling government action in EU matters. The government is required to submit an annual report on Portugal in the EU to the Committee. The chairman then asks the various permanent committees in the Parliament to prepare opinions on the policies discussed and analysed in the report. The first exercise was undertaken in 1994 under the supervision of Jorge Braga de Macedo. At the end of the process, the Committee of European Affairs publishes an annual report, 'Portugal in the European Union in [year]—a parliamentary evaluation' (Magone 1995). In addition, the new President, José Medeiros Ferreira, supervised the process in 1995 and 1996. One of the criticisms made is that the government tended to ignore the work done by the Committee of European Affairs during the 1996 IGC (which led to the publication of two volumes comprising the opinions of civil associations and economic groups) and that there was also an absence of feedback from Amsterdam during negotiations. Nevertheless, the relationship between government and the Parliament, in terms of exchange of information, has improved over the past six years, making it a genuinely two-way relationship. The strong commitment of the Committee of European Affairs in the Conference of National Parliaments has strengthened the self-confidence of this Committee which is supported by a tiny staff of two researchers (Assembléia da República 1997: 21–45).

Portugal is a unitary country, so no other tier of government is included in the decision-making process. The referendum on regionalization on 8 November 1998 did not change this situation. Over two-thirds of the voters decided against the regionalization of the country in eight regions. This was a big defeat for the Socialist government. Only the Alentejo region voted for regionalization. Furthermore, 52 per cent of the registered voters did not bother to cast their vote.[6] Even if the results of the referendum were not binding, because less than 50 per cent of the registered voters voted, it was a serious blow for the pro-devolution parties PS and PCP, while it was a considerable boost to the right–centre coalition between PSD and CDS–PP. For the moment only representatives of the autonomous regional governments of Madeira and Azores are included in the overall EU policy co-ordination process.

Interest groups do not directly approach the administrative unit dealing with EU policy co-ordination. They normally lobby the respective ministry

---

[6] Diário de Notícias, 9 Nov. 1998.

which takes their concerns to the CIAC. One can see strong lobbying activity in the Ministry of Agriculture, which during the Cavaco Silva years was close to a *clientela* relationship, a strong dependency of certain departments within the Ministry of Agriculture in relation to the expertise or knowledge of certain interest groups.

On the whole, parliament, subnational actors, and interest groups have played a relatively minor role in EU policy co-ordination in Portugal. However, their influence has increased in the 1990s, with the rise of the Assembly of the Republic's Committee of European Affairs particularly noticeable. After almost twenty-five years of democracy, one has again to refer to the point that making democracy work is a long-term process and that a stronger civil society can only emerge with time.

Administrative opportunity structure

It is difficult to determine precisely how many people are involved in EU policy co-ordination because of the flexible nature of the process. The permanent staff within the DGAC numbers around 250. Including the officials involved in EU policy making in other departments, the total may be between 350 and 400. Adding the members of the Permanent Representation and the civil servants in other ministries leads to a figure of about 450. Not all are active at the same time, but this gives an idea of the human resources in the Portuguese administration involved in EU policy co-ordination. Most of are centrally allocated to the DGAC and the Permanent Representation with the rest scattered among the other fifteen to seventeen ministries depending on which party is in power. The administrative system related to EU policy co-ordination is relatively well integrated, as is the whole administration since the early 1990s. The administrative reforms introduced by the Secretariat for the Modernization of the Administration (*Secretariado para a Modernização da Administração*) during the Cavaco Silva era were quite important in making the Portuguese civil service more integrated. In terms of competence, in the past decade, EU policy co-ordination has been dominated by the DGAC and this remains uncontested internally. Informal networks both in Portugal as well as in Brussels are used to smooth the already well-functioning formal channels of EU policy co-ordination. Informal networks are used particularly where there is need for a quick answer due to the legislation proposals coming from the commission or working group.[7]

On the whole, the DGAC is the uncontested site of EU policy co-ordination. Most of the administrative staff dealing with EU policy co-ordination are located within the DGAC. The Permanent Representation is

[7] Interview with Dr Josefina Carvalho, CIAC, 22 Sept. 1998.

directly formally linked to the DGAC and, only informally, sporadically linked with the other ministries.

Conclusion: Keeping the Golden Mean of EU Policy Co-ordination

From the run-up to accession, Portugal has had a light and flexible structure for EU policy co-ordination, which is able to adjust rapidly to the challenges of a dynamic multifaceted process, such as the European integration process. In normal periods, the DGAC guarantees the smooth running of EU policy co-ordination, the dissemination of information to and from the ministries and to and from the Permanent Representation. In cases of specific events, temporary working groups are established to guarantee the success of the Portuguese intervention. Most actors within the DGAC see the present structure as appropriate for the EU policy co-ordination tasks assigned to them: there is always scope for improvement, but the basic structure remains the same. Civil servants learned a great deal from the experience of EU policy co-ordination of other countries, but at the same time developed their own approach, being conscious of the fact that Portugal is a middle-sized country. In spite of being a member since only 1986, Portugal has learned quickly how to cope with the incrementalism of EU decision making. One of the reasons for its pragmatic approach is the fact that, like the European Union, the Portuguese political system is still in the making. This convergence of two incomplete systems and their adjustment to each other since 1986 has ensured that the Portuguese public administration sought a very flexible machinery of EU policy co-ordination, which would be able to respond quickly and efficiently to questions of further European integration.

References

Assembléia da República (1993), *Assembléia da República e o Tratado da União Européia* (Lisbon: Comissão de Assuntos Europeus).

——(1994a), *Portugal na União Européia: Lei de acompanhamento e apreciação* (Lisbon: Comissão de Assuntos Europeus).

——(1994b), *Portugal na União Européia em 1993: Apreciação parlamentar* (Lisbon: Comissão de Assuntos Europeus).

——(1995), *Acompanhamento parlamentar da revisão do Tratado da União Européia na Conferência Intergovernamental de 1996*, 2 vols. (Lisbon: Comissão de Assuntos Europeus).

——(1997), *Portugal na União Européia em 1995 e 1996: Apreciação parlamentar* (Lisbon: Comissão de Assuntos Europeus).

——(1998). *Opções européias de Portugal: União econômica e monetária* (Lisbon: Comissão de Assuntos Europeus).

Bandeira, C. L. (1996), 'The Portuguese Parliament in the Cavaco Era', Hull: Centre for Legislative Studies, University of Hull, Research Paper 3/96.

——(1998), 'The Relationship between Parliament and Government in Portugal: An Expression on the Maturation of the Political System', in P. Norton (ed.), *Parliaments and Governments in Western Europe* (London: Frank Cass).

Bruneau, T. C. (1984), *Politics and Nationhood: Post-revolutionary Portugal* (New York: Praeger).

Direcção Geral de Assuntos Comunitários (DGAC) (1998), 'La Commission Interministeriel de Affaires Communautaires (CIAC)', photocopied document.

Eaton, M. (1994), 'Regional Development Funding in Portugal', *Journal of the Association of Contemporary Iberian Studies*, 7: 36–46.

Eisfeld, R. (1984), *Der sozialistischer Pluralismus in Europa: Ansätze und Scheitern am Beispiel Portugal* (Cologne: Verlag Wissenschaft und Politik).

European Union (1998), *Who's Who in the European Union: Interinstitutional Directory* (Luxembourg: Office of the Official Publications of the European Communities).

Giddens, A. (1993), *Modernity and Self-Identity: Self and Society in the Late Modern Age* (Oxford: Polity Press).

Hayes-Renshaw, F., and Wallace, H. (1997), *The Council of Ministers* (London: Macmillan).

Kommission der Europäischen Gemeinschaften (1978), 'Stellungnahme zum Beitrittsantrag Portugals (von der Kommission am 19. Mai 1978 dem Rat vorgelegt)', *Bulletin der Europäischen Gemeinschaften*, 5.

Lequesne, C. (1996), 'French Central Government and the European Political System: Change and Adaptation since the Single Act', in Y. Meny, P. Muller, and J.-L. Quermonne (eds.), *Adjusting to Europe: The Impact of European Union on National Institutions and Policies* (London: Routledge) 110–20.

Magone, J. (1995), 'The Portuguese Assembléia da República: Discovering Europe', *Journal of Legislative Studies*, 1: 152–65.

——(1996a), *The Changing Architecture of Iberian Politics: An Investigation on the Democratic Structuring of Political Systemic Culture in Southern European Semiperipheral Societies* (Lewiston, NY: Edwin Mellen Press).

——(1996b), 'Portugal', in J. Lodge (ed.), *The European Parliament Elections of 1994* (London: Pinter) 147–56.

——(1997), *European Portugal: The Difficult Road to Sustainable Democracy* (Basingstoke/New York: Macmillan/St Martin's Press).

——(1998a), 'A integração européia e a construção da democracia portuguesa', *Penelope*, 18: 123–63.

——(1998b), 'Portugal: Party System Installation and Consolidation', in D. Broughton and M. Donovan (eds.), *West European Party Systems* (London: Pinter) 232–54.

Manuel, P. C. (1995), *Uncertain Outcome: The Politics of the Portuguese Transition to Democracy* (Lanham, NY: University Press of America).

Martins, V. (1993), 'Introdução', in *Ministério dos Negócios Estrangeiros: Portugal nas*

Comunidades Européias 1992, sétimo ano (Lisbon: MNE).

Ministério dos Negócios Estrangeiros (1987), *Portugal nas Comunidades Européias, primeiro ano 1986* (Lisbon: MNE).

——(1989), *Portugal nas Comunidades Européias, terceiro ano, 1988* (Lisbon: MNE).

——(1990), *Portugal nas Comunidades Européias, quarto ano, 1989* (Lisbon: MNE).

——(1991*a*), *Portugal nas Comunidades Européias, quinto ano, 1990* (Lisbon: MNE).

——(1991*b*), *Rumo a União Européia* (Lisbon: MNE).

——(1992*a*), *Portugal nas Comunidades Européias, sexto ano, 1991* (Lisbon: MNE).

——(1992*b*), *Presidência portuguesa no Conselho de Ministros das Comunidades Européias* (Lisbon: Casa da Moeda).

——(1993), *Portugal das Comunidades Européias, sétimo ano, 1992* (Lisbon: MNE).

——(1995), *A restruturação do Ministério dos Negócios Estrangeiros* (Lisbon: MNE).

——(1996), *Portugal e a Conferência Intergovernamental para a revisão do Tratado da União Européia* (Lisbon: MNE).

Pires, L. M. (1998), *A política regional européia e Portugal* (Lisbon: Fundação Calouste Gulbenkian).

Poulantzas, N. (1976), *Die Krise der Diktaturen: Portugal, Griechenland und Spanien* (Frankfurt: Suhrkamp).

Pridham, G. (1991), 'The Politics of the European Community: Transnational Networks and Democratic Transition in Southern Europe', in G. Pridham (ed.), *Encouraging Democracy: The International Dimension of Regime Transition in Southern Europe* (London: Pinter) 211–54.

Secretária do Estado da Integração Européia (1992), *Guia para o exercício da presidência* (Lisbon: SIE).

Seixas Costa, F. (1997), 'Tratado de Amsterdão: História de uma negociação', *Política internacional*, 1: 23–47.

——(1998), 'Portugal e o desafio europeu', *Nação e defesa*, 85: 15–27.

Wallace, H. (1996), 'Relations between the European Union and British Administration', in Y. Meny, P. Muller, and J.-L. Quermonne (eds.), *Adjusting to Europe: The Impact of the European Union on National Institutions and Policies* (London: Routledge) 61–72.

Wessels, W., and Rometsch, D. (1996), 'German Administrative Interaction and European Union: The Fusion of Public Policies', in Y. Meny, P. Muller, and J.-L. Quermonne (eds.), *Adjusting to Europe: The Impact of European Union on National Institutions and Policies* (London: Routledge) 73–109.

7

Greece

Calliope Spanou

A Truncated Pyramid?

Co-ordination depends upon the ability to define priorities and the capacity to ensure compliance with these priorities in the face of centrifugal tendencies. In that sense, co-ordination has to do with the *steering capacity* of individual political-administrative systems. Unless priorities are specified, co-ordination is problematic, even if the apparatus designed to achieve co-ordination is physically in place.

The analysis of the Greek case will seek to show that in terms of formal arrangements the country has little to envy, being more or less in tune with other EU members. Still, co-ordination deficiencies are often apparent and pronounced. This chapter will highlight the 'inanimate' character of these arrangements and their neutralization by the absence of clear priorities set at the political level and diffused throughout the political-administrative system. The co-ordination scheme looks like a truncated pyramid where everything is in place apart from the unifying element at the top.

It is further argued that although the existing arrangements are apparently well entrenched, they are not unalterable. What is required essentially is leadership from the centre and for government to lay down general orientations in the European policy domain. The core executive must take daring decisions and mark clear priorities. Ultimately it then becomes possible to give a sense of direction, compensating for the 'political cost' argument used by centrifugal forces.

Prerequisites of Co-ordination

The nature of co-ordination

The search for *mutual predictability* is a direct consequence of increased interdependence within the complexities of the EU environment[1] and the European policy process. It constitutes a vital precondition for further integration. Given that within the EU a number of different—often diverging—rationales meet, the governability of the whole depends on co-ordination systems which reduce complexity and uncertainty regarding the behaviour of their component states. Co-ordination serves predictability; it represents an integration mechanism concerning more particularly the interface between the EU and domestic structures and policies. Co-ordination constitutes a systemic function of the EU, involving EU as well as member states' policies. In that sense, difficulties arise on both sides (Wright 1996).

A fundamental question actually consists in what co-ordination is. Its meaning is not self-evident. Metcalfe (1988) considers it to be a slippery concept and a 'standing temptation to academic eclecticism'. Co-ordination may be conceived in terms of a Guttman scale composed of nine cumulative steps[2] going from zero co-ordination to overall governmental strategy implying a unitary rational actor model (Metcalfe 1988: 4–7). Wright (1996: 148) reminds us of the various forms of co-ordination and of the lack of a framework integrating them. Nor is it always clear what is sought by co-ordination. The answers to the question oscillate between the extremes of a minimal avoidance of mishaps on one hand and of overall steering on the other.

The issue of co-ordination is often presented as a technical matter, as a *technique* of pulling together centrifugal forces, tendencies, and policies. It is seen as a matter of organizational arrangements susceptible to preventing or handling divergence and conflict. It focuses on designing the appropriate structures and procedures to carry out this function, thus shaping and even reducing the scope for debate.

The key to the concept of co-ordination lies in its *political nature*. If the goal of co-ordination is to introduce a minimum of coherence into governmental policies, it cannot be reduced to organizational techniques. It is a 'strategy for reducing conflict, for treating tensions with a view to preserve the

---

[1] It has been argued that political and administrative patterns of interaction within the EC are indeed characterized by a high degree of 'fusion', increasing 'mutual calculability and confidence in the actions of partners' (Wessels 1990: 238).

[2] The steps on the scale are the following: (1) independent ministerial decision making; (2) establishing governmental priorities; (3) consultation with other ministries; (4) avoiding divergence among ministries; (5) interministerial search for agreement; (6) arbitration of interministerial differences; (7) setting parameters for ministries; (8) establishing governmental priorities; and (9) overall governmental strategy.

unified model upon which the modern state has been implicitly based' (Timsit 1975). It is widely acknowledged, though, that the ideal of the monolith is little more than a myth. Segmentation and fragmentation are the everyday reality of governmental action and machinery, exacerbated by the European integration process (Dehousse 1996: 59) and tolerated to various degrees within different national contexts.

There is no need to insist on the widely known phenomena of administrative competition and overlapping; they are the inescapable result of interrelation and interdependence between policy sectors and their links with different social groups and interests. Co-ordination is as limited as the division of labour between government departments and agencies is complex.

Ensuring co-ordination involves 'a mixture of hierarchical authority and dialogue, of capacity to convince and arbitrate' with variable efficiency (Sfez 1970: 238). It definitely necessitates *setting and diffusing priorities throughout a system*. Co-ordination is therefore a highly political process, involving conflicts, disagreements, divergent interests, etc. and shaping these interests according to certain priorities. Because of its political dimensions, co-ordination involves pressure and constraints on the individual political-administrative systems. It should therefore not be confused with the specific mechanisms and organizational arrangements that are supposed to make it possible.

Domestic co-ordination of EU policy has nevertheless come to be seen as an organizational-managerial problem of the EU political-administrative system and its component states. Seen as a technical matter of mere organizational arrangements, co-ordination implies that there is a common starting point for all EU countries and that these arrangements are the necessary and sufficient condition for effectiveness. Still, this functional imperative puts different pressure on different EU members, depending on the extent of the adjustment required by EU policies (Wright 1996: 163; Spanou 1998).

Therefore, what criteria should we use in order to assess domestic EU policy co-ordination? *Who* is to conduct this effort, to act as an arbitrator, to convince and pull together centrifugal trends? How is the necessary unifying element, around which co-ordination is possible, shaped? It seems that these questions converge on the essential functions of leadership.[3] To phrase it differently, the wider and deeper precondition for co-ordination is *steering capacity*, in the sense of 'the exertion of goal directed influence bringing a system from one state to another' (Mayntz 1993: 11) and of 'consolidating the

[3] In an attempt to clarify what is sought by co-ordination, Wright (1996) refers to Selznick's analysis of the functions of leadership: goal setting, embodiment of purpose into an organization, maintaining values and institutional identity, reconciling competing interests. Still, these four functions are bound together by an internal logic, all stemming from the first.

integration of the system through the necessary adjustments' concerning more particularly the logic of one sector in relation to more global objectives (Jobert and Muller 1987: 16).

Steering does not necessarily involve a high degree of centralization. On the contrary, it may suffer from it. It does not predetermine organizational arrangements. It goes further and touches upon the nature of the political system, state–society relations, and the issue of governance.[4] Co-ordination as a matter of vertical or horizontal structures, procedures, and communication flows is, therefore, only the vehicle for steering. What is more broadly at stake is the degree of *integration* of the system.

Organizing co-ordination

Various formal arrangements seem to work well and point to no 'one best way' for co-ordination (Wright 1996). Furthermore, different countries present varying efficiency levels at different stages of the EU policy-making process. The domestic co-ordinating capacity 'must be judged according to the issue, the policy type, the policy requirements and the policy objectives'. Hence, 'merely to examine the machinery of co-ordination is to confuse the means and the outcomes' (ibid. 165).

A comparative study conducted in the late 1980s showed that a 'lack of capacity to serve one's own interests effectively' seems to be the rule in the EC context (Metcalfe 1988). But this generally low co-ordination capacity may stem from diverse reasons, including a federal structure, insufficient preparation, competition between strong sectoral priorities, or an inability to formulate priorities. Grading different countries according to their co-ordination capacity does not, therefore, advance beyond the obvious. Furthermore, countries that seem to have effective co-ordination systems sometimes present other features, including a politically or economically strong position in the EU. On the contrary, countries that are not considered paradigms of effective co-ordination may have a strong presence and a successful record within the EU (Germany, for example).

The potential for any government to influence EU decision making does not depend exclusively on organizational arrangements. The size of the state and its importance to particular negotiations, the desire and capacity of the government to play an active role and to build alliances are important parameters determining its success (Nugent 1994: 413–14). Wright (1996: 165) concludes that 'whilst co-ordination may be important in some respects, its absence does not appear to be disruptive or dysfunctional'.

A successful record cannot be explained exclusively by the state of co-ordination systems. It may be attributed to the fact that (*a*) they pursue clear

[4] Governance refers to patterns emerging from governing activities (Kooiman 1993: 2).

objectives efficiently and priorities taking advantage of opportunities offered generally and within the EU, and (*b*) they are often able to shape EU priorities and invite other EU members to follow them by 'co-ordinating' their efforts and policies. Is then co-ordination a word for 'homogenization'? Furthermore, is co-ordination the right way to approach the issue? Are we, in fact, still talking about co-ordination?

In this perspective, it is important to take into account the role of the government of the day and, especially, how it sees the role of the country in EU policy making. Two main views can be distinguished: a mainly 'domestic' perception of EU affairs and policies leading to a defensive, introverted, and self-serving attitude or a broader extroverted perspective, where national interests, goals, and policies are offensively pursued in relation to the EU dynamics. They represent two different 'mind frames' that largely condition a country's co-ordination and intervention capacity impregnating the whole political-administrative system. In light of this framework, the configuration of domestic co-ordination of EU policy in Greece will be examined and its shortcomings analysed.[5]

The Truncated Pyramid

Langrod's description of the Greek administrative system as the sum of 'isolated fortresses' holds as true today as it did in the 1960s. Public administration, traditionally centralized and dominated by the party in government, is incapable of ensuring continuity. Co-ordination has been notably deficient, as demonstrated by a low level of planning and failure to make use of relevant mechanisms. Political and administrative centralization is thus cause and effect of the low degree of system integration. Centrifugal political forces resist formal co-ordination obligations and they perpetuate a high degree of fragmentation along with a selective respect for formal rules (Spanou 1996). The constraints imposed by EU membership on the Greek political-administrative system involve a major revision of its mode of operation. They imply a shift, transforming it from introverted to extroverted (policy oriented, responsiveness and accountability, pluralism and consistency) (Spanou 1998).

Greece is often said to have not yet found 'a workable formula' for ensuring co-ordination of EU policy. This is seen as a lack of a proper *structure*, which might take the form of a collective standing body at ministerial level

[5] Some of the empirical data and examples are informed by research conducted within a postgraduate seminar on 'Greek Administration in the EU System' organized by the author in 1996–7.

capable of formulating and co-ordinating European policy, resolving conflict, and, more generally, setting policy guidelines and orientations (Ioakimidis 1994: 146–9). Almost from the start of membership a junior Minister of Foreign Affairs was entrusted with responsibility for European affairs. Abolished between 1990 and 1993, this post was recreated after 1993. Though the appointment of a minister on each occasion was considered as a possible start for the creation of a specialized European affairs department, this has not materialized so far. The questions of a lead ministry and of intersectoral co-ordination remain central.

A lead ministry?

A mapping of the organizational arrangements illustrates that bureaucratic politics obstructs the concerned ministries. The leading role in EU policy co-ordination has oscillated between two main ministries: the Ministry of Co-ordination (MCo) (later Ministry of National Economy—MNE) and the Ministry of Foreign Affairs (MFA). While the former started the negotiation period in 1976, the centre of gravity changed later.[6] The grounds cited were the 'political dimensions of the issue' (Ioakimidis 1993: 212–13), which implied an increased role for the MFA in European matters.

The scheme adopted at the start of full membership consolidated this change. In contrast to the 1976 format, Law 1104/80 assigned to the MFA general responsibility for representing Greece *vis-à-vis* the EC. As a result, the Permanent Representation, initially under the MCo, was transferred to the MFA, which was further granted a monopoly over communications between the Permanent Representation and the Greek administration.[7] At this stage, the MFA succeeded in asserting its role as the lead ministry in European affairs.

The bipolar scheme was, however, partly preserved. The MCo/MNE is by definition a horizontal structure with the mission to plan and co-ordinate economic development.[8] In this capacity it was already involved from the start in the negotiations for accession to the EC. It gradually lost its general competence in favour of a strictly economic one. In 1980 it was entrusted with the *domestic* elaboration and co-ordination of the governmental economic policy in the framework of the EC. It explicitly had to co-ordinate the actions of tech-

---

[6] In 1977, a minister without portfolio was appointed with a responsibility for Greece–EC relations. Moreover, the Central Negotiations Committee (CNC) was reformed and put under the responsibility of a diplomat. Last, a Directorate of European Communities was also created in the MFA in order to assist the CNC (PD 200/77).

[7] Ioakimidis (1993: 213) notes that the idea of a more collective scheme was rejected as dysfunctional in the Greek context.

[8] This ministry was created in 1945. Since 1977, it has included a General Directorate for the Relations of Greece with the European Communities (PD 816/77).

nical ministries and to monitor the adjustment of the Greek economy to EC requirements.[9]

Despite the apparently clearly distinguished orientation, tension and antagonisms were part of the relations between these two ministries. The division of labour (inward and outward co-ordination/representation) was coupled with the 'technical' or 'political' character of the issues and the necessary expertise to handle them. Delineating their respective responsibilities has proved to be an extremely delicate task (Ioakimidis 1993; Tsinisizelis 1996).

This fragmented scheme is nevertheless not unique in the EU (Wright 1996: 156). Two further observations can be made. First, EU policy co-ordination was integrated within the existing framework of ministerial architecture. Despite the rivalry between the two main ministries, no new structure was created. Second, the oscillation and the occasional shifts of balance between the two ministries are due to the very existence of a Ministry of Co-ordination, to bureaucratic antagonisms, the organizational resources available, and influential personalities involved. In fact, the apparent lack of clarity in their respective competencies can be seen as a means to preserve the conditions for further mutual claims.

In any case, the leading role of the MCo was often qualified as provisional, concerning the negotiations and pre-accession period (A. Papaligouras, Minister of Co-ordination, Parliamentary Proceedings, 21 Sept. 1976: 1389 and 8 Dec. 1980). The transfer of the general competence to the MFA was justified by reference to rules at the European level, governing the General Affairs Council, and the increasingly political character of the EC, but was criticized on the grounds that the experience and knowledge accumulated by the MCo would be wasted. No explicit borrowing from other countries can be identified, but borrowing would not answer the question as to why one model had been preferred to another. Though each has sought legitimizing arguments to support its claim for predominance, the success of the MFA has to be seen in the light of other parameters.[10]

---

[9] The MNE is competent for ECOFIN issues and the implementation of Community Support Frameworks, both of which present highly technical aspects.

[10] The parliamentary proceedings reveal the main stages of this bureaucratic antagonism. In 1976, the then minister of co-ordination was an important personality in government and an expert in economic matters (A. Papaligouras). He used the argument of the economic character of the EC and of the adjustments needed for Greece to become a full member (Introductory Report, law 445/1976, and Parliamentary Proceedings, 21 Sept. 1976). In the same year, however, the Parliament adopted a law (419/1976) defining the competences of the MFA that included European Affairs. This inconsistency shows that the new policy field was claimed by both ministries. The antagonism involved the diplomatic corps—favoured by the 'political character' argument—and the group of experts and technocrats that was gradually formed for the negotiations, primarily located in the MCo. In 1979, the role of the MCo was confirmed (Law 992/1979). When, later in 1980, general

The co-ordinating role of the MFA is currently ensured by the General Directorate of the EU, and comprises four directorates (External Affairs; European Integration and Economic and Monetary Policy; Internal Market, Agriculture, and New Community Policies; and Justice and Internal Affairs) and a European Parliament Bureau.[11] A special legal service of the EC (ENY), under the direct authority of the minister, includes a European law division responsible for legal incorporation[12] and transgressions of Community law.[13] Similarly, the current structure of the MNE (PD 138/1993) includes a (horizontal) Directorate of Relations with the EC, responsible for the preparation and representation of the country in the European Council of Ministers for matters falling into its scope of competence.[14] Furthermore, an Office of Legal EC Issues is entrusted with the monitoring and co-ordination of the incorporation and implementation of European legislation.[15] In 1987, a highly regarded Council of Economic Experts was created (Law 1682/1987). It was placed directly under the minister and given a consultative role in ECOFIN matters.

Intersectoral co-ordination

Within both ministries, high-level interministerial committees were set up under the 1980 law: the Committee of European Affairs in the MFA and the

responsibility shifted towards the MFA—thus upgrading its role in European matters while restricting the MCo to a more domestic, economic role—the then minister of co-ordination was appointed Minister of Foreign Affairs (C. Mitsotakis). Last, it is significant that during the discussions, the primacy (and priority) of the diplomats over other experts was explicitly noted in relation to senior positions in the General Directorate of the EC. (See Parliamentary Proceedings, 8 Dec. 1980: 2150–1; Introductory Report to Law 1104/1980.)

[11] This organizational structure is based on Presidential Decrees 11/1992 and, 98/1994 and, more recently, Law 2594/1998 and Presidential Decree 230/1998.

[12] Incorporation of EU legislation as a rule takes place via Presidential Decrees or ministerial decisions issued on the initiative of the relevant ministry.

[13] A special legal service of the EC (ENYEK) was initially created by Law 1640/1986. It corresponded to the concern for handling the rising number of non-compliance cases and to the pro-European turn of the PASOK government that took place in the mid-1980s. It has provided the central impulse for compliance and achieved visible results (see Tsinisizelis 1996). The recent revision of the internal organization of the MFA led to the merging with the Special Legal Service that had a more general competence.

[14] Equally important for domestic co-ordination of EU policy, is the General Directorate of Public Investment, Regional Policy, and Development. It co-ordinates the elaboration and implementation of the Community Support Framework, regional development programmes, and Community initiatives.

[15] The minister of NE always countersigns incorporation acts.

Interministerial Co-ordination Committee in the MCo. However, they were dissolved two years later.

Beyond the political aspects of EU membership, the MFA claimed and received a role in intersectoral co-ordination, that is as an intermediary between the other ministries and the EU. In theory, the MFA transmits national positions on specialized, sectoral issues to the Permanent Representative. Sectoral representation runs counter to its monopoly of representation but is tolerated on the condition that it is carried out in co-operation with the MFA. This is ensured mostly by personnel specializing in various policy fields and ensuring contacts with the technical ministries and the Permanent Representative. Weekly meetings take place at the MFA with representatives of other ministries in order to prepare the agenda of the COREPER (often already at an advanced stage of negotiation) and to transmit guidelines and instructions to the Permanent Representative. Ad hoc meetings and personal contacts are equally frequent. Sometimes, preparation takes the form of 'briefings' at the Permanent Representation in Brussels (Passas 1997).

From the Permanent Representation in Brussels to the MFA and then to the technical ministries, the communication chain seems quite long and time-consuming. Sometimes, the technical infrastructure is insufficient to support it (Minakaki 1992). Information overload is a real risk for the MFA. In light of the breadth and technical nature of sectoral issues, it is not surprising that the role of the MFA as the main communication channel for all EU policies and issues is contested. The MFA's attempts at unifying and scrutinizing the positions to be presented on specialized councils when preparing the CO-REPER meetings can be problematic (Ioakimidis 1993: 218). Policy issues are managed more or less successfully, but are dealt with directly by the relevant ministry and the Permanent Representation or the Commission in Brussels.

The organizational strategy that led to the victory of the MFA was bound to prove fragile. The argument of the 'political dimensions' of Greece–EC relations, based on a strict separation between high and low politics, seems to have sustained the MFA's claim for a long period (Ioakimidis 1993: 222). It is, however, only formally speaking that it managed to survive. The reality of European policies is at odds with the MFA's centralization aspirations. The volume and the increasingly technical character of the issues, as well as the intertwining of their technical and political aspects, have led to the development of a direct line of communication between sectoral ministries and the Permanent Representation (Galatsinou 1996; Minakaki 1992). This readjustment, though informal and non-systematic, seems to correspond more closely to the actual needs of the EU policy process.[16]

---

[16] The co-ordinating role of the MNE equally attracts criticisms from sectoral ministries (Minakaki 1992; Anastopoulos 1988).

The Permanent Representation

The Permanent Representation is headed by a diplomat and comprises about 100 representatives, most of whom (about 60) come from technical ministries.[17] It serves as the main channel of communication between Greek public administration and Brussels. Its principal correspondent is the Ministry of Foreign Affairs, which has the responsibility for the outward representation of the country.

Problems in the Permanent Representation's own operation do not allow it to exercise influence during the informal stages of policy formation. Some of these difficulties have to do with its mode of staffing, others with the lack of networking with Greek nationals in the Commission and with Greek MEPs (Galatsinou 1996; Passas 1994). Others are linked to the lack of preparation of policy alternatives and goals, and of the absence of a negotiating strategy.

Greek governments seem not to have realized the need to promote high-quality staff from Greece to the Permanent Representation or Community posts. Politicization of staff selection at the expense of expertise and their having the appropriate qualifications, and frequent changes in personnel, result in a discontinuity in representation (Ioakimidis 1993; Makridimitris and Passas 1993). Additional problems include the disregard of the opportunities offered by personnel exchange programmes (Passas 1994; Giataganas 1990) and the marginalization of staff upon return, preventing them from contributing their expertise and experience to the service. Greek governments seem to neglect opportunities to influence these informal avenues for promoting their interests.

Sectoral co-ordination

After 1976, within each individual ministry, special European (and often international) affairs units were created for the internal co-ordination of European policy and as intermediaries for communication with the Permanent Representative, the Commission, and the MFA. Co-ordination problems persist as European affairs units are often marginalized. Their role is not always understood within the ministry. Far from being an in-house think-tank on European affairs, they are regarded at best as a 'conveyor belt', unable to

---

[17] It is organized into divisions (External Affairs, Economic Affairs, Agriculture, other policies Third Pillar Issues, European Parliament, Administrative Affairs, Legal Office). The relatively high number of representatives is justified by the geographical distance of the country from EU decision-making centres and the time and costs involved in ensuring communication and travelling.

influence decision making in the technical directorates (Minakaki 1992). Still, the situation may vary according to the policy field and the bureaucratic interests at stake.

The Directorate of Agricultural Policy, for instance, is a horizontal structure and includes a European affairs and international relations unit. Its mission involves the co-ordination of goal setting among the vertical directorates within the wider context of the single market, the elaboration of an appropriate strategy, and the comprehensive and consistent formulation of the country's position in agricultural policy. This Directorate communicates with the Permanent Representation, and transmits information to the technical divisions. In practice, however, it is kept in the dark, circumvented both by the Permanent Representation in Brussels and technical experts in the ministries in Athens, and ignored by the minister and his or her office (Galatsinou 1996). Deficiencies in policy formulation add to these weaknesses. Insufficiently clear priorities, not linked with, or related to, wider national priorities, and an absence of 'information hunting' in Brussels, result in insufficient preparation for meetings and a difficult position for the minister in negotiations (Louloudis 1993; Galatsinou 1996).

The social security policy field is characterized by the extreme fragmentation of social security funds, and lack of co-ordination and a comprehensive approach to policy. The European affairs unit of the Ministry of Labour and Social Security follows developments at the EU level and diffuses uniform information and implementation guidelines. However, the vertical directorates of the ministry do not readily accept what they regard as its interference. They tend to make direct contact among themselves and with the relevant social fund on how to interpret EU legislation. Not every fund has a European affairs unit, nor do they tend to consult on matters concerning the implementation of EU legislation. 'Variegated implementation' (Richardson 1996) is unsurprisingly the result. The intermediary role of the MFA is equally deficient.

The situation for research is somewhat different. The European affairs unit has a more important role, no doubt reflecting the importance of EU funding in this area. Its collaboration with the other divisions is much smoother. The same is true for third pillar issues where the relationship between the ministry and the MFA works well.

General weaknesses extend beyond organizational structures to the process of negotiation itself. Technical ministries often formulate positions without a sense of priorities and alternatives in the wider context of the country's European policy. Each individual minister or service, under the impression that this better serves their constituency, does not normally make concessions in order to build alliances or in order to be in a better position to negotiate. Therefore, negotiations become more difficult and neither the horizontal role of the MFA nor the Permanent Representative can reverse the situation.[18] The question of 'how important is this issue for Greece?' receives a rather limited response.

Difficulties in co-ordination frequently mean that national positions are often decided at the eleventh hour in Brussels between officials at the Permanent Representation and the minister concerned. Insufficient preparation at the domestic level and lack of clear sectoral priorities account for this. Furthermore, representation of the interests of technical ministries can be problematic, since they are not always present at the various working groups and committees (Makridimitris and Passas 1993: 56; Galatsinou 1996; Ioakimidis 1998: 139). Those are further reasons for the lack of influence during the initial stages of policy making.

If the capacity of the MFA to be the main communication channel with Brussels is widely contested, technical ministries themselves have not necessarily established the mechanisms or developed the capacities to substitute for it. They do not seem in a position to promote their objectives while keeping in perspective the wider context of national priorities. The tensions between the MFA and the technical ministries take place at a low capacity level on both sides.

Governmental co-ordination

At the political level, EU policy co-ordination is equally low. In 1980, the task of governmental co-ordination was assigned to the already existing Economic Committee with an enlarged composition (to include the ministers of foreign affairs and transport) and later to the Governmental Committee. Once again, no specialized structure was set up.

The significance of the lack of a specialized body at the political level seems, however, to have been overstated. A more important question is whether the function is performed or not. Existing governmental committees could play this role perfectly adequately.[19] A more general question needs to be posed. The inactivity or lack of institutional, collective decision making, though they did not originate at the time, became the striking feature of the Papandreou governments of the 1980s. The cabinet seldom met, and decisions would be taken by the Prime Minister and his close collaborators and then presented to the other members of the cabinet. It is therefore not surprising that there has been no collective body for the domestic co-ordination of EU policy. More-

---

[18] The Permanent Representation may also be short-circuited by direct contacts between ministers and Commissioners or Commission staff. As a result, the Permanent Representative cannot offer a global view of the developments and issues.

[19] The French SGCI, seen as a successful—but possibly overrated—co-ordination structure, was not specifically created in view of EU affairs. Since 1948 it has performed a similar function (Lequesne 1996).

over, had it been set up, there is no reason to suppose that anything would have happened differently.

An Interministerial Committee for the Co-ordination of Greece–EU Relations was set up only in 1993 after Papandreou regained control of the government. The Committee highlighted a new awareness of the need to improve co-ordination. It is presided over by the Minister of Foreign Affairs and brings together the economic and main technical ministries. It also meets at the more junior level of Secretary General, which is indeed what occurs most often. For major issues, such as IGCs, ad hoc meetings take place under the supervision of the Prime Minister.

More important is, however, a change in government priorities. Until 1995, the Prime Minister and the government did not show a great interest in EU affairs. The situation has changed since Simitis became Prime Minister. The Council of Ministers now deals far more often with EU matters (Ioakimidis 1998: 138).

A conclusion drawn from these organizational arrangements, and especially the central role of the MFA, is that the EC has been considered as part of the country's foreign relations architecture (Ioakimidis 1993: 215; Makridimitris and Passas 1993). Turning the argument on its head, it could be observed that the above organizational arrangements constitute what might be described as the 'domestication' of European policy, since no special structure at ministerial or governmental level was created. To put it differently, this is the symbolic translation of an introverted way of dealing with the EC; it reveals a short-term and self-serving perspective, where political and economic priorities of the country within the EC were defined by strictly Greece-centred politics. Finally, there has been no explicit copying of a specific prototype. References to other countries' experience have occasionally served as a vague legitimizing argument for bureaucratic claims and antagonisms. Such a parochial attitude inevitably neglects the more complex dynamics of European integration, its ambitions, and the position of Greece in it and on it. This approach to the European experiment was bound to prove inadequate.

The summary of co-ordination arrangements shows that in terms of organizational arrangements, everything is more or less in place. What is missing then? Though this scheme was supposed to be centralized, it has been qualified as 'loose and decentralized' (Metcalfe 1988)[20] or even fragmented and disorderly. Co-ordination often relies on ad hoc meetings and seems rather a

---

[20] According to a comparative study of the twelve member states (Metcalfe 1988), the policy co-ordination scale used showed Greece, Portugal, Spain, but also Germany, each with low co-ordination capacities. Greece was placed among countries exhibiting loosely coupled systems of European policy co-ordination, together with Italy, Belgium, and Germany. The very diversity of this grouping shows the different factors accounting for a loosely coupled system (e.g. federal structure). 'Institutional inertia' is in these conditions an insufficient explanatory factor.

matter of personalities than of institutional mechanisms (Makridimitris and Passas 1993).

The configuration of domestic EU policy co-ordination shows that more general characteristics of the Greek political-administrative system have visibly left their mark on the organizational adjustments undertaken: a low degree of institutionalization, a gap between formal rules and informal practices, the fragmentation and importance of personal initiatives and networks, the politicization of recruitment at the expense of merit, and the lack of continuity. Reform proposals tend to underestimate the profound causes of this unsatisfactory situation, by suggesting that responsibility for EU policy should be centralized in a ministry or minister for European affairs, or in specialized interministerial bodies (Anastopoulos 1988; Makridimitris and Passas 1993; Ioakimidis 1993). As has been noted, 'co-ordination is a property of a system not the prerogative of one part of a system' (Metcalfe 1988); none of the above solutions is, therefore, adequate by itself, as long as the preconditions allowing co-ordination are not present throughout the system.

Parliament and parliamentary committees

What is the role for Parliament in this context? Apart from its traditional ways of influencing governmental policies, Parliament hardly plays a role in the domestic co-ordination of European policies. The extensive use of delegated legislation for the incorporation of European legislation—often of a technical nature—sidelines Parliament, thus limiting its access to information and the opportunity to debate EU subjects. Strong single party majorities have dominated Parliament since 1974 (with the exception of 1989–90) and have not stimulated the exercise of parliamentary oversight functions (Ioakimidis 1994: 149–51). Parliament has not shown any particular interest in EU affairs, while other available opportunities have not been exploited.[21] It is, however, observed that Parliament is *indirectly* involved in the process of European integration by promoting structural reforms resulting from EU membership (Pliakos 1996).

As a reaction to the perceived 'democratic deficit' within the EU, the Parliamentary Committee for European Affairs (CEA) was established in 1990, based on a decision of the President of the Chamber. The decision referred explicitly to a motion of the European Parliament recommending the creation of such a body and the fact that Greece was the only member state not to

---

[21] Between 1974 and mid-1995 only seven 'pre-agenda' discussions took place. In fact, all of these discussions occurred after 1990 and only involved party leaders. Moreover, only in 1989 did the government submit the (annual) report on EC developments despite a law, dating back to 1979, which mandated this procedure.

have such a Committee. It brings together MPs and MEPs on an equal footing.[22]

Its mission is to monitor European Community affairs with particular attention paid to the action taken by the Greek authorities, and to express its opinion in reports submitted to Parliament and the government. The government should transmit to the CEA all documents and legislative proposals of the EU as well as to other interested parliamentary committees.[23] Since 1993, the Committee has presented two reports a year expressing its opinion on developments at the European level.[24] These reports can be discussed in Parliament but do not lead to a vote.[25]

The political visibility of this Committee is low, largely because of the rather technical character of the issues and its consensual mode of operation (Yannis 1996). Its establishment reduces, however, the introverted character of the Greek Parliament, promoting its 'Europeanization'.

The institutional equipment of the Parliament is sufficient to allow the constant or ad hoc monitoring and influencing of EU–Greece relations. The 'democratic deficit' in the Greek context is not the result of inappropriate or deficient organizational arrangements. On the contrary, Parliament does not make enough use of the possibilities offered (Papadimitriou 1995: 143) and does not constitute an essential part of a comprehensive approach to European policies. This observation, like others made above about the executive, underscores the profound need for steering as a prerequisite for co-ordination.

The Missing Link: Governmental Steering

Co-ordination systems cannot be understood on their own terms. Organizational arrangements and operating procedures come as an explicit or implicit response to policy problems, political and bureaucratic antagonisms, leadership styles, and various current or long-standing constraints. They constitute a reflection of broader political-administrative characteristics and policy-making styles (Richardson, Gustafsson, and Jordan 1982). Domestic co-ordination of EU policy has to be placed in context. Hence, two questions arise: first, is there a common thread linking up the features described above?

---

[22] It comprises 31 members (15 + 15 plus the president, who is one of the vice-presidents, appointed by the President of the House).

[23] This possibility was nevertheless not used until the end of 1996.

[24] The CEA holds on average seven to eight meetings per year with the regular presence of the Minister of Foreign Affairs. It represents the Greek Parliament at the Conference of Corresponding Committees (COSAC).

[25] This procedure was not used until the end of 1995.

And, second, what is the broader policy framework and style that gave birth to this configuration of EU policy co-ordination? Two factors which account for these shortcomings can be identified as follows: the circumstances surrounding the early years of membership; and particular features of the Greek political system.

The formative years

Accession to the European Community coincided with a major political change in Greece. The PASOK government of that time initially held hostile positions *vis-à-vis* the EC. No doubt, EC membership was not a priority for the government, giving a direction and orientation to policy. This is reflected in the delays, the lack of preparation, and more generally, the poor responsiveness of the Greek political-administrative system towards the Community at that stage.

Among the factors usually cited in accounting for this stance are: the initial lack of consensus on the role and place of the country in the EC; the frequent changes in officials dealing with EC affairs; more general perceptions within the public administration relative to the EC resulting in an ethnocentric approach; the weight of financial issues in the negotiations; and a generally defensive attitude (Ioakimidis 1993: 223 ff.; Makridimitris and Passas 1993). However important, these factors seem to be only the *symptoms* of a more profound cause always to be found behind co-ordination difficulties. They point to a deficiency in the government's ability, and willingness, to define political and policy priorities. Though the hostile position of PASOK governments of the 1980s gradually changed, it remained limited to trying to gain time and take advantage of the resources offered. In short, the apparent change of position did not trigger any change of priorities or of policies.

To sum up, this formative period of Greek membership was marked by a striking lack of priority given to EC matters. This had important implications in the way the role of the country in the Community was perceived by the government and, subsequently, by lower political-administrative levels. In other words, despite the participation of Greece in a wider community, the dominant perception and orientation have been 'introverted'. In that sense one could talk about a form of *domestication* of European policy, as opposed to promoting national interests in line with European integration dynamics. This situation has changed, however, since the beginning of the 1990s.

The steering capacity

The inactivity of collective decision-making bodies at the governmental, as well as at the administrative level, and the more general underdevelopment of planning mechanisms, staff services, and functions in the Greek political-administrative system, provide the wider context in which any description of the co-ordination structures has to take place. A summary of the main characteristics of policy making in Greece—beyond sectorization and issue specificity—includes strong centrifugal tendencies, fragmentation and lack of continuity, corporatism and constituency driven decisions, reactive problem solving, centralization and imposition, low institutionalization and consultation. A weak civil society (Sotiropoulos 1995), vulnerable to state intervention, meets a weak state, unable to shape priorities and guide developments. What is at stake is the steering capacity of the state. Part of the co-ordination problem goes therefore beyond EU policy to touch upon more profound features of the Greek political administrative system.

In this context, the concept of an intellectual and normative referential framework (*référentiel*) is extremely apposite (Jobert and Muller 1987: 52–78). At the sectoral level, it refers to the representation of a sector and its place and role in the wider society. It is a social construct shaped by sectoral operators, a compromise among sectoral elites. Policy inconsistencies and administrative anarchy result from the segmented way in which public policies introduce certain adjustments between the various dimensions of social integration. The maintenance of global social cohesion operates through political action (Jobert 1985: 662) and involves a dynamic process of relating sectoral referential frameworks to the global one.

The *global* intellectual and normative framework is an image of the whole, an overall representation around which the various sectoral representations can be ordered. The norms it contains are closely linked to prevailing values. Shaped by ruling elites, it does not constitute a universal consensus but marks the scope within which conflicts and confrontations take place. Building a relationship between sectoral and global frameworks is required for achieving social integration. This becomes possible through alliances between sections of the ruling elite and certain sectoral elites; it requires the meeting of sectoral and political leadership, though the boundaries between sectoral mediators and ruling elites are not all that clear (Jobert and Muller 1987).

This is where the co-ordination process seems to stumble in the case of Greece. As previously noted, insufficient co-ordination is not necessarily linked to strong sectoral priorities in conflict between them; *it can also originate from the absence of clearly set priorities.* Steering is undoubtedly the responsibility of the political level, but shaping the intellectual and normative framework involves social actors more broadly. In Greece, interest groups seem unable to promote objectives that go beyond corporatist claims and to assess realistically broader constraints. The specific mode of interest aggregation and of their articulation with the state traditionally favours fragmentation and ad hoc decisions. The emergence of sectoral priorities—as shown by last minute decisions about national sectoral positions—is therefore problematic. At the same time, weak governments, prone to clientelism, tend to lose their sense of direction under the pressure of present political cost at the expense of future rewards. A global referential framework seems equally weak, preventing the timely ordering of national priorities.

In other words, the deficient steering capacity is a result of a specific configuration of state–society relations. The lack of clear priorities concerning the place and role of the state in the EU is an expression of a wider weakness of the steering role of governments in Greece and penetrates the whole political-administrative system. This is why the system of co-ordination seems more like a *truncated pyramid*. Given the absence of a clear referential framework either for the country or for the sector, steering at the top is insufficient. This can be observed in the deficiencies of sectoral as well as horizontal policies (Spanou 1996). Co-ordination is inherently horizontal and requires cross-sectoral integration. If steering is deficient, co-ordination cannot follow. In that sense, the political approach to co-ordination supplements the organizational one.

More specifically, the weakness of an established framework and the lack of adequate steering help to contribute to the apparent inertia of the collective co-ordination bodies. This further affects the whole co-ordination system: lower level co-ordination seems unnecessary, and meaningless, since there is no underlying imperative or capacity establishing higher-level priorities and objectives. National positions for the preparation of specialized councils are therefore seen in isolation and contacts take place directly between technical ministries and the Permanent Representation leaving out co-ordination bodies. Co-ordination is then expected at a higher (political) level—which is supposed to be able to link sectoral issues to wider considerations—only to be confronted with the reproduction of the same phenomena. Deficient organizational arrangements, neglect of staff functions and the marginalization of relevant services, the frequent change of personnel in dealing with technical matters in Brussels, and the absence of an appropriate personnel policy as described above, are side effects of this lack of strategy and political orientation. A bureaucracy weak in expertise and autonomy further aggravates co-ordination difficulties encountered. Personal qualities, networks, and contacts come into play as a fire alarm mechanism, and in the short run, may be extremely important and efficient in remedying deficiencies, but they lack predictability and are thus unable to overturn the general characteristics of the system.

Conclusion

A question that necessarily arises is whether it is possible to remedy this steering deficiency. Though, with a few exceptions, it can be considered a long-standing feature of the Greek political-administrative system, the answer is surprisingly, in the affirmative. This is not a metaphysical situation, any change in which is beyond human efforts to achieve. Rather, it is a result of specific social and political conditions, which can be gradually reshaped. The web of constraints currently placed upon political administrative systems works in this direction.

What is needed is strong political leadership or entire preneurship from above in the domain of European policy, representing the global referential framework, pursuing consistently and persistently the relevant set of priorities, and willing to make daring decisions. Such an entrepreneur undertakes an action involving risk and uncertainty, has the willingness to defer immediate gratifications for future gains (Schumpeter 1962), and can mobilize public sentiment and social groups that have historically been peripheral. Building alliances with segments of society and sectoral elites that have similar normative frameworks can thus compensate for centrifugal forces (interests and their various advocates, electoral contests, and political rivalries). The policy entrepreneur is not a traditional charismatic leader, but requires consistency and political courage. The role of enabling circumstances is important to provide the challenges and constraints and for shaping potential individual and institutional allies vital to the whole experiment.

Greece is currently undergoing a process of transition, moving from a referential framework dominant during the 1980s to a new one, explicitly informed by and directed towards European perspectives and priorities. Determined political steering is trying to shape and diffuse the new normative framework, giving the country a different place, role, and recognition in the EU from those of the past decade. Priorities tend to become clearer and credibility is being built inside and outside the country. The process will be anything but easy, as the March 1998 decision of the Simitis government to re-enter the EMS illustrates. The shift of referential framework takes place within the context of social values that are being tested by tough decisions in dire economic constraints. Strong corporatist reactions and sectoral centrifugal tendencies coupled with political rivalries are expected at every turn, as was illustrated in legislation aimed at preparing the national flag carrier, Olympic Airways, for privatization. Persistence in the pursuit of objectives, unambiguously defined, makes it possible to introduce a new coherence and direction into a system that has historically been fragmented, and increases the chances of making membership of the Union a success.

References

Anastopoulos, J. (1988), 'Greece', in H. Siedentopf and J. Ziller (eds.), *Making European Policies Work* (Brussels: Bruylant).

Dehousse, R. (1996), 'Les États et l'Union Européenne: Les Effets de l'intégration', in V. Wright and S. Cassese (eds.), *La Recomposition de l'État en Europe* (Paris: La Découverte).

Galatsinou, M. (1996), 'Organisational and Operational Adjustments of Greek Admin-istration for the Co-ordination of Agricultural Policy in the EU' (unpublished Master's thesis, University of Athens: Department of Political Science and Public Administration).

Giataganas, X. (1990), *Europe and the Left* (Athens: Themelio).

Ioakimidis, P. C. (1993), 'Greek Administration and European Policy Formation', in L. Tsoukalis (ed.), *Greece in the EC: The Challenge of Adjustment* (Athens: EKEM/Papazissis).

—— (1994), 'The EC and the Greek Political System: An Overview', in P. Kazakos and P. C. Ioakimidis (eds.), *Greece and EC Membership Evaluated* (New York: St Martin's Press).

—— (1998), *The European Union and the Greek State* (Athens: Themelio).

Jobert, B. (1985), 'L'État en action: l'apport des politiques publiques', *Revue française des sciences politiques*, 35/4: 654–82.

—— and Muller, P. (1987), *L'État en action* (Paris: PUF).

Kooiman, J. (1993), 'Social-Political Governance: Introduction', in J. Kooiman (ed.), *Modern Governance* (London: Sage).

Lequesne, C. (1996), 'French Central Government and the European Political System', in Y. Mény, P. Muller, and J.-L. Quermonne (eds.), *Adjusting to Europe* (London: Routledge).

Louloudis, L. (1993), *CAMAR Project: The Greek Report* (Athens: Agricultural Uni-versity of Athens: Department of Agricultural Economics).

Makridimitris, A., and Passas, A. (1993), *Greek Administration and European Policy Co-ordination* (Athens: Sakkoulas).

Mayntz, R. (1993), 'Governing Failures and the Problem of Governability', in J. Kooiman (ed.), *Modern Governance* (London: Sage).

Metcalfe, L. (1988), 'Institutional Inertia versus Organisational Design: European Policy Co-ordination in the Member States of the EC', paper presented at ECPR joint sessions, Rimini, 5–10 Apr.

Minakaki, T. (1992), 'The Communication of Central Administration with the EC and the Role of the European Affairs Units of the Ministries in Greece', *Administrative Reform* [Dioikitiki Metarrithmissi], 51–2: 33–56.

Nizard, L. (1980), 'Les Dynamiques contradictoires en œuvre dans l'administration française', *Revue française d'administration publique* 15: 571–91.

Nugent, N, (1994), *The Government and Politics of the European Union* (London: Macmillan).

Papadimitriou, G. (1995), 'European Integration and National Constitution', in N. Maraveyas and M. Tsinisizelis (eds.), *The Integration of the European Union* (Athens: Themelio).

Passas, A. (1994), 'National Administrations and their Relations to the European Par-liament', *Parliamentary Review* [Koinovouleftiki Epitheorissi], 17–18: 162–9.

—— (1997), 'L'Expérience de la Grèce en matière de réforme de l'administration publique dans la perspective de l'intégration européenne', unpublished paper, Mul-ticountry Seminar, SIGMA-OECD, Athens, 8–10 Oct.

Pliakos, A. (1996), 'The Legislative Production of Parliament', *European Expression* [Evropaiki Ekfrassi], 20: 18–19.

Richardson, J. J. (1996), 'Eroding EU Policies: Implementation Gaps, Cheating and Re-steering', in J. Richardson (ed.), *European Union: Power and Policy-Making* (London: Routledge).

—— , Gustafsson, G., and Jordan, G. (1982), 'The Concept of Policy Style', in J. J. Richardson (ed.), *Policy Styles in Western Europe* (London: Allen & Unwin).

Schumpeter, J. (1962), *Capitalism, Socialism and Democracy* (New York: Harper).

Sfez, L. (1970), *L'Administration prospective* (Paris: A. Colin).

Sotiropoulos, D. (1995), 'The Remains of Authoritarianism: Bureaucracy and Civil Society in Post-authoritarian Greece', Madrid: Juan March Institute, Working Paper 1995/66.

Spanou, C. (1996), 'On the Regulatory Capacity of the Greek State: A Tentative Approach Based on a Case-Study', *International Review of Administrative Sciences*, 62: 219–37.

—— (1998), 'European Integration in Administrative Terms: A Framework for Analysis and the Greek Case', *Journal of European Public Policy*, 5: 467–84.

Timsit, G. (1975), 'Le Concept de co-ordination administrative', *Bulletin de l'IIAP* 36: 1085–108.

Tsinisizelis, M. (1996), 'Greece', in D. Rometsch and W. Wessels (eds.), *The European Union and the Member States: Towards Institutional Fusion* (Manchester: Manchester University Press).

Wessels, W. (1990), 'Administrative Interaction', in W. Wallace (ed.), *The Dynamics of European Integration* (London: Pinter/RIIA).

Wright, V. (1996), 'The National Co-ordination of European Policy-Making', in J. J. Richardson (ed.), *European Union: Power and Policy-Making* (London: Routledge).

Yannis, N. (1996), 'Greek Parliament: The Quest for Participation in European Policy', *European Expression* [Evropaiki Ekfrasi], 20: 20–7.

8

Belgium

Bart Kerremans

Introduction

At the Amsterdam Summit of June 1997, the Belgian delegation attracted the attention of many observers. This was due, first, to its radically pro-integrationist stance and, second, to the visible frustration of the Belgian Prime Minister at the lack of German support for its position.

This Belgian approach to the process of European integration is nothing new.[1] It has existed since the beginning of the EEC itself. What was different about the Amsterdam Summit was the fact that Belgium seemed to have been isolated at one extreme of the continuum between the supranational and the classic intergovernmental approach towards European integration. In this sense, one could say that Belgium has become the most pro-federalist state in the European Union if 'pro-federalist' means being in favour of a European Union shaped by federalist principles. Indeed, in the very first sentence of the Belgian position on the 1996 IGC, a federalist European Union is stated as 'the principal objective of Belgium's European policy' (Kerremans 1995).

It is remarkable then that such a pro-European country has at the same time developed a poor reputation for implementing EU legislation, as confirmed by Commission reports.[2] The reasons for this are partly related to the problems with which Belgium has to cope when it tries to define its position on EU matters in day-to-day decision making. This has to do with the large

---

[1] Cf. the Belgian approach to the IGCs on EPU in 1991 (de Wilde d'Estmael and Franck 1993).

[2] The September 1998 report on the implementation of the single market directives, for instance, gives Belgium as the member state with the highest percentage of non-transposed directives (7.2% against the average of 4.3% for all the member states). In 1997 Belgium, with Germany, was among the member states with the worst implementation record—an exception being made for Austria on the grounds that it had only just acceded to the Union. In 1998, Belgium was alone in this category (European Commission 1998).

number of actors involved in this process—as in the process of implementation—together with the tradition of consensus, which has resulted in a complicated, time-consuming, and often cumbersome co-ordination process. Despite attempts in the 1970s to address these problems, arrangements have become more complicated as a consequence of a process which is completely peculiar to the Belgian situation: the radical federalization of the Belgian state during the 1980s and the early 1990s. It is not a coincidence that Belgium is the only EU member state that refers to its subnational authorities in its signature of the Amsterdam Treaty.[3] Though necessary to keep the country together in the longer run, this radical process further complicated the process of co-ordination on EU matters and negatively affected Belgium's record on implementation.

Belgian politicians have not, however, remained idle. Many attempts have been made to simplify co-ordination whilst respecting and maintaining the autonomy of each of the participants. This is not an easy task. The central principle in this whole endeavour has been and remains consensus building. This is not just for the sake of Europe. Consensus building has become a central feature of Belgium's political culture despite, or perhaps because of, profound social divisions. The latter is to a certain extent correct. But the effect of this has been that the process of consensus building has become more complicated and cumbersome, not that the principle of consensus has been given up. This is as true for domestic Belgian politics, as it is true for Belgium's policies in the European Union.

This chapter discusses the theory and practice of consensus building and how it affects Belgium's European policy. It examines the principles that inform the system of EU policy co-ordination in Belgium, and assesses the impact of Belgian state reforms.

Political Culture and Co-ordination

The political culture of co-ordination

Although it is sometimes difficult precisely to assess the effect of political culture on decision making on concrete issues, it is none the less interesting and important. As EU member states have to cope more or less with the same pressures as a consequence of their membership of the Union (see Kassim,

---

[3] Indeed, below the Belgian Foreign Minister's signature, there is a statement that says in three languages (Dutch, French, and German): 'This signature equally commits the French Community, the Flemish Community, the German-Speaking Community, the Walloon Region, the Flemish Region, and the Brussels Capital Region.'

Peters, and Wright, in this volume), their differing responses can be attributed at least in part to differences in political culture. In the Belgian context, the following cultural features tend to exert an influence on these reactions: the tradition of consensus, ministerial autonomy, and an inclination towards informal and ad hoc decision-making devices.

The tradition of consensus

The tradition of consensus to a large extent reflects the fact that Belgian society is deeply divided. This is true not only because of the well-known cultural-linguistic division between flemish- and French-speaking communities, but also because of the importance of two other cross-cutting cleavages: the philosophical-religious divide (between Catholics and free thinkers), and the socio-economic divide (between employees and employers). The existence of these divisions not only resulted in the involvement of at least four political parties in each federal government coalition, but also in the erection of different organizational structures, in which people are supported, helped, and protected from 'the cradle to the grave'. This process of 'pillarization', which in itself is not peculiar to Belgium, has made consensus building a precondition for social, economic, and government stability as each cleavage has a strong capacity for mobilization (Lijphart 1981). The whole range of legal and constitutional devices to protect minority views stems from this.[4]

Ministerial autonomy

Ministerial autonomy is partly related to the foregoing although it seems to contradict it (Kerremans and Beyers 1997). It arises from three factors. The first principle is consensus building, which, because time-consuming, is limited to politically sensitive issues. Other issues are dealt with by each of the ministers separately and will only reach the government agenda when other government members have contested them, that is when they have been politicized. In such cases, however, the issues concerned will be integrated in package deals in which the coalition parties exchange concessions on numerous issues. This process puts a brake on the politicization of issues and promotes respect for ministerial autonomy, as no party wants to grant concessions in exchange for concessions from the other on relatively minor issues.

   Second, ministerial autonomy is a consequence of the fact that the distribution of government functions and responsibilities is the result of a subtle balancing process among the coalition parties. Whenever one of these parties

---

   [4] Note that such devices also exist inside the Flemish and the Walloon regions, which show that the linguistic cleavage in Belgian society is only one of three, albeit increasingly the most important.

politicizes the issues on which a particular minister of another party has decided, this will be perceived as an act that disturbs the balance among these parties. This can easily jeopardize government stability.

Third, respect for the autonomy of each of the partners is a precondition to consensus building. It is only from the assurance that each participant's role in the process will be respected that a culture conducive to consensus building can be developed. This is true not only of ministerial autonomy at the federal level but applies even more to the action of regional ministers when they interact with each other and with their federal counterparts (see below).

Informal and ad hoc decision making

In Belgian politics there exists a very strong tendency towards secretive decision making by way of informal and ad hoc decision-making channels (Kerremans and Beyers 1997). This is partly related to the complicated compromises that political leaders construct and which they want to present to their rank and file when the decision has already been taken. The losses then can be excused by referring to the gains that have been achieved through the use of package deals. In this way, Belgian politics is like EU policy making (or vice versa, see Bursens and Kerremans 1997: 24), and is typical of consociationalist political systems. Therefore, the existence of deep-rooted social cleavages goes hand in hand with consensus building based on elaborate compromises reached in 'smoke filled rooms' by a relatively small number of participants. The state reforms (discussed below) may have made it more difficult to limit the number of participants, but they have not affected the covert character of decision making.

The impact of culture on co-ordination

The three major features of the Belgian political culture have, each in its own way, affected the co-ordination process concerning European integration. Consensus building has entailed the creation of an increasing number of devices at different levels. This happened as the number of participants in co-ordination increased steadily in response to the state reforms—which resulted in the participation of the subnational governments in the determination of Belgium's EU policies—and in response to the scope of EU competencies.

Ministerial autonomy has affected Belgian co-ordination in two ways. First, almost no central co-ordination system exists to determine how each of the ministries should organize itself in order to deal with issues on the EU agenda. Belgium's poor implementation record has led to efforts to reinforce central control on implementation by each of the ministries, but this has proved difficult as no ministry (not even the Prime Minister's Office) can impinge too much on the autonomy of the others.

Second, ministerial autonomy has resulted in the creation of specialized networks of co-ordination, in many cases without the existence of a legal framework to structure or to rule them. Due to ministerial autonomy, the structure of these networks differs from sector to sector, and has been largely determined by the sensitivities and priorities of the ministers or officials involved.

As far as ad hoc decision making is concerned, its effect on the Belgian co-ordination process has proved to be important, especially as it is based on consensus building between an ever larger number of actors. Many Belgian positions in the EU are decided by informal contact (often over the telephone) before they reach the stage of formal co-ordination. This permits formal co-ordination to proceed more smoothly, while overload and politicization are also avoided. It has also allowed Belgium to be involved in the early stages of EU decision making (that is after the initiation of a Commission proposal or during the decision making in the working groups of the Council) as Belgian representatives can take a position based on an informal consensus, even in the absence of formal instructions.

EU Policy Co-ordination in Belgium

The horizontal and vertical dimensions

The reforms that have fundamentally transformed the Belgian state in the last twenty years make it necessary to approach the Belgian co-ordination on EU issues from a horizontal and vertical perspective (Kerremans and Beyers 1995, 1997; Hooghe 1995). The horizontal perspective stems from the fact that the Belgian co-ordination process is to a large extent an intergovernmental one, as it includes different governments, which are legally on an equal footing. This last aspect—which is the reason why we define this perspective as horizontal—is a central feature of the current Belgian state. From a constitutional point of view, no hierarchy exists between the federal government and its subnational counterparts. No federal law can overrule a subnational decree. Nor can a federal government decision or a federal law overrule a subnational government decision. If Belgium wants to take a position on issues that belong either partly or completely to the competencies of its subnational entities, the consent of each of these entities is required. If such a consent, albeit just from one entity, is lacking, the Belgian delegation in the Council cannot take a position. In case of a vote, this means that Belgium has to abstain. Consensus building is thus not only a central element of Belgian political culture, but has the status of a legal or even a constitutional requirement. As ever more EU issues fall—either completely or partly (which is more often the case)—within the realm of Belgium's subnational authorities, the requirement for consensus building has steadily increased, and with it the search for co-ordination devices.

The vertical dimension refers to the fact that EU decision making takes place at different levels: the political (ministers in the Council), the ambassadorial (COREPER), and the administrative (working groups). This vertical organization of Council business is reflected in the process of internal co-ordination in Belgium, where the co-ordination effort differs at each level. In addition, as far as the official level is concerned, the nature of the horizontal co-ordination processes differs from sector to sector. In some sectors, co-ordination is structured and routinized. In others, arrangements tend to be more ad hoc.

Horizontal co-ordination at the political and ambassadorial level

Horizontal co-ordination

Whenever Belgium has to take a position in the Council, the decision is arrived at by horizontal co-ordination at the political level. Both federal and subnational ministers participate, with the (federal) Foreign Ministry acting as the co-ordinating agency. The Permanent Representation is also closely involved.

Co-ordination takes place on a weekly basis, through the so-called P.11 meetings (see Fig. 8.1).[5] This system, which has been in place since 1974,[6] was created due to the increasing importance of European integration for Belgium's foreign policy (Franck 1987: 70–1).[7] It reflected a strong desire to improve the effectiveness of Belgium's input into EU decision making.

P.11 refers to the Directorate European Affairs inside the federal Foreign Ministry, which organizes the concerned meetings (Ingelaere 1994). These meetings are attended by interested ministers,[8] depending on which sectoral Councils are due to convene the following week and the items on their agendas. When an Agricultural Council meets, representatives from the agricultural ministries (both federal and subnational) will participate. Some actors, though, are entitled to attend all P.11 meetings. These include

---

[5] Figure 8.1 refers to co-ordination that concerns issues belonging to the competencies of both the regions (Brussels, Wallonia, and Flanders) and the federal government. A similar way of co-ordination takes place whenever the communities are involved. In that case, the reference to the three regions has to be replaced by a reference to the French, the German-speaking, and the Flemish Community.

[6] Before 1985, the P.11 Co-ordination was called 'European Co-ordination'.

[7] Before 1974, no centralized co-ordination system existed. Co-ordination was informal and ad hoc.

[8] Each minister works with a large group of personal advisers called a cabinet. In P.11 meetings, these cabinet members act as personal representatives of their ministers. This system exists for the members of both the federal and the subnational governments.

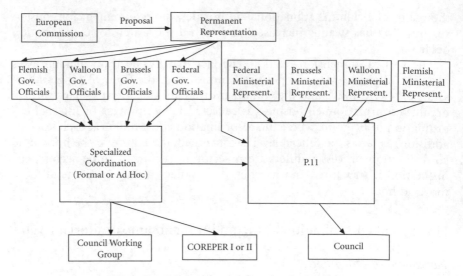

FIG. 8.1. National co-ordination in Belgium

representatives at the federal level of the Prime Minister and the deputy Prime Ministers, representatives of the Minister-Presidents, who head the subnational governments, and officials from the Belgian Permanent Representation.

Although the federal Foreign Ministry chairs the P.11 meetings, one has to avoid overestimating its role. Its role as co-ordinating agency is largely secretarial and logistical. It provides a room, and coffee! Moreover, it mails out invitations and it proposes an agenda (largely based on the agenda of the upcoming EU Council meetings). Otherwise, the Foreign Ministry is only one participant among many, though it does play a special role in preparing for the General Affairs Council.

The purpose of P.11 meetings is to transmit instructions to the minister who will represent Belgium in the EU Council. Instructions can only be issued if they have been approved by consensus in the P.11 meetings.[9] The P.11 meetings play a similar role concerning the positions that the Belgian Permanent Representatives defend in the COREPER I and II.

[9] Whenever consensus on such instructions can be reached among the different administrative departments (without the direct involvement of the personal representatives of the ministers), the P.11 meetings will be involved in such matters. In such cases, co-ordination takes place under the aegis of the Economic Ministry in the Interministerial Economic Committee (IEC). Its composition is analogous to that of P.11, the only difference being that senior officials, not the personal representatives of the ministers, participate and that the Secretary General of the federal Economics Ministry chairs the sessions instead of the Director of P.11. Decisions of the IEC concerning the EU have to be rubberstamped, however, by the P.11. Indeed, officially all Belgian positions in the councils and the COREPERs have to be approved unanimously by the P.11 co-ordination.

Horizontal co-ordination and the state reforms

The current system of horizontal co-ordination has existed since 1974, but has been reformed to take account of the changes in the Belgian state structure. Since 1970, four successive constitutional reforms (1970, 1980, 1988, and 1993) have transformed Belgium from a centralized state into a federal one. The last two sets of measures have been especially far-reaching and have affected the way in which Belgium's EU policies are determined. Two developments have been particularly significant: the equality enjoyed by subnational authorities with the federal government; and the right of subnational governments to conduct a foreign policy in the areas in which they enjoy policy competence. These changes have increased both the number and the diversity of participants in the co-ordination process, which involves both federal and subnational ministries. A regional perspective and an intergovernmental dimension have been added. As some subnational governments are extremely sensitive about their role and legal prerogatives, their involvement has increased the political salience of co-ordination.

The adaptation of the Belgian co-ordination process to the state reforms reflects a general concern that the larger autonomy of the Belgian subnational entities should be compatible with Belgium's ability to define a clear proactive EU policy. It therefore reflects the desire of both federal and subnational governments to reconcile regional autonomy with the requirements of European integration.

Three aspects of the adaptation of the co-ordination system to the new architecture of the Belgium state are important to highlight: the broadening of P.11 co-ordination, the creation of additional consensus-building devices, and the establishment of a mixed system of representation in the EU itself that allows for 'on the spot co-ordination'.

The broadening of the P.11 process

P.11 meetings have been expanded to include subnational ministries and the personal representatives of the Minister-President have a permanent seat. Before 1994 participation was largely based on an informal arrangement. Since 1994 it has been based on an agreement between the federal government and all five subnational governments, the Co-operation Agreement (CA) of 8 March 1994.[10]

Article 2 of the Co-operation Agreement gives a central role to the P.11

[10] As in Belgium the distinction is made between personally related matters—for which the communities are responsible—and territorially related matters—for which the regions are responsible—and as the Flemish Community and the Flemish Region have merged, it concerns the following five governments: the Flemish government, the government of the French Community, the Walloon regional government, the government of the Brussels Capital Region, and the government of the German-Speaking Community.

process. Under this provision, co-ordination concerning any issues dealt with in the Council which fall under the competencies of the subnational governments takes place in P.11 meetings. Moreover, P.11 can—whenever it considers it to be necessary—call for *ad hoc* meetings on technical issues to prepare for formal meetings of the P.11 committee. During the 1996 Intergovernmental Conference, for instance, many ad hoc meetings were organized.

The creation of additional consensus-building mechanisms

Additional co-ordination mechanisms have been established to deal with issues that arise when P.11 meetings fail to reach agreement due either to conflicts between the subnational governments and the federal government, or to differences among the subnational governments. As a lack of consensus would mean that Belgium would have to abstain in a Council vote,[11] and that the Belgian representative in the Council would be unable to participate in the negotiations, the absence of agreement is perceived as detrimental to Belgium's interests. The creation of additional consensus-building mechanisms in the form of the Interministerial Conference for Foreign Policy (ICFP) and the Concertation Committee derives from the desire on all sides to avoid such a contingency.

The ICFP and the Concertation Committee are bodies on a higher political level than the P.11. Whereas P.11 meetings involve ministers' personal representatives, the ICFP brings together the ministers themselves.[12] Failure to reach consensus in the P.11 results in the transfer of the issue to the ICFP. If the ICFP fails to reach an agreement, the issue will be submitted to the highest possible political level, the Concertation Committee. In this committee the federal Prime Minister and his vice prime ministers will discuss the matter with the minister-presidents of the subnational governments. Just as in the P.11 meetings and in the ICFP, a decision can only be taken when all participants have approved it. If this is not possible at this level, Belgium will have no choice but to abstain and the Belgian representative in the Council will be unable to negotiate on behalf of his country.

It has to be added that it is not by definition that a failure to agree in the P.11 means that the issue will be automatically transferred to the ICFP or Concertation Committee. P.11 can decide that Belgium will abstain, thereby ending the internal co-ordination process. If it refers the question to the ICFP—which normally happens—and if no agreement can be reached there, the ICFP decides whether the issue will go to the Concertation Committee.

---

[11] Whenever unanimity is required, a Belgian abstention has no consequence for Council decision making as such. It can only have a consequence as far as the five Belgian votes are necessary to reach the qualified majority. Although it has already happened that Belgium had to abstain because of a lack of internal consensus, it has never happened that this jeopardized a possible qualified majority in the Council.

[12] It concerns all the ministers that are directly involved in foreign policy making.

This only happens if the question is 'mature enough' to enable a political breakthrough to be made at the highest political level. It has to be added, however, that in reality, in most of the cases, P.11 succeeds in reaching a consensus. This is largely due to three factors: the perception that abstaining in the Council brings Belgium and its subnational governments into a 'lose–lose situation', the practice of package deals by which every government can be satisfied on at least something, and the development of an atmosphere conducive to consensus building. The last depends on the dense informal networks (and often personal relations) that connect the representatives of the various governments and arises because decision making, due to the extensive reach of the EU agenda, is an iterated game.

Representation and on-the-spot co-ordination

The amendment of Article 146 of the EEC Treaty following Maastricht allows member states to be represented in the Council by ministers from subnational, as well as central, government.[13] Nevertheless, these representatives have to represent their member states as a whole, not just parts of it.[14] For Belgium, the new Article 146 opened the door to the direct participation of its subnational governments in Council meetings, and created the possibility for 'on-the-spot co-ordination'. To make use of this opportunity, a new system was introduced in Belgium by the Co-operation Agreement mentioned above.

In the Council, the Belgium delegation consists of two members at the ministerial level: the leader of the delegation and the assessor. The leader of the delegation is allowed to speak on behalf of Belgium and is entitled to vote. The assessor attends the meeting and will—if necessary—consult the governments that are not participating in the meeting. Depending on the kind of council, the leader of the delegation is either a member of the federal or of a subnational government. The same holds for the assessor.

In cases which involve matters that fall exclusively within the federal government is area of responsibility, for example, the General Affairs Council, Belgium will be represented by a federal minister only. No assessor will accompany him or her. These Councils are designated 'Category I'. With respect to Councils that deal with matters that lie wholly within the competence of the subnational authorities, for example, the Education Council, Belgium will be represented only by a minister from a subnational government (Category IV). No assessor will accompany him or her. In most cases, however, the Council deals with issues that are the responsibility of both levels of government. Where policy concerns federal government more than subnational government, which is the case will the Social Affairs Council, for example, the

---

[13] These changes were proposed by the German and the Belgian delegation in the 1991 IGC on EPU.
[14] This requirement was included in the new Article 146 by explicit French demand.

delegation is led by a federal minister and the assessor comes from the sub-national tier (Category II). In areas where the responsibility of subnational government is primary, a subnational minister leads the delegation and is accompanied by a federal assessor (Category III).

In order to allow for some predictability, it has been determined in advance which Council falls within which category. This means that the composition of the Belgian delegation is not determined by the issues on the agenda of a particular Council, but by its type.[15] In addition, when the subnational governments can participate, and as they can only be represented by one minister, a system of rotation has been created. During each semester, in each of the Councils, a particular subnational government will send a minister either as leader of the delegation or as assessor.

The function of the assessor is to allow for on the spot co-ordination. As bargaining has become a fundamentally important aspect of Council decision making, Belgium has had to look for a system where it could reconcile the intergovernmental nature of its internal co-ordination with the need to negotiate in the Council. Indeed, since every instruction of a particular Belgian delegation is the result of a delicately constructed compromise amongst six governments,[16] the problem for the Belgian representatives is to assess how far one can go in granting concessions to the other member states without running into problems with one of those six. Two ways to approach this problem exist. First, the members of the Belgian delegation have been involved in the internal co-ordination process, which allows them to know how far they can go in 'taking their responsibilities'. Otherwise stated, they interpret their instructions as a mandate that allows them some leeway and requires them to defend the possible use of such leeway afterwards.

The *modus operandi* of the P.11 committee has promoted this approach, as quite often, the co-ordination process does not end in a clear instruction but in a 'tour de table'. Each government puts forward its concerns and objections so as to allow the delegation in the Council to know what can be and what cannot be defended or accepted.

The role of the assessor is also important. During Council negotiations, the head of the Belgian delegation consults the assessor—who is sitting beside him—about whether some or other concession is likely to be accepted by the Belgian governments that are not present. This is the 'on-the-spot co-ordination'. If there is any doubt, the assessor consults other governments over

---

[15] A Council is put into a particular category by looking at its activities and assessing which division of competencies in Belgium is predominant. In cases where a Council deals mostly with issues largely belonging to the subnational competencies and only to a lesser extent to those of the federal level, the Council will be put in Category III.

[16] The federal government, the Brussels regional government, the Walloon regional government, the French Community government, the government of the German-Speaking Community, and the Flemish government.

the telephone, the theory being that their representatives will be on 'stand-by' for as long as the Council meeting lasts. The combination of 'on-the-spot co-ordination' with 'co-ordination over the phone' allows the Belgian delegation to represent several governments at the same time and to adapt its position accordingly as Council negotiations progress.

In practice, however, the operation of the system is not quite as smooth as the theory suggests. One problem is that ministers do not like to be assessors, since their precious time is wasted in playing a secondary role. The result is a weakening 'on-the-spot co-ordination' and a strengthening of the head of delegation, as well as the risks of assuming such responsibility. Why is this so?

Whenever a minister does not attend the meeting as an assessor, he or she is replaced by a senior official from the same government. However, in such instances, the problem of status arises. The job of the assessor is to ask, and sometimes to urge, the minister that is the head of delegation to abandon negotiations temporarily and to switch attention to the search for a compromise position that is domestically acceptable. This is not easy, where the senior member of the delegation is a minister and the assessor 'merely' an official. In addition, where the assessor considers it necessary to consult other governments, he or she must convince the head of delegation to ask the Council presidency to suspend deliberations in order to allow internal Belgian co-ordination to take place. It is clear that in the midst of hard negotiations, a ministerial head of delegation will feel less inclined to co-ordinate and more inclined to assume his responsibilities. This makes it more difficult for the high official to urge the minister to do what he or she asks him to do, that is, to ask for the suspension of an issue in order to allow for some co-ordination. This has increased the probability that one or more of the non-participating governments will reject a position taken by Belgium in the Council afterwards, making it more difficult for the other member states to adjudge the value of agreements entered into by the Belgian delegation.

The weakness of the assessor system has put more pressure on *ex ante* co-ordination, and therefore, on P.11. That makes the task of P.11 even more difficult.

Vertical co-ordination

The P.11 process has a number of weaknesses. First, there is the problem of the number of participants. About twenty-five officials attend an average P.11 meeting. Federal and subcentral government levels are represented, as are the relevant ministries, reflecting the fact that an item of EU business is typically of interest to both levels of government and to several departments. Some issues, for example, may involve three federal ministries and six subnational departments (two for each region). The process of co-ordination, therefore, becomes extremely cumbersome, and inevitably generates informal mechanisms that short-circuit formal procedures, but restrict real influence to only a small number of actors.

A second problem in P.11 co-ordination relates to the scope of its agenda. As P.11 co-ordination covers in principle all business that reaches the Council or COREPER, overload is a very real possibility. Consequently P.11 meetings tend to concentrate only on the controversial issues and to rubber-stamp the others.

Another weakness concerns the stage in the EU policy process at which P.11 co-ordination actually takes place. The aim is to decide the position that Belgium will adopt in meetings of the Council or COREPER, P.11 as a central co-ordinating mechanism becomes operative late in the day. This makes it very difficult for a department or a government to bring its influence to bear. In order to be effective, such objections would have to be made much earlier in the process. In other words, what is missing is a technical preparatory stage in which co-ordination takes place on issues that are dealt with in the working groups of the Council. This problem has been resolved by the emergence, in some cases very recently, of a battery of specialized co-ordination mechanisms, though this differs from sector to sector. There has been no attempt by the federal government either alone or in association with the subnational governments to introduce or standardize these structures or procedures across all policy areas. Where they have emerged, the forms taken by co-ordination mechanisms have been shaped by a variety of sector- and issue-specific factors.

Before turning to these technical arrangements, it should be noted that one central attempt at communication—not co-ordination—was made by the federal government. In the early 1990s, the federal government decided to create a system of European co-ordinators. Within each ministry an official was designated as a co-ordinator, and known to all other departments, to be responsible for the co-ordination of EU business in the department. The intention was to improve Belgium's implementation record. The idea was that it would be easier, if a specific individual were named, for the Foreign Ministry to know who to contact where insufficient steps had been taken by a department to implement a particular directive.

With the formal inclusion of the subnational governments in the co-ordination process, two additional decisions have been taken. First, the subnational governments decided to appoint a European co-ordinator in each of their departments as well. Second, the federal and the subnational governments jointly created the post of federal correspondent. These correspondents are federal officials[17] charged with securing the co-ordination among the

---

[17] In practice, the European co-ordinators of the federal ministries have been selected for this function.

different governments for the issues for which their ministry is responsible.[18] As intended, they play a central role in the different specialized co-ordination to which we shall now turn.

As noted, there is considerable variation in sectoral arrangements for technical co-ordination, ranging from the extremely formalized and structured to the informal and largely sporadic. This prompts two questions: why is there no uniformity, and what is the effect on the effectiveness of co-ordination? A partial answer can be found by looking at the experience of four sectors—environment, agriculture, transport, and social affairs—which exhibit a variety of approaches.

Co-ordination at the technical level: variations

The hubs

Despite the differences between sectors, the central role of two figures is constant: the federal correspondent and the specialized representative in the Belgian PR.[19] The technical representative is important because he or she represents Belgium in the working groups of the Council. In many cases, he or she will be accompanied by officials from other departments and subnational governments, but, with the federal correspondent, is the only member of the Belgian delegation that has the right to speak and, if necessary, vote. Moreover, these two officials dispatch the documents that arrive from EU institutions to the European correspondents in the federal and subnational departments. Finally, they are responsible for briefing the Permanent Representative or his deputy before meetings of COREPER on dossiers falling within their area of expertise.

The federal correspondent is responsible for deciding whether co-ordination is necessary and for triggering the procedure. Whether the arrangements are formal or ad hoc, the federal correspondent is at the centre of the networks that exist or emerge from the technical officials from federal and subnational ministries, and the anchor for his or her federal and subnational counterparts. Beyond the presence and function of these two actors, however, the similarity between sectoral arrangements comes to an end.

[18] This decision did not deal with the question of co-ordination on issues that belong to the exclusive competencies of the subnational governments. In such cases no federal correspondent exists and co-ordination largely takes place by way of informal meetings between the European co-ordinators of the concerned subnational departments.

[19] The official in the Permanent Representations is likely to have been seconded from one of the technical-ministries (e.g. environment, social affairs, transport, agriculture) at the federal level. As in other member states, the Belgian PR is not exclusively staffed with diplomats. About half of its staff consists of officials from different federal ministries. In addition, each of the communities and regions is entitled to have a representative (called an attaché) in the PR.

The extent of formalization

To explain the different levels of formalization, it is useful to think in terms of demand and supply. On the demand side, the sensitivity of leading officials or ministers has led to a formalization of co-ordination. In other words, there has not been any attempt at formalization from the centre. However, even if the demand for formal co-ordination has been raised in a particular sector, there is no guarantee of success. Despite attempts at formalization, co-ordination in some sectors has remained informal.

What appears to have been decisive is either the workload of the EU or the international agenda (i.e. supply). In those sectors where co-ordination has to take place frequently, that is on a weekly or bi-weekly basis, co-ordination has been formalized. In the other cases, co-ordination has remained ad hoc and informal. An important factor here is that in case of formalization, an agreement on the exact nature of co-ordination and on the competencies and responsibilities of the participating governments is necessary. This requires an 'investment' on the part of governments, and it is only when the pressure from the EU or international level increases that these governments have proved themselves prepared to make that investment. In other cases, agreement is lacking because of resistance and no investment is made from the federal or the subnational level.

In the case of the environmental sector, where international organizations and the EU are very active, co-ordination is extremely formalized. A Co-operation Agreement—signed and ratified by each of the six governments and parliaments—was concluded in 1995, and a co-ordination body was created, which meets every Tuesday morning.[20] The very full agenda at international (e.g. Montreal, Rio, Kyoto) and EU level, and the need to implement the measures agreed, ensures that this weekly meeting is extremely busy. All decisions are taken by consensus. These meetings determine the instructions for Belgian representatives in international negotiations or in Council working groups. A failure to find a consensus results in the transfer of the issue to the P.11 meetings. But according to the people involved, this rarely happens for three reasons. First, referring an item to the P.11 meeting rarely results in a better outcome for the government that blocked the issue. Therefore, a government needs to be extremely careful in deciding when to submit a matter to the P.11 process, and to 'prioritize its priorities'. Second, as co-ordination takes place on a regular basis, the representatives tend to know each other well, which is conducive to consensus building. Third, decision making is an iterated game (just like in the P.11) where the expectation of getting concessions tomorrow promotes or eases the acceptance of concessions today.

In the case of agriculture, a similar pattern can be distinguished. A special

---

[20] This is the Co-ordination Committee on International Environmental Policy (CCIEP), created in Apr. 1995.

co-ordinating body[21] has been set up to deal with the heavily loaded agricultural agenda of the EU and to determine the Belgian standpoint in the numerous agricultural working groups.[22]

The situation is different in the cases of transport and social affairs. In both, demands—mainly from the subnational governments—have been made to set up a formal co-ordinating system, but have not been met. This was due to the federal government's opposition in the case of transport and to disagreement among different governments as to the exact provisions of a specialized Co-operation Agreement in the case of social affairs. In both areas, co-ordination takes place even in the absence of formal institutions in the form of telephone calls and faxes. The sustainability of this system is largely due to the fact that the EU agenda on these issues is not very demanding in terms of the number of EU proposals and the frequency of EU Council or working group meetings. This is also why the different governments do not really feel under pressure to create a formal system. There is no need to create formal mechanisms when informal channels are able to cope and when there are barely sufficient items to fill an agenda for a meeting.

But informal systems do have certain shortcomings. The quality of co-ordination depends on the openness of the federal correspondent who is at the hub of the informal system of phone calls and faxes, though any failure to meet the co-ordination needs of the subnational governments will lead to problems at the P.11 level—which has been known to happen—and an increasing demand on their part for a more formal system. In the meantime, however, the current way of working is likely to survive.

Conclusion

The Belgian system of co-ordination is highly decentralized with different arrangements in each policy sector. This does not mean that there has been no attempt to create or to improve Belgian co-ordination on EU policy making. At the political level the system of the P.11 co-ordination has been established. But at the lower levels of COREPER and the working groups, the only traces of a central attempt at improving co-ordination can be found in the presence of European correspondents in each of the federal ministries. These correspondents play an important, if not central, role at the technical level, but technical systems differ from sector to sector for two main reasons. First, there is the constitutional equality between the subnational and federal

---

[21] This is the Permanent Working Group (PWG) of the Interministerial Conference on Agriculture. The PWG was created in Feb. 1990.

[22] It equally prepares the meetings of the Special Committee on Agriculture (SCA).

level. This prevents the federal government from deciding unilaterally on the form to be taken by arrangements at the technical level, since this would conflict with the privileges of the regions and the communities. As a result, co-ordination depends on securing agreement between all governments, federal and subnational. Second, the principle of ministerial autonomy at both the federal and regional level makes technical co-ordination problematic. That technical systems came about at all was due to the shortcomings of co-ordination on the political level (P.11) on the one hand,[23] and to the consensus requirement on the other.

As noted above, the need for specialized co-ordination combined with the relative autonomy of ministries and authorities has resulted in a variety of arrangements at the technical level ranging from the highly formalized and regularized (e.g. environment) to the extremely informal and infrequent (e.g. social affairs). The differences between sectors depends on two main variables. The first is the significance of international and European agendas in the area concerned. The greater the frequency of international or European activity, the more formalized the technical co-ordination system in Belgium. This is due to the fact that creating and maintaining a formalized co-ordination system requires a cost in terms of time, money, organization, and commitment. Where there are insufficient grounds for incurring these costs, expensive mechanisms are not created and co-ordination continues to be informal.

There is also the question of the benefits that can be reaped from formal co-ordination. The major benefit is the fact that formal co-ordination increases the capacity of consensus building, of channelling information, of interpreting information, and of channelling both regional and federal concerns on the related issues. This allows Belgium, as a representative of its several governments, to intervene quickly at all stages (from initiation by the Commission to the adoption of the decision by the Council) in EU decision making or in decision making in international negotiations outside the EU.

The balance between the costs and the benefits is to a large extent the outcome of the extent to which there really is an international or EU agenda on the issues concerned. If there is barely anything to discuss in the EU or internationally, the incentive to bear the political costs of creating and maintaining a formal co-ordination system is relatively weak. If, on the other hand, either international negotiations or EU decision making on the issues concerned is important and frequent—as it is for agriculture and environment—the incentive to co-ordinate frequently on a large number of issues will be strong.

This does not mean, however, that formal co-ordination automatically follows from a large international or EU agenda in a particular field. The

---

[23] As has been indicated above, the shortcoming of the P.11 co-ordination is that it brings the regions into the co-ordination process very late. This negatively affects the consistency of Belgian positions in Council decision making.

assessment of the costs and benefits of such co-ordination is a political one. It depends on the perception of each of the governments that it has a direct interest in—moreover, that it is necessary to—formalizing co-ordination.[24] In addition, a certain consensus on this need has to exist among the governments concerned. If there is a lack of such consensus (as was originally the case in agriculture, and still is in social affairs), the need for more co-ordination tends to be fulfilled by informal devices such as faxing more information or calling particular representatives more regularly.

The second factor is the role of the federal correspondent. In cases where no formal co-ordination exists, the complexity of technical co-ordination depends largely on the role played by the European correspondent and his or her personal assessment of the need to co-ordinate more often, more frequently, and more collectively. Some correspondents show greater openness to the subnational governments and try to involve them actively in the decision-making process, even if they show a low level of interest. Others, however, enjoy their role and position at the centre of co-ordination. In these situations, they count on the likelihood that regions will raise objections late in the day, namely, when the issue reaches P. 11. In other words, the lower the international or European salience of an issue, the more that personal characteristics will determine the way in which Belgium co-ordinates EU business among its several governments. As the scope of European integration expands, the greater will be the pressure for a formalization of sectoral co-ordination at the technical level in Belgium. However, any such development will have to find a balance between the need to preserve domestic consensus building, on the one hand, and the demands of a European environment which requires swift reaction to, and extensive involvement in, complex negotiations with other countries and institutions, on the other.

References

Bursens, P., and Kerremans, B. (1997), 'Loose and Tight Policy Networks in EU Decision Making', *PSW-Papers*, 3: 2–29.

[24] In the case of the regional governments such a perception has stemmed from the feeling that the federal government tries to keep them out of EU decision making. The Flemish government especially has been very sensitive on this point. In the case of the federal government the interest stems from its dependence on the regions for the implementation of the EU directives. Since Belgium has been involved in a disproportionately high number of infringement procedures because of the failure of one or more of its regional governments or parliaments to take implementation seriously, the federal government has increased its efforts to involve them more formally in the process of EU decision making. This reflects the interdependence between the federal and the regional governments on many EU issues, and the related interdependence between decision making and implementation.

De Wilde d'Estmael, T., and Franck, C. (1993), 'Du mémorandum belge au Traité de Maastricht', in C. Frank et al. (eds.), *Aux tournants de l'histoire: La Politique extérieure de la Belgique au début de la décennie 90* (Brussels: De Boeck).

European Commission (1998), *Implementation of Internal Market Directives as of September 15, 1998* (Brussels: European Commission, DG XV, available on internet).

Franck, C. (1987), 'La Prise de décision belge en politique extérieure: Cohésion, tensions, contrôle et influences', *Res publica*, 29: 61–84.

Hooghe, L. (1995), 'Belgian Federalism and the European Community', in B. Jones and M. Keating (eds.), *The European Union and the Regions* (Oxford: Clarendon Press).

Ingelaere, F. (1994), 'De Europeesrechterlijke draagvlakken van de nieuwe wetgeving inzake de internationale betrekkingen van de Belgische Gemeenschappen en Gewesten', *Sociaal-Ekonomische Wetgeving*, 2: 67–82.

Kerremans, B. (1995), 'Europeser dan Europees: Het Belgische standpunt voor de IGC van 1996', *Samenleving en Politiek*, 2: 22–5.

——and Beyers, J. (1995), 'De plaats van de federale overheid, gewesten en gemeenschappen in de Europese Unie: Consequenties van de staatshervorming en de wijziging van artikel 146 EG', *Tijdschrift voor bestuurswetenschappen en publiek recht*, 50: 647–57.

——(1997), 'Belgian Adaptation to EU-Membership: The Dilemma between Autonomy and Cohesion', in R. B. Soetendorp and K. Hanf (eds.), *Small States and the European Union* (Harlow: Longman).

Lijphart, A. (1981), *Conflict and Coexistence in Belgium: The Dynamics of a Culturally Divided Society* (Berkeley: Institute of International Studies).

9

Austria

Wolfgang C. Müller

Introduction: EU Membership and the Challenge of Co-ordination

Austria became a member of the European Union in the post-Maastricht period. Although the relevant actors had gained experience with the European institutions and processes when preparing and conducting membership negotiations, Austria faced a situation which was quite different from that of the established EU countries which had had the possibility of gradually adapting to, and shaping, an 'ever closer Union' (Dinan 1994). It was clear to all actors that major challenges would result from membership and that they would include domestic co-ordination.

Austria is a small country, but its political structure is very elaborate, resulting in 'big government' or rather 'big politics'. To begin with, Austria, though smaller even than many of the subnational units in traditional federal states (except Switzerland), is a federal country comprising nine *Länder*. At the national level the framework of political institutions includes a directly elected president with considerable powers, including the power to 'represent the Republic internationally' (Article 65). However, no one doubts that the parliamentary aspect of Austria's constitutional framework is the dominant one. Here a two-chamber legislature exists. It consists of the dominant first chamber, the Nationalrat (which I refer to as Parliament), and the second chamber, the Bundesrat, which had been designed to represent *Land* interests at the national level and can, with few exceptions, only delay legislation. In practice, however, the cabinet is the major institutional player in Austrian politics. Due to the effects of proportional representation (almost none) on the one hand and the political parties' desire for government office (which means that minority governments have been hitherto unknown), cabinets are coalitions.[1] Since 1987 the Social Democrats (SPÖ) and the People's Party (ÖVP) have formed these coalitions. They have been the country's major parties throughout the post-war period, holding between them up to 95 per cent of the seats in Parliament. Although their combined share has recently declined to roughly two-thirds of the seats, the government coalition is still a 'grand' one. This, in turn, means that the major line of division often can be found within government rather than between government and opposition.

Finally, post-war Austria has developed a system of comprehensive interest group participation in policy making, which is referred to as 'social partnership' (in Austria) or corporatism. In this system most of the major interest groups enjoy chamber status, that is recognition by law and obligatory membership of all potential members. Three of the chambers—business, labour, and agriculture—and the trade union congress (ÖGB) and, to a lesser extent, the federation of industry (VÖI), participate in all stages of policy making, from the drafting of legislation to implementation.

While power shifted back and forth between political actors and institutions over the whole post-war period, membership of the EU has constituted a major challenge to the power balance within the Austrian system of government. Although the major actors agreed that membership would be necessary from a national point of view, some of them were concerned that the transfer of powers from Austria to the EU would affect them more than others (Schaller 1994, 1997; Karlhofer and Tálos 1996: 50–72). Their loss of formal competences or de facto decision-making power to Brussels would not be compensated by participation in the decision-making bodies of the EU. This discussion was fuelled by the fact that the 'democratic deficit' of the EU was already a public issue when Austria, a latecomer to the process of European integration, approached membership.

In order to win or maintain the support of the major political actors for membership in the EU, the government's policy was to offer compensation for their anticipated loss of power. On 26 June 1989, shortly after Austria's membership application, the government parties signed a party agreement on the further steps of integration policy.[2] Accordingly, a council for integration policy was established, which included the cabinet, representatives of all parliamentary party groups, the *Länder*, local communities, and the major interest groups.[3] The 1989 party agreement also committed the SPÖ and ÖVP to work towards the maintenance of the interest groups' 'proven participation'

---

[1] There were exceptions in the 1960s and 1970s. In 1966, 1971, 1975, and 1979, elections gave a single party parliamentary majorities, enabling them to form single party administrations. In 1970–1, there was a brief period of minority government.

[2] The agreement dates from 26 June 1989 and is reprinted in Rauchenberger 1989: 144–51.

[3] *Bundesgesetzblatt* 368/1989.

in economic and social policy decision making under the condition of EU membership and the way towards it. This claim was made with respect to both domestic and EU policy. In 1994, after the successful completion of membership negotiations with the EU but before the referendum, the SPÖ and ÖVP hammered out another party agreement.[4] It renewed the promise that the major interest groups would fully participate in the preparation of EU decisions. It was even claimed that they would be entitled to do so not only in the domestic arena but also in official EU bodies.

In 1992 the government agreed in principle to a major reform of the division of tasks between the national and *Land* levels in the context of European integration. It would strengthen the *Länder* and thus compensate them for the loss of competences they would suffer from the transfer of decision-making powers to Brussels.[5] In the same year, a treaty according to Article 15a of the constitution (*Bundes-Verfassungsgesetz*) between the national level and the *Länder* laid down the rules for the participation of the *Länder* and local communities in position taking in EU matters.[6] The core of these rules was later included in the amendment which adapted the Austrian constitution to membership in the EU (see below) (Schreiner 1992; Weber 1994; Morass 1994).

In short, by participating in working out the position Austria would take in EU bodies, the collective actors outside the framework of national political institutions —in particular the major interest groups and the *Länder*— could enjoy the same position in areas that now fall under the jurisdiction of the EU as they had occupied at the national level before accession. This strategy has resulted in high ambitions concerning EU co-ordination. Given the country's long tradition of wide consultation, grand coalition government, parliamentary consensus seeking, and corporatism, it seems fair to say that this co-ordination ambition is supported by a policy-making culture which values co-ordination and integration.

In the remainder of this chapter the various actors will be looked at individually, briefly pointing out in which way membership in the EU constitutes a challenge. Then the respective actor's formal role in the co-ordination process will be mapped out. Finally, an evaluation of the actor's impact on Austria's position taking in the EU will be provided. In so doing, I begin with the central players—the cabinet and the central administration. Then the roles of Parliament and the President, the *Länder* and the interest groups will be discussed. The conclusion aims at an overall evaluation of the EU co-ordination process from a political power perspective.

[4] The agreement dates from 22 Apr. 1994 and has been reproduced fully in Rauchenberger 1989: 243–9 and partially in Karlhofer and Tálos 1996: 214–17.

[5] The text dates from 8 Oct. 1992 and is reprinted in Rauchenberger 1989: 179–82 and Schreiner 1992: 203–7.

[6] *Bundesgesetzblatt* 775/1992.

EU Co-ordination in the Cabinet and Central Administration

Each coalition cabinet is faced with two major 'centrifugal forces', which Rudy Andeweg (1988) has called departmental and political heterogeneity. As elsewhere, government departments often differ over policies; appropriate examples may be the departments of environment and economics, health and social security, finance and all others. In coalition cabinets, departmental heterogeneity is paralleled by political heterogeneity, resulting from the different policy preferences of the coalition parties. Grand coalition government pushes political heterogeneity to an extreme. There are two parties of almost equal strength. Both have a stake in each policy field, and their policy preferences tend to differ substantially.

The particular challenge in EU matters results from the constitutional framework of decision making. Austria participates in European rule making primarily via *individual* cabinet members or their subordinates: the relevant minister in the Council, the permanent representative in the COREPER meeting, who is a subordinate to the Foreign Minister, and the many civil servants who serve in working groups of the Commission or the Council and who are accountable to their respective minister. Compared to their responsibilities at the national level, the competencies ministers enjoy at the European level are huge. While ministers need the unanimous consent of cabinet and subsequent majority support in parliament for their proposals at the national level, constitutionally the constraints imposed by Austrian institutions and procedures when it comes to position taking in Brussels are extremely loose. Within cabinet, ministers need to co-ordinate only to the extent that there are differences in the distribution of competences between the Austrian ministries on the one hand and the various councils on the other hand, that is, when one particular council deals with issues falling into the competences of two or more ministries. In these cases only one minister represents Austria in the Council but has to co-ordinate with those ministers who are in charge with regard to Austrian law.[7]

In practice, however, the government parties and departments have agreed to a co-ordination mechanism which, by and large, seems to work quite well. The details of this mechanism were fixed in party agreements between the SPÖ and ÖVP and by government guidelines.

To begin with, all government departments are actively involved in EU co-ordination. For each EU matter there is one leading government department which represents Austria. According to the 1994 'Europe agreement' between

---

[7] Given the government parties' concern about co-ordination in practice it remains an open question why the cabinet *de jure* hardly has a role in European position taking.

the SPÖ and ÖVP the ministry which according to Austrian law provides the bulk of the funds for the respective task is the lead ministry. This agreement also allocated specific competences (for example, the distribution of EU funds) to specific government departments.

It is worth noting that EU membership has not led to changes in the Austrian ministerial structure. In particular, there was no attempt to adapt it to that of the Council. Even worse, the Council's structure did not have an impact on the last major changes in the Austrian ministerial structure which were made after the 1994 general elections, which took place after the successful EU referendum. This has led to very imbalanced demands on Austrian ministers in terms of participation in Council meetings. While the Minister of Science and Transportation has to serve on four different councils, the Minister of Women's Affairs (until 1997, when consumer protection was added to her tasks) did not participate in any council. Not surprisingly, at least one Minister of Science and Transportation has complained repeatedly about the huge demand participation in EU bodies has made on him. It is particularly pressing, since he has no junior minister who may deputize for him at some of the Council meetings. It is also worth noting that the Council structure influences the relative weight of ministries. The Environment Council, for instance, has a much larger jurisdiction than the Austrian Ministry of Environment has at home. Representing Austria at this Council has positive spill-over effects for this ministry when it comes to the preparation of EU decisions in the domestic arena (Steiner and Trattnigg 1998: 156–60).

In its respective fields each ministry is actively involved in EU co-ordination in several ways. First, it has to keep those other government departments informed which, according to the Austrian division of competences, also have a competence in this field. Second, it has to co-ordinate the position to be taken in various kinds of EU bodies with these departments (but also with other actors, see below). If the government departments cannot agree the lead one is entitled to make the decision. According to the government guidelines, each department should hold at least one general co-ordination meeting per month for the preparation of the Council's and Commission's working groups and the Council meeting. In any case, each Council meeting is preceded by a co-ordination meeting. The results of the pre-Council meetings have to be reported to the two chief departments of EU co-ordination, the Chancellery and the Foreign Ministry.

Having two (rather than one) chief departments of EU co-ordination springs from the fact that both government parties want to be involved. While the Chancellor is from the SPÖ, the Foreign Minister is from the ÖVP. Initially, both parties were keen to maximize their influence in EU co-ordination. While the SPÖ claimed that EU matters would be 'domestic' affairs now (and hence no longer would fall into the Foreign Ministry's jurisdiction), the ÖVP argued that it would be the Foreign Minister (rather than the Chancellor) who would be the *primus inter pares* in the European arena. None of these positions was politically viable, nor could the parties agree on having a special minister for European affairs. Therefore, the pragmatic solution was to apply in principle the existing constitutional division of labour to the new tasks of government. Accordingly, the Chancellor is in charge of co-ordination within Austria while the Foreign Minister represents Austria in the General Affairs Council and is responsible for Austria's Permanent Representative at the EU. A clear-cut division of labour along these lines, however, would hardly have been functional. Fortunately, functional requirements met with political ambition. While the Foreign Ministry wanted to acquire a stake in co-ordination within Austria, the federal Chancellery was interested in acquiring one in the more visible representation in the EU's general Council. Hence, the agreement is that intra-Austrian co-ordination is under the joint direction of the Chancellery and Foreign Ministry and that the Foreign Minister is deputized in the EU general Council by the junior minister of the federal Chancellery who is in charge of EU co-ordination.

As mentioned above, the federal Chancellery and Foreign Ministry receive reports on ongoing co-ordination processes between ministries. Their genuine task in long-term co-ordination, however, is the preparation for the European Council, which involves both of their heads. Otherwise, the chief co-ordination departments become actively involved only very late in the EU co-ordination process. This is just before the COREPER meeting.

Towards the end of the working week, Austria's Permanent Representation at the EU provides the agenda for the upcoming COREPER meeting for all government departments. The agenda refers to documents which already have been provided by EU institutions. Co-ordination within government departments takes place on Monday and Tuesday mornings. It is followed by a weekly *jour fixe* on Tuesday afternoon. This is the central co-ordination meeting at the civil service level. The chair alternates between civil servants from the federal Chancellery and the Foreign Ministry. All government departments participate as do the major interest groups, the national bank, the central statistical office, the federation of local communities, and the joint national office of the *Länder*. Most government departments are represented by civil servants from the EU divisions, though occasionally members of the personal cabinets of the ministers act as the departments' representatives. The task of this meeting is to agree on the positions Austria's Permanent Representative will take in the next COREPER meeting. If no agreement can be achieved, the government department in charge of the respective issue makes the decision. The sense and decisions of the meeting are summarized by the representatives of the Chancellery and Foreign Ministry in the form of an order to the Austrian Permanent Representative in Brussels which is then officially given by the Foreign Ministry (Morass 1996; Karlhofer and Tálos 1996: 136, 146; Müller 1997a: 80–1).

The civil servants involved in the co-ordination attempts of line ministries are first and foremost those who serve in the specialized divisions (*Abteilung*). It is they who represent their department in Council or Commission working groups and who co-ordinate with other government departments. All ministries now have an EU division and generally it belongs to the presidial department (*Sektion*). Typically, EU divisions take over from specialized divisions once an issue reaches Council stage, and on the whole they closely co-operate with the personal *cabinet* of the minister.

EU divisions play a more central role in preparing the individual departments for the EU presidency.[8] Naturally, the specialized ministerial departments lack the required overview when it comes to selecting issues to be pushed during the presidency. Again, the EU divisions closely co-operate with the *cabinets* of the ministers when this selection is made and the minister is briefed. Otherwise, in bottom-up processes, the political level, which in practical terms primarily means the minister's *cabinet*, may become involved when co-ordination fails. In these cases civil servants of those departments which are not in the lead position of the co-ordination process appeal to the political level if they feel that important departmental goals cannot be achieved. Then, the respective minister's *cabinet* or the minister himself or herself contacts their counterpart in the lead ministry and tries to exercise influence.

There are also provisions for regular co-ordination in EU matters at the political level. The coalition agreements of 1994 and 1996 and a more detailed later paper have established rules for co-ordination within the cabinet. Accordingly, ministers have to report to the cabinet on these matters both in written form and orally. The latest possible date for these reports is the last cabinet meeting before the decision is supposed to be taken in the Council. These reports identify the content of the issue, the Austrian position and the supporting arguments, as well as the respective positions of the other EU countries. Reports to the cabinet are also envisaged on issues at an early stage of the EU decision-making process. In order to allow the other participants to prepare for the discussion of these issues in cabinet (which meets on Tuesday mornings), they need to be announced, at the latest, at the coalition's weekly co-ordination meeting on Mondays.

One specific incentive to co-ordinate within cabinet results from the constitutionally strong position of Parliament (see below). Within specified limits,[9] the opposition has the right to demand the discussion of each EU item in the Parliament's main committee. When the main committee functions as the EU committee its meetings are largely public. They might be used to drive

---

[8] The first Austrian EU presidency took place in the second half of 1998.

[9] While a quarter of the MPs can always demand the discussion of a specific issue in the main committee of parliament, each parliamentary party group can select one issue for each of its meetings.

a wedge between the coalition partners if they have not agreed beforehand on the positions to be taken on the items which will be discussed. Therefore, the government parties have agreed that it is necessary to have a joint position when going to the main committee.

As a consequence, the nature of cabinet meetings has changed. First, the leaders of the parliamentary groups of the government parties have become official (though non-voting) members of this meeting. To be sure, they have always attended the cabinet's preparatory meeting, in which cabinet deliberations were held and decisions made *de facto*, leaving only their formalization to a very short formal cabinet meeting (Müller 1997*b*). Concerning domestic policies, the most important cabinet decisions are those on government bills which are then channelled through Parliament, providing the parliamentary groups of the government parties with the opportunity to demand and indeed enforce amendments. This is not the case with respect to the bulk of EU matters which are never dealt with in formal parliamentary meetings. Indeed, Parliament could demand this (see below). However, the coalition partners prefer to bypass this process by participation of their parliamentary groups' leaders in cabinet decision making. Given the general dominance of the executive in the EU decision-making process, it was considered necessary to define the positions of the parliamentarians in the cabinet minutes. Therefore, the party group leaders became official participants in the cabinet meeting. Second, cabinet meetings have a new permanent item on the agenda: EU matters. Ministers report on Council meetings which they have just attended as well as on their plans for future meetings. As a consequence, on average the cabinet meetings last roughly one hour longer than before EU membership.

Naturally, there is some leeway for the ministers about the extent to which they report to the cabinet on EU matters. Personal interviews with cabinet ministers and other insiders conducted between 1995 and 1997 suggest that major issues are indeed approved before a minister takes a position in Brussels. As one minister has put it:

Although it is true that constitutionally there is a difference (between domestic and EU matters), as EU matters have not to be agreed by the cabinet, in practice there is no real difference. I have continued to co-ordinate my position on important questions with the coalition partner—of course! Not on questions such as whether the EU passport will be red or green, but whether the Schengen agreement will be fully implemented in 1998 or in 2000. This is a deeply political question with financial consequences.

The fact that the government is a coalition, and especially a 'grand coalition', creates pressure towards cabinet co-ordination of EU matters. As one of the architects of the intracabinet co-ordination mechanism has pointed out:

Of course, we have seen the danger of ministers breaking away. Therefore it is quite good that we are in a coalition government. If it were a one-party government, each minister would work for himself and the chancellor would have the task of keeping it together. Being party chairman, he can do it, but it is very cumbersome, because it is a huge territory. But in a coalition, the 'blacks' check the 'reds' and the 'reds' the 'blacks' and all have an interest that important issues are processed through cabinet.

Checking one another, however, partly occurs outside the co-ordination framework set up for EU matters. While major issues are processed through cabinet, ministers may use other means of co-ordination with regard to issues of lesser importance. Rather than going through cabinet, ministers may inform the coalition partner's relevant parliamentary spokesperson, the leader of the parliamentary party group, or a specific minister on the position to be taken in the Council. If they do not object, the minister goes to Brussels without involving the cabinet. While these co-ordination mechanisms were used extensively before EU membership (Müller 1997*b*), they did not prevent but rather smoothed cabinet treatment of the respective issue. Hence, it is fair to conclude that the co-ordination between the coalition parties has become more informal when it comes to EU matters. As already indicated, cabinet insiders are generally rather satisfied with the amount of co-ordination which is actually achieved at the political level. However, there are dissenting opinions, as the following quotation reveals:

It has become the practice that ministers always work in pairs. A minister of the ÖVP talks to a related minister from the SPÖ before he goes to Brussels. After the decision had been made we are told: the issue had been agreed with your party. Previously (i.e. before EU membership) a government proposal required unanimous acceptance by the cabinet and the proposals were exactly worded. Now the cabinet gets informed after the event, mostly only orally.

Notwithstanding this criticism, successful co-ordination, as understood in the preceding paragraphs, is largely 'negative', meaning that one party manages to prevent the ministers of the other party pursuing damaging policies in Brussels and vice versa. 'Positive' co-ordination, that is the interparty and interministerial attempt to maximize Austrian influence in Brussels, tends to be the exception rather than the rule. It would appear that Austria has a positively co-ordinated strategy concerning the EU decision making on trans-Alpine transit policy. This had been a matter of great concern for Austria already in the membership negotiations, and the goals Austria wishes to achieve come close to a national consensus. Both government parties probably would face electoral punishment if Austria spectacularly fails to succeed with regard to EU decision making concerning this vital issue. In other cases, however, the incentive structure is more complex. This is particularly true when it comes to making cross-sectoral package deals. Then one minister would suffer a disadvantage for the gain of another minister. While departmental interests always work against cross-sectoral package deals, coalition government in many cases provides another disincentive to engage in this kind of deals. One party would be able to claim credit for being successful in Brussels while the other would have to carry the blame for not doing well at the EU level. Consequently, Austria hardly ever attempts package deals. As one minister has stated: 'I have the impression that other countries make more use of this strategy.' Likewise, a ministerial adviser in EU matters has told the author: 'I have never come across a package deal.' In principle, the problem could be solved by strong leadership which guarantees each party a fair share in such gains from trade—a kind of super co-ordination. However, it seems that this would place too strong a demand for co-ordination on the coalition leadership.

To summarize, EU membership has increased the powers of individual ministers *vis-à-vis* the cabinet. This moves the Austrian case closer to the ideal type of ministerial government, as proposed by Laver and Shepsle (1994, 1996) in their seminal work.

Parliament and EU Co-ordination

The transfer of many legislative powers to the EU has presented a major challenge to Parliament. MPs estimate that about 70 per cent of their law-making powers have been lost to Brussels. In this context, that Parliament in general, and the opposition parties in particular, would have looked for strategies to minimize the impact of this transfer of competences on their power was only to be expected. The fact that the government parties—the SPÖ and ÖVP—did not enjoy the two-thirds majority in the Nationalrat which was required for constitutional amendments when it came to adopting Austria's institutional framework to EU membership in 1994 constituted a window of opportunity for the opposition parties, in particular the Liberal Forum and the Greens. Together with the government parties they provided the required two-thirds majority. In exchange, they extracted concessions from the government concerning the role of Parliament in determining the positions Austria takes in EU decision making.

Accordingly, in contrast to co-ordination within cabinet, ministers are constitutionally obliged to co-ordinate position taking in the EU with Parliament or rather to give Parliament the possibility of demanding this (Khol 1995; Körner 1994; Schäffer 1996: 40–9). According to the new Article 23e of the Constitution (B-VG),[10] the relevant ministers are obliged in good time to inform the Nationalrat about EU proposals concerning all three pillars. It is up to Parliament to issue its opinion on these matters or not. If it does so, the

---

[10] *Bundesgesetzblatt* 1013/1994.

minister is bound by the Parliament's will[11] and may deviate from it only for 'cogent foreign and integration policy reasons' and only after having consulted Parliament again. Parliament acts through its main committee, which is permanent in the sense that it remains in office even if Parliament is dissolved. A 1996 amendment to the Parliament's rules of procedure provided for a subcommittee for EU affairs, to complement the main committee, which two years later had not yet been created.[12] The main committee is chaired by the President of Parliament, and its composition varies, meaning that parties can send their specialists in certain policy fields to the respective meetings.

Constitutionally, the position of the Austrian Parliament is stronger than that of any other parliament in the European decision-making process (Bergman 1997). In practice, its direct impact has remained rather limited. In 1995, Austria's first year within the EU, the Nationalrat was informed about 17,317 EU proposals. About 100 were selected for consideration by the main committee which issued an opinion in no more than 18 cases. In the first two years of the following Parliament (1996 and 1997) 37,624 EU proposals were submitted to Parliament, and of those, 106 were dealt with by the main committee in nineteen meetings. The committee eventually issued an opinion in eleven cases. This is less than in the first year of Austria's membership and indicates that Parliament has not made a major impact.[13]

The decline in the number of opinions the Parliament issues may be explained by learning and changes in the political environment. Learning refers to the early experience that it may be counterproductive to bind a minister too strictly. In 1995, a minister could not accept any compromise in the negotiations in Brussels and since total victory was not possible had less influence and returned with a worse result than otherwise would have been possible (Griller 1995: 171–4). The changed political conditions relate to the fact that the government parties regained a two-thirds majority in 1995. Although decisions on position taking in EU matters do not require a two-thirds majority, MPs and Parliament insiders generally agree that the government parties

[11] In the case of matters which need also the consent of the second chamber, the Bundesrat (Article 44 (2)), this applies to both chambers.

[12] *Bundesgesetzblatt* 438/1996. According to parliamentary convention, permanent subcommittees are taken into consideration when committee chairmanships are allocated among the parliamentary parties according to proportional rules. The party which would be entitled to claim the next committee or subcommittee is the strongly anti-EU FPÖ. This has created a major disincentive for the government parties to set up an EU subcommittee.

[13] Moreover, interviews with civil servants and interest group representatives in the social policy and environment policy fields suggest that Parliament has not necessarily selected the most important issues. These interviews were conducted by the authors of sector studies and case studies—Martina Eder, Karin Hiller, Gerhard Steiner, and Rita Trattnigg—which are published in Falkner and Müller (1998).

need to find support among the opposition parties for constitutional amendments and other matters requiring such a majority had 'positive spill-over
effects' on position taking in the EU. In other words, the government parties
needed to be accommodating with the opposition parties in order to win their
support in constitutional and other matters: and they 'paid' for the opposition parties' support also by giving them (or some of them) a greater influence in EU affairs.

The discovery that Parliament does not directly influence Austrian
position taking in the EU to a great extent, however, should not be interpreted
to mean that Parliament is irrelevant. As mentioned above, the anticipated
discussions in the main committee exert pressure on the government parties
to reach an agreed position in EU matters. Indeed, the opposition parties have
made many more proposals for binding ministers in the main committee,
which have been rejected by the government parties. Given the policy
differences between the government parties, it might be thought that at least
occasionally one of them would be tempted to join forces with the opposition. However, this has not happened so far. Coalition discipline has been
maintained also in EU affairs (Müller 2000). This indicates that the pre-
parliamentary co-ordination between the two government parties works.
The question is, therefore, in which situations do the government parties
themselves find it useful to issue opinions via the Parliament's main
committee?

Between 4 October 1996—the date since which the proceedings of the main
committee have been published[14]—and 18 November 1997 the main committee issued opinions on Austria's position concerning:

- employment policy at the EU level;
- economic and currency union;
- Europol;
- preparation of Austrian position for the World Trade Organization's
  minister conference;
- human rights;
- the relations between the EU and Iran;
- trans-Alpine traffic;
- biotechnical inventions.

These are issues which have a direct impact on domestic politics or which are
otherwise of great importance. By issuing an opinion through the main committee the government parties send signals to the electorate and formalize
their deals. As a minister explained to the present author:

[14] See *IV-1–IV-12 der Beilagen zu den Stenographischen Protokollen des Nationalrates XX.
PG.*

Central themes are dealt with within the parliament's main committee. They are also agreed beforehand between the government parties. On central themes such as foreign and security policy we have negotiated Austria's position for Brussels and its precise wording over many days.

In the same way that the absence of successful censure motions in West European parliaments does not indicate the irrelevance of these assemblies, the absence of open conflicts between Parliament and the government in EU affairs and of strict parliamentary orders on how cabinet members have to behave in Brussels does not indicate the irrelevance of the Austrian Parliament in this respect. It has been argued in this section that the potential channelling of all EU issues through the Parliament's main committee helps to enhance coalition discipline and to foster agreement at the cabinet level. As mentioned above, the parliamentary groups of the government parties participate in the pre-parliamentary cabinet and coalition processes. Nevertheless, it is fair to conclude that the power of Parliament is less direct and detailed and more difficult to enforce than before EU membership. Hence, it has declined due to membership of the EU.

The President and EU Co-ordination

According to the 'logic' of the Constitution the President should have important appointment powers with respect to Austria's positions in EU bodies, mirroring those in the domestic arena. However, the constitutional amendment adapting Austria's institutions for EU membership does not create any new role for the President. The President 'does not exist' with regard to EU affairs, as Manfried Welan (1997: 56) has put it. Indeed, the most important appointments to EU positions are made (or, to be technically correct, prepared) by the cabinet, with the main committee of Parliament exercising veto power.

The President might nevertheless be important for EU co-ordination, since the constitution boldly states: 'The Federal President represents the Republic internationally' (Article 65). Constitutional lawyers have interpreted this clause differently. In the most extensive interpretation (Koja 1993), the President has a constitutional monopoly for Austria's *formal* representation in acts under international law. In this interpretation, the Chancellor or the Foreign Minister can represent the country in a formal sense only on the President's delegation. Based on this specific interpretation, President Klestil claimed that it was his role to represent Austria in the European Council, when Austria became a member in 1995. The Chancellor disagreed, and eventually the President gave in, while maintaining the claim that he only has delegated this task to the Chancellor.

What may have eased President Klestil's concession is the *material* side of foreign policy making. Here even advocates of a strong President agree that the Constitution gives precedence to the government and Parliament. All foreign policy acts of the President require a proposal of the cabinet or a cabinet minister who is entrusted by the cabinet. Thus, the President is not allowed to initiate foreign policy. Rather he has to wait for a proposal which he can only accept or reject (Koja 1993: 631). It is easy to understand that this would be a rather impractical method when it comes to decision making in the European Council. In short, the role of the President has been reduced (Schäffer 1996: 50–1).

The Länder *and EU Co-ordination*

The *Länder* are even more affected by EU membership than the national Parliament. Even before the accession, their jurisdiction was very narrow. Now hardly anything is left. Indeed, the *Land* diets meet only infrequently and sessions are short. Most of their time is devoted to hearing and debating reports of the *Land* government. Having a stake in the national co-ordination process might, therefore, be particularly important.

According to the new 1994 Article 23d of the Constitution the political institutions at the national level (the *Bund*)—in practice the cabinet—are obliged to inform the *Länder* about EU proposals which affect the jurisdiction of the *Länder* or might be of interest to them. It is up to the *Länder* to issue their opinion on these matters or not. If they provide a common position, the national-level institutions are bound by the will of the *Länder* if the matter falls under *Land* jurisdiction. In these cases Austrian representatives in EU institutions may deviate from the position of the *Länder* only for 'cogent foreign and integration policy reasons', which have to be reported to the *Länder* as soon as possible. In cases of EU proposals affecting *Land* jurisdiction, Austria may be represented in the Council by a representative of the *Länder* (Schäffer 1994, 1996; Schambeck 1997: 171).

In practice, the *Länder* have done less well than on paper. To begin with, the major reform of the division of competences between the federal *Land* and community levels, which had been promised to the *Länder*, has not yet been carried out (Öhlinger 1994; Pernthaler and Schernthanner 1994). The government parties failed to enact it before the 1994 elections. While it was good for the Parliament's position in EU co-ordination that the SPÖ and ÖVP lost the two-thirds majority required for constitutional amendments in the 1994 elections, it was not good for the *Länder*. The SPÖ and ÖVP chose to enlist the support of the Liberal Forum and the Greens, which also provided the required votes for the constitutional amendment which, among other things, regulates position taking in the EU. However, the compromise ultimately achieved was so watered down that the *Länder* rejected it in December 1994. Negotiations have continued since then, but had not produced a result by late 1999.

In contrast, the participation of the *Länder* in EU co-ordination, as outlined above, is constitutionally guaranteed. However, it has turned out not to be very effective. To begin with, the *Länder* have to agree on a joint position. Given the important differences between the *Länder*, this often is difficult. What might be good for the Burgenland, the economically backward *Land* bordering Hungary, might not be good for the prosperous *Länder* in the west of Austria. Moreover, as a study of the environmental policy community has demonstrated, it has turned out to be difficult for the *Länder* to co-ordinate within the parameters of EU decision-making processes (Steiner and Trattnigg 1998: 163–5). In particular, they lack the time and resources to make full use of their right of participation, even when there is no conflict of interest between them.

Corporatism and EU Co-ordination

As mentioned in the introduction to this chapter, over the whole post-war period the major interest groups have traditionally participated in law making and policy making in general via regular consultation mechanisms. Moreover, interest group representatives in cabinet and a strong parliamentary representation of interest group officials (elected on party lists) have enabled them to support their positions within the formal institutions of government. Many political decisions have de facto been left to the major interest groups. In any case, a joint proposal of the major interest groups was one which was hard to defeat, though less so in the 1980s and 1990s than at any time since the late 1950s. In this context, EU membership might have meant a further acceleration of the decline of the major interest groups' power. Nevertheless, interest groups have supported Austrian membership in the EU and have received the government parties' promises that their participation in policy making would be maintained, even with regard to position taking in EU bodies. Strictly speaking, interest group participation is more a question of concertation than co-ordination. However, given the traditional importance of corporatism in post-war Austria a brief discussion is warranted.

The right of the chambers of labour and business to participate in the regular consultation process which precedes law making was extended to EU matters in 1994. Interestingly, this right was extended to the trade union congress and the association of the chambers of agriculture (Karlhofer and Tálos

1996: 141–2) which do not enjoy chamber status.[15] According to law, these interest groups are informed about all proposals which aim at making rules at the EU level and have the right to be heard on these matters. Moreover, they became members of new advisory boards and the *jour fixe* which prepares the COREPER meeting. Finally, interest group representatives may become members of Austrian delegations (without the right to speak) in EU bodies (Karlhofer and Tálos 1996: 141–3). Although this falls short of the government's initial commitment, it is more than interest groups have achieved in any other EU member state.

How does interest group participation in EU co-ordination within Austria work in practice? The few studies which have been conducted so far demonstrate that interest groups are indeed comprehensively involved in working out Austria's position to be taken in all kinds of EU bodies (Karlhofer and Tálos 1996: 143–51; Falkner and Müller 1998). The greatest problems they face are their lack of resources for the big new tasks as well as the agenda control by the EU which establishes the deadlines of the decision process. Compared to domestic decision making in the pre-EU period, this tends to increase the impact of the bureaucrats and their political masters.

Conclusion

This chapter has dealt with the case of a latecomer to European integration, facing a post-Maastricht European Union from the very beginning. Adaptation to the new, multi-level way of conducting politics has been a huge task. Austria's way into the European Union was smoothed by the support of the major political parties, interest groups, and governmental institutions. In this process, the government made considerable commitments to co-ordinate its position taking in EU bodies with other domestic actors once Austria had achieved membership.

Most of these commitments have indeed been realized by changes to the institutional framework. The constitution and ordinary laws have been amended and new advisory bodies have been set up to satisfy the demands of Parliament, the *Länder*, and the major interest groups. They all have a stake in the co-ordination process before position taking in EU bodies. One of them—Parliament—can also impose its position on the government. Constitutionally, it has a stronger position in this process than any other Parliament in the European Union. In practice, however, time pressure and lack of

[15] According to the Austrian constitution agriculture falls into the competences of the *Länder*. The chambers of agriculture therefore are at *Land* level. These have formed a voluntary association, the presidial conference of the chambers of agriculture, which represents them at the national level.

resources have proved to be important factors influencing the co-ordination process. Despite the real attempts by the bureaucracy and ministers to co-ordinate EU position taking, membership in the EU has led to a considerable shift of power between the central actors in Austrian politics. At the risk of oversimplification, power has been shifted from the President to the Parliament and the cabinet, from the Parliament to the government, from the major interest groups to the government, and from the *Länder* to the government. While government is the main winner of power through membership in the EU, it is fair to say that the Austrian system of co-ordination has contained its gains.

Finally, it is worth recalling that EU membership has also led to important changes within government. Despite the attempt to keep these changes at bay by party agreements and new tasks for the cabinet, the decision-making process has become more informal. Individual cabinet ministers generally have gained power and some of them have also benefited from having a more important role in the Council than in domestic politics. However, it is again fair to conclude that the grand coalition's system of political co-ordination has limited these gains.

References

Andeweg, R. B. (1988), 'Centrifugal Forces and Collective Decision Making: The Case of the Dutch Cabinet', *European Journal of Political Research*, 16: 121–51.

Bergman, T. (1997), 'National Parliaments and EU Affairs Committees: Notes on Empirical Variation and Competing Explanations', *Journal of European Public Policy*, 4: 373–87.

Dinan, D. (1994), *Ever Closer Union? An Introduction to the European Community* (Basingstoke: Macmillan).

Falkner, G., and Müller, W. C. (eds.) (1998), *Österreich im europäischen Mehrebenensystem* (Vienna: Signum).

Griller, S. (1995), 'Zur demokratischen Legitimation der Rechtsetzung in der EU', *Journal für Rechtspolitik*, 3: 164–79.

Karlhofer, F., and Tálos, E. (1996), *Sozialpartnerschaft und EU* (Vienna: Signum).

Khol, A. (1995), 'Demokratieabbau durch EU-Regierungsgesetzgebung?', in G. Schefbeck (ed.), *75 Jahre Bundesverfassung* (Vienna: Verlag Österreich).

Koja, F. (1993), 'Wer vertritt die Republik nach außen?', *Juristische Blätter*, 115: 622–31.

Körner, M. (1994), 'Das EU-Begleit-Bundesverfassungsgesetz: Die Mitwirkung der Parlamente von Bund und Ländern bei der Schaffung von neuem EU-Recht', *Österreichischer Jahrbuch für Politik*: 513–41.

Laver, M., and Shepsle, K. A. (eds.) (1994), *Cabinet Ministers and Parliamentary Government* (Cambridge: Cambridge University Press).

——(1996), *Making and Breaking Governments* (Cambridge: Cambridge University Press).

Morass, M. (1994), *Regionale Interessen auf dem Weg in die Europäische Union* (Vienna: Braumüller).

—— (1996), 'Österreich im Entscheidungsprozeß der Europäischen Union', in E. Tálos and G. Falkner (eds.), *EU-Mitglied Österreich* (Vienna: Manz).

Müller, W. C. (1997*a*), 'Das Regierungssystem', in H. Dachs et al. (eds.), *Handbuch des politischen Systems Österreichs* (Vienna: Manz).

—— (1997*b*), 'Regierung und Kabinettsystem', in H. Dachs et al. (eds.), *Handbuch des politischen Systems Österreichs* (Vienna: Manz).

—— (2000) 'Austria Tight Coalitions and Stable Government' in W. C. Müller and K. Strøm (eds.), *Coalition Governments in Western Europe* (Oxford: Oxford University Press).

Öhlinger, T. (1994), 'Das Scheitern der Bundesstaatsreform', *Österreichisches Jahrbuch für Politik*: 543–58.

Pernthaler, P., and Schernthanner, G. (1994), 'Bundesstaatsreform 1994', *Österreichisches Jahrbuch für Politik*: 559–95.

Rauchenberger, J. (ed.) (1989), *Entschedung für Europa* (Vienna: PR-Verlag).

Schäffer, H. (1994), 'Die Länder-Mitwirkung in Angelegenheiten der europäischen Integration', in J. Hengstschläger et al. (eds.), *Für Staat und Recht* (Berlin: Duncker & Homblot).

—— (1996), 'Österreichs Beteilung an der Willensbildung der Europäischen Union, insbesondere an der europäischen Rechtssetzung', *Zeitschrift für öffentliches Recht*, 50: 3–73.

Schaller, C. (1994) 'Die innenpolitische EG-Diskussion seit den 80er Jahren', in A. Pelinka, C. Schaller, and P. Luif (eds.), *Ausweg EG?* (Vienna: Böhlau).

—— (1997), 'Österreichs Weg in die Europäischen Union—E(W)G/EU/EU-Diskurs in Österreich', in H. Dachs et al. (eds.), *Handbuch des politischen Systems Österreichs* (Vienna: Manz).

Schambeck, H. (1997), *Regierung und Kontrolle in Österreich* (Berlin: Duncker & Humblot).

Schreiner, H. (1992), 'Die Mitwirkung der Länder im Zuge der EG-Integration', *Österreichisches Jahrbuch für Politik*: 183–210.

Steiner, G., and Trattnigg, R. (1998), 'Sektorstudie Umweltpolitik', in G. Falkner and W. C. Müller (eds.), *Österreich im europäischen Mehrebenensystem* (Vienna: Signum).

Weber, K. (1994), 'Österreichs kooperativer Föderalismus am Weg in die Europäische Integration', in J. Hengstschläger et al. (eds.), *Für Staat und Recht* (Berlin: Duncker & Humblot).

Welan, M. (1997), *Das österreichische Staatsoberhaupt* (Vianne: Verlag für Geschichte und Politik).

10

Denmark

Thomas Pedersen

Introduction

One of the curious things about European integration is the combination of a very high degree of regional institutionalization and the continuing importance of states and their concern for relative gains. There are several aspects to this phenomenon. EU constitutive politics may to a certain extent be seen as an attempt on the part of influential member states to extend their own national systems and rules beyond their national borders (Pedersen 1998). Page has shown convincingly that 'features of intergovernmentalism are ubiquitous in the EU political system'. Notably, 'bureaucratic and intergovernmental-interinstitutional worlds are very closely linked in the European Union' (1997: 163, 158). Similarly, several authors have argued that the EU policy-making process tends to strengthen the national executives *visà-vis* legislatures and that Europeanization may be used as an alibi against the domestic opposition (Moravcsik 1993; Taylor 1991: 109–25). Wright has pointed out that lack of national co-ordination or inadequate coordination of EU policy may be functional to European integration (1996: 165). These factors provide all the more reason to study national institutions and the various ways in which member states attempt to influence EU policy making.

The Danish position within the EU is somewhat contradictory. On the one hand, Denmark has acquired the image of a 'Eurosceptic' having obtained several opt-outs from the Maastricht Treaty. On the other hand, Denmark's day-to-day performance in the EU is widely regarded as positive, its rate and speed of implementation of EU legislative acts being one of the highest. This performance is partly due to Denmark's EU co-ordination system, combined with its internal emphasis upon consensus. The Danish EU co-ordination system is centralized but also displays some decentralized features. Compared to normal domestic procedures for co-ordination, EU co-ordination in

Denmark is very formalized, although co-ordination also is achieved informally through consensus.

Centralization and Decentralization

In Denmark there is a clear ambition to co-ordinate EU policy, horizontally
as well as vertically.[1] Like other older nation states in Europe such as
France and the UK, Denmark has a centralized EU policy-making system.
A study carried out by Les Metcalfe of the European Institute of Public
Administration found that Denmark and the UK had the highest co-
ordination score followed by France, Holland, Belgium, and Ireland (Nedergaard 1994: 281). Other surveys have been conducted, but the rankings remain
the same. The fact that over the years, this centralization has been modified
by the phenomenon of sectorization does not change the overall conclusion (see below). In part centralization is due to the strength of the national
bureaucracy which dates back to the strong absolutist state created in the
seventeenth century. The emphasis on co-ordination in Denmark may
also reflect the fact that Denmark is a small country. The Danish view is
that co-ordination is particularly important in small countries because they
cannot afford to be seen to present contradictory negotiating positions.
Large countries, such as Germany, on the other hand, can get away with
presenting loosely co-ordinated and often contradictory views (see Derlien,
this volume).

Member states where European policy is highly politicized also put a
premium on co-ordination. From the early days of Denmark's membership
the Community was a controversial issue. Centralized control was needed not
only because of the risk of dangerous domestic political fall-out from EU
policy making, but also as a way of ensuring that long-term considerations
prevailed over short-term clientelism in EU policy (Pedersen 1996). The fact
that in Denmark the government position on European issues has to be
presented to the European affairs committee in the Danish Parliament, the
Folketing, also makes early co-ordination imperative.

It is probably fair to say that co-ordination in Denmark is facilitated by
the existence of a politico-administrative culture supporting co-ordination.
Danish pragmatism and informality facilitates co-ordination in that the distance between the top and bottom of the pyramid is not very great. On the
other hand, socialization of EU civil servants is probably less complete
in Denmark than in certain other member states. In Denmark there is no

---

[1] To a large extent this chapter is based upon interviews with civil servants in the Danish
administration. The sources have wished to remain anonymous.

equivalent of the French ENA or the British public schools to ensure the diffusion of a set of common values and techniques in the administration. Danish civil servants involved in EU affairs are normally trained as lawyers, economists, or especially as political scientists. Thus in terms of educational background Danish civil servants are a heterogeneous group.

EU Policy Co-ordination: Structure and Procedures

The Danish system of EU co-ordination is highly formalized. However, as already indicated a pragmatic outlook helps oil the wheels of the somewhat rigid procedures.[2] Danish civil servants point out that the Danish system of co-ordination is mainly inspired by the French system, but that some inspiration from the British system can also be detected. The Danish co-ordination system is essentially French in inspiration, with a bit of British pragmatism thrown in. Compared to the French system the Danish system of co-ordination suffers from the drawback that the central co-ordinating actor, the Ministry of Foreign Affairs, is not a neutral arbiter to the same extent as the SGCI in France.[3] The Ministry of Foreign Affairs is likely to find it more difficult to impose its views on other ministries than the SGCI (though see Menon, this volume).

The Danish co-ordination philosophy furthermore emphasizes consensus. In part the search for consensus reflects a general corporatist tradition in Denmark. It also reflects a wish to ensure that EU decisions are effective and enjoy wide support. Nedergaard draws attention to the dilemma between elite consensus on the one hand and social legitimacy on the other. In order to reach a high level of consensus, the policy-making process has to remain relatively closed, which in turn tends to undermine the legitimacy of the process (1994: 283).

The standard procedure in EU policy making is portrayed in Fig. 10.1 There are four levels: (1) the special committees (at present thirty-two), (2) the EC committee, (3) the government's foreign policy committee, and (4) the European committee in Parliament.

The Danish EU co-ordination process mirrors the policy-making process at the EU level. The special committees are involved at the preparatory stage, whereas the EU committee and the government's foreign policy committee only make their presence felt in the Council stage. The time pressure is quite strong. The special committees typically convene three weeks before a Council meeting.[4]

Although all legislative acts go to the top of the co-ordinating structure, in

[2] Interview, Ministry of Foreign Affairs, Apr. 1998.   [3] Ibid.   [4] Ibid.

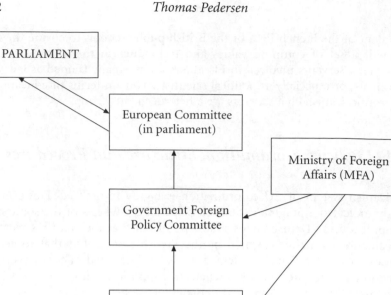

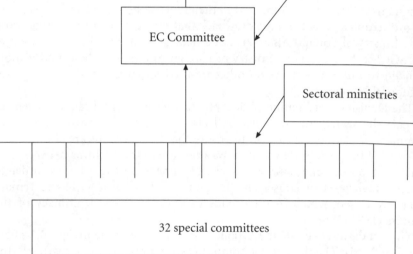

FIG. 10.1. Simple model of Danish EU co-ordination

practice most decisions are made at the lower levels. A civil servant in the Ministry of the Environment estimates that some 95 per cent of EU acts are *de facto* decided at special committee level; some 4 per cent are decided in the EC committee and only 1 per cent are subject to a substantive debate in the government's foreign policy committee.[5] The equivalent figures for the Ministry of Agriculture are roughly similar.[6]

[5] Interview, Ministry of the Environment, May 1998.
[6] Interview, Ministry of Agriculture, May 1998.

The special committees are the first tier in the interministerial co-ordination system. They seek to balance the sectoral ministries' wish for the highest degree of decentralization and specialization and the MFA's wish for centralization (Nedergaard 1994: 294). The special committees, which play a key role in the preparatory phase of EU policy making, largely reflect the division of policy areas in the Commission's general directorates. The committees are composed of civil servants from the ministries most concerned and representatives of various interest groups. The EC committee decides which interest groups are to be involved, and on what basis. It draws up lists which are revised time and again, sometimes on suggestion from interest groups themselves.

The special committees are often very large. Thus the special committee for environmental affairs has seventy-five members.[7] The Ministry of Foreign Affairs is a member of all special committees. The Prime Minister's Office (*statsministeriet*) is only a member of some of the committees. Meetings of the special EU committees are chaired by the ministry most concerned. The special committee undertakes the technical analysis of the legislative act in question. The ministry most affected by the EU initiative in question produces a position paper (*notat*), on the basis of which the deliberations in the special committee take place. The work in the special committee tends to concentrate on identifying positive and negative consequences of a proposal for Denmark.[8] Some specialists point out that in recent years co-ordination has become less frequent at the preparatory stage. National experts taking part in the Commission's working groups now sometimes act under instruction from their home ministry only (Hagel-Sørensen and Rasmussen 1985: 276). In addition to the thirty-two ordinary special committees there are ad hoc committees; at the moment, for example, there is an *ad hoc* committee on ASEM-II.[9]

Not all EU acts pass through special committees. Issues taken up by the general affairs council typically either bypass the special committees altogether or pass through several such committees, as do foreign policy issues.[10] Nor are ECOFIN matters co-ordinated in special committees; exceptional committees may deal with ECOFIN matters only in a few cases.

In practice the EC committee does not play a very significant role in the co-ordination process. Only when the special committees are unable to reach agreement, does the EC committee play an active role. The committee appears to have lost some power to the government's foreign policy committee in recent years. This is due to the fact that it has become customary to decide all politically sensitive acts in the government's foreign policy committee (Christensen et al. 1994). Originally, the committee was composed of senior civil servants, but now street-level officials often run the committee meetings.

---

[7] Interview, Ministry of the Environment, May 1998.   [8] Ibid.
[9] Interview, Ministry of Foreign Affairs, Apr. 1998.   [10] Ibid.

Overall, the EC committee has three tasks: (1) it helps the government distinguish technical and administrative issues from political issues—in a sense then the committee serves as a filter; (2) it makes decisions in areas where the government has already laid down the Danish line; and (3) the committee follows EU development (Nedergaard 1994: 298).

The chairman of the EU committee, who comes from the Foreign Ministry, is also secretary for the government's foreign policy committee and is present at the meetings of the European committee in Parliament. He or she will also normally attend all meetings of the Council of Ministers and thus follow the legislation through all stages, which helps to establish continuity and gives the Foreign Ministry a key role in the EU policy-making process (Pedersen 1996: 202).

The government's foreign policy committee consists of the Prime Minister, the Foreign Minister, and the eight ministers most affected by the EU. The committee is chaired by the Ministry of Foreign Affairs. The committee does not meet very frequently. The government committee deals with issues covering all three pillars of the Maastricht Treaty. The agenda of the meetings are divided into two parts, part I covering EC matters and part II covering CFSP and JHA matters. The committee's composition varies in the two parts. In part I the former members of the Common Market committee take part. In part II a smaller circle of ministers directly affected take part. At the administrative level both CFSP issues and JHA issues are dealt with by the so-called foreign and security committee, the equivalent of the EC committee.[11] Normally, the government foreign policy committee has a very short deadline for reacting to EU legislation and often the committee uses a written procedure, whether in order to save time or because the matter is regarded as uncontroversial.[12] Notwithstanding the rather rigid standard procedure, there is scope for some *ad hoc* improvisation. Thus, the circle of participants in EU coordination may be enlarged on an ad hoc basis. Junior officials enjoy considerable freedom of action and are rarely found hanging around waiting for directions from above. In part this is due to the socializing effect of junior officials attending the meetings of the European committee on a regular basis.

In matters of high politics special procedures are applied. There is a summit committee headed by the Prime Minister and his ministry. Likewise, preparations for intergovernmental conferences are chaired by the Ministry of State.[13] In this respect the Danish system differs from that of other EU member states, in which the Foreign Ministry normally prepares summits and IGCs. In recent years the Ministry of State (Prime Minister's Office) has strengthened its foreign policy staff. The relationship between the Ministry of State and the MFA has at times been strained, the MFA feeling that the Ministry of

---

[11] Interview, Ministry of Foreign Affairs, Apr. 1998.   [12] Ibid.
[13] Interview, Ministry of State (Prime Minister's Office), May 1998.

State usurped its natural leading role in EU policy. Sources in the ministries play down the rivalry, pointing out that the shift in the balance of power between the two ministries is mainly due to the personalities of the two ministers and that the foreign policy staff in the Ministry of State remains very limited.[14] A division of labour is also visible with the Ministry of State concentrating on strategic policy and domestic political aspects of EU issues. In crisis decisions seen to affect the interests of Denmark as a nation, informal meetings will typically be held in smaller circles. Attempts will also normally be made to include the EU spokesmen from the major parties represented in the European committee in such meetings. Prior to IGCs, informal meetings will also be held with key personalities in the European committee.[15]

The decision-making process typically starts when a draft position paper formulated by a sectoral ministry is sent to one of the special committees, where it is co-ordinated with the views of other ministries as well as relevant interest groups. The number of ministries represented in special committees is normally quite extensive. The special committee may approve the draft paper or revise it in collaboration with the sectoral ministry. One interviewee describes the special committee as a kind of radar that seeks to spot problems at an early stage.[16] If one or more members of a special committee raises a problem with the ministry in the chair, a separate meeting with the critics will typically be held. The Ministry of Foreign Affairs (MFA) is often active prior to the special committee stage, although the initiative lies with the ministry most affected by the legislative act in question. The act is subsequently submitted to the EC committee, which will normally just take note of the position reached in the special committee. The legislative act then moves on to the government's foreign policy committee, which is likely to pay particular attention to the domestic political aspects of the matter. The government committee lays down the Danish negotiating position, which is subsequently presented to the European committee. Unless the European committee objects, this will become Denmark's negotiating position in the Council (Nedergaard 1994: 301).

Throughout the co-ordinating process the Ministry of Foreign Affairs supervises discussions. One civil servant from a sectoral ministry describes the MFA as a 'valuable sparring partner' and as 'a service agency' for sectoral ministries.[17] It is not unusual for the MFA to hold informal preparatory meetings prior to EC committee meetings. At the administrative level the final responsibility for co-ordination resides in the head of the northern group in the MFA. All papers and letters from sectoral ministries to the European committee in the Folketing must go via the Ministry of Foreign Affairs.[18] Likewise, the Ministry of Foreign Affairs formulates the important negotiation

---

[14] Ibid.   [15] Interview, Ministry of Foreign Affairs, Apr. 1998.
[16] Interview, Ministry of the Environment, May 1998.   [17] Ibid.
[18] Interview, Ministry of Foreign Affairs, Apr. 1998.

instruction to the ambassador at the Danish EU representation (Nedergaard 1994: 285).

Generally, the Danish EU co-ordination system functions as a 'police-patrol' system with the MFA in the policing role.[19] The ministry supervises all current issues. Thus, to take but one example the MFA reads all minutes from sectoral meetings regarding EU matters. The purpose is first to ensure consistency in the Danish negotiating position, consistency being particularly important for a small country. A second task is, when necessary, to establish linkages between different sectoral issues so as to maximize Denmark's negotiating performance. Thirdly, the MFA also takes into consideration the need for alliance building and the accumulation of good will. It should be added that the co-ordinating style of the MFA depends to a certain extent on the strength of the incumbent Foreign Minister. The Prime Minister's Office normally assists the MFA in its endeavours to discipline sectoral ministries and make them tow the 'country line' (as defined by the MFA).[20] In a comparative perspective, the prominent role of the Foreign Ministry in Danish EU co-ordination stands out.

The EU representation in Brussels employs thirty-eight civil servants with academic training drawn from the various ministries.[21] Table 10.1 shows the composition of the staff in the Danish representation to the EU.

The relative weight of the various ministries in the representation is reasonably stable, but adaptations are made in response to constitutional changes in the EU or reorganizations of ministries in Denmark. Thus recently the representative of the Ministry of the Interior took over health affairs, which used to have its own representative.

At present, the EU ambassador is a top civil servant from the Ministry of Foreign Affairs, formerly second in command to Niels Ersbøll in the Council Secretariat. A certain tension is detectable between the Foreign Ministry on the one hand, which tends to emphasize domestic political aspects of issues, and the Permanent Representation in Brussels on the other, which is more inclined to stress the country's general foreign policy interests, not least the need to maintain and enhance Denmark's goodwill within the EU and considerations relating to coalition politics. One civil servant has observed a tendency for domestic political considerations to absorb more and more time within the EU co-ordination process, which tends to strengthen the role of the leading civil servants in the MFA back home in Copenhagen.[22]

Given the emphasis on centralization one might have expected the Ministry of Foreign Affairs to have set up a policy planning staff on the British model. This has not been the case. Various attempts have been made to go down that road but in vain. Thus, Denmark lags behind both the Netherlands

---

[19] Interview, Ministry of Foreign Affairs, Apr. 1998..   [20] Ibid.
[21] Ibid.   [22] Ibid.

TABLE 10.1. *Staff in Denmark's Permanent Representation to the EU, 1998*

Origin	Number
Ministry of Foreign Affairs	15
Ministry of Labour	1
Ministry of Business and Industry	2
Ministry of Finance	2
Ministry of Research and Information Technology	2
Ministry of Food, Agriculture, and Fisheries	5
Ministry of the Interior	1
Ministry of Justice	1
Ministry of Culture	1
Ministry of Environment and Energy	3
Ministry of Taxation	1
Ministry of Social Affairs	1
Ministry of Transport	1
Ministry of Economic Affairs	2
Total from national ministries	38
Faroe Islands	1
(Technical-administrative staff)	13

and Sweden in policy planning, both of which have a large policy-planning section. It is difficult to account for this lag except for the fact that one or two powerful personalities at the top of the Ministry of Foreign Affairs may have wished to reserve the strategic function for themselves. A beefed-up Ministry of State has tried to fill the vacuum, but with only some seven full-time employees in the foreign policy section, it has been difficult to create a genuine think-tank.[23] As a result, there is precious little 'rubbing of noses in the future' within the Danish EU administration.[24]

A certain diffusion of expertise and responsibility has occurred in the EU area in recent years (one civil servant from the MFA observed dryly that 'we are no longer the only ones who read French').[25] Whereas in the early days of Danish EU membership the Foreign Ministry adopted a hands-on approach, setting up a 'common market unit' predominantly staffed by civil servants who had taken part in accession negotiations, EU problem solving has since been

[23] Interview, Ministry of State (Prime Minister's Office). May 1998.
[24] The metaphor is borrowed from Douglas Hurd, who used it to describe Edward Heath's think-tank (see Hennessy 1990: 221).
[25] Interview, Ministry of Foreign Affairs, Apr. 1998.

decentralized with the Foreign Ministry increasingly playing the role of back-stop (Nehring 1998: 61). The MFA retains a crucial co-ordinating role. One can say that the overall model of co-ordination with the MFA at the top is reflected in individual sectoral ministries, where it is now typical to have general co-ordinating EU offices alongside the normal technical offices. In addition, attempts are made to introduce an informal division of labour, allowing the Ministry of Foreign Affairs to set aside some time for longer-term issues. But in this endeavour the MFA competes with the Prime Minister's Office.

The case of the Ministry of the Environment is illustrative. Here there is a specialist office and a co-ordinating unit with responsibility for EU affairs. The co-ordinating unit has several tasks. It ensures that the ministry addresses EU issues in a consistent manner. It supplies a certain professionalism as regards how to prepare EU negotiations. Finally, the co-ordinating unit handles the political aspects of an issue, notably the relationship with the European committee.[26]

The normal method of conflict resolution in Danish EU policy is negoti-ation. At all levels one tries to reach consensus. A civil servant in a special EU committee cannot easily block a decision, as he or she risks seeing the matter being referred to the ministerial level.[27] This involves the possibility of expo-sure and there is always a risk that the minister in question is not 100 per cent behind his or her civil servants. Civil servants in the MFA point out that there is a certain fixed circuit of EU posts, within which national EU specialists cir-culate.[28] Civil servants with EU experience are not normally regarded as Trojan horses, but as valuable resources. But clearly there are differences from one ministry to another. The Ministry of Foreign Affairs attempts to improve the career prospects of personnel returning from Brussels, while other ministries also seek to make better use of EU expertise.[29] An indicator of the prestige attached to Brussels experience is that several of the senior civil servants in the Danish Ministry of Foreign Affairs have reached the top via EU posts.

Notwithstanding the formalized vertical co-ordinating structure in Danish EU policy, in practice most decisions are taken at the lower and lowest admin-istrative level. An interview-based study from 1994 found that three factors in particular tended to involve the higher levels of the policy-making machinery actively in the EU process: first, the higher levels of co-ordination are involved whenever decisive national interests are at stake; secondly, they are involved whenever there are clashes of interest between sectors leading to open con-troversy regarding the handling of an issue; and thirdly, there is involve-ment whenever there are internal problems of co-ordination in the ministry concerned (Pedersen 1996: 200).

---

[26] Interview, Ministry of the Environment, May 1998.   [27] Ibid.
[28] Ibid.   [29] Interview, Ministry of the Environment, May 1998.

Sectorization

Despite conspicuous centralization in Danish EU co-ordination, the process also has important decentralizing features. Increasingly, national civil servants contact EU institutions directly.[30] But the typical pattern is still that contacts with the EU apparatus are channelled through the Permanent Representation in Brussels.[31] Incidentally, the Danish EU ambassador is now normally called back to Copenhagen prior to meetings in the General Affairs Council, a practice reminiscent of the British.[32] More importantly, the Danish EU co-ordinating process displays some of the same sectorizing tendencies as does the domestic legislative process. By sectorization we mean a decision-making process in which the decisive influence is located in an alliance between a sectoral ministry and important interest groups in an area (Grønnegaard, Germer, and Pedersen 1994).

The sectoral ministry has the initiative in the preparatory phase and retains considerable influence in the decision-making phase:

- Sectoral ministries send representatives to the Commission's expert committees, where draft legislation is commented upon (Pedersen 1996: 202). Depending on the Commission's receptivity the sectoral ministry thus has a certain influence upon the Commission's original proposal.
- They not only handle consultation of interest groups but also integrate responses from interest groups in a basic draft position paper relating to the EU proposal in question.
- This position paper forms the basis of the meeting in the special committee, where the sectoral ministry is chairman.
- In the decision-making phase it is the sectoral ministry that appoints Denmark's representatives to the Council's working groups.
- The sectoral ministry maintains contact with the sectoral attaché in the Permanent Representation in Brussels.
- The sectoral ministry drafts the Permanent Representative's negotiating instruction, which is subsequently approved by the Danish co-ordinating organs and given its final form by the Ministry of Foreign Affairs.
- Finally, the sectoral ministry is represented by its minister at council meetings.

The precise balance between the centralizing and decentralizing features can only be established by means of case studies.[33] The nature of decisions appears to be as important if not more important than the nature of the ministry. Thus the so-called oil directive (KOM (92) 110) was mainly dealt with in informal cabinet meetings, the formal EU co-ordination system

---

[30] Ibid.   [31] Interview, Ministry of Foreign Affairs, Apr. 1998.   [32] Ibid.
[33] For four such case studies see the report Grønnegaard, Germer, and Pedersen 1994.

having been largely bypassed. Decentralized policy making in the sense of sectorized policy making should not be confused with democratic policy making.
While a decentralized process does invest the policy-making process with an
element of subsidiarity, the risk is that EU policy will be decided by special
interests without broader public backing.

The Role of Parliament and the European Committee

Denmark has created an arrangement for parliamentary scrutiny of EU
legislation, which from a comparative perspective is very advanced. It should
be understood, however, that a major part of the explanation for the setting
up of the European committee (previously the 'market relations committee')
was that Danish governments are normally minority governments. The
committee thus serves as a kind of 'early warning' system for minority
governments fearing to be voted down in the Folketing. The committee is
composed of seventeen Members of Parliament, reflecting the party distribution in Parliament. The Danish government is obliged to present all 'important' EU legislation in the European committee. Over time the word
'important' has been defined ever more broadly so that now almost all EU
proposals are presented to the European committee. The government does not
have to be able to muster a positive majority for a given negotiating position;
it only must be sure that there is not a majority against. The government tends
to anticipate the attitude of the European committee when adopting its position on EU legislation. If the state of play changes at council meetings, the
government has a duty to inform the committee about the new situation,
before a decision is made in council. The government may thus need a new
mandate. After the negotiations have ended the government presents the result
in the European committee including the government's own minutes of the
council meeting.

   The European committee has access to all confidential documents relating
to EU acts. Even in cases where the document involves another country's
security affairs the members have the right to read the document in the chairman's office. However, it is not handed over to committee members. The committee members are bound by a rule of confidentiality. The European
committee is regularly informed about EU acts. The Foreign Ministry sends
standardized forms, containing the proposal's title, information about its itin-
erary through the EU institutions, and a brief description of its content as well
as estimated national legislative consequences. These forms are now sent to
the European committee once a week. Apart from this the committee receives
brief analyses of proposed legislative acts.

   The quality of the information provided to the European committee has improved in recent years due to pressure from the committee and Parliament. In 1994 it was decided that the Foreign Ministry should produce 'basic papers' (*grundnotater*) on all new legislative acts relating to the internal market. In 1996 this obligation was extended to include all areas of EU legislation.[34] During the same year it was also decided that the government every six months should inform the European committee about important issues to be dealt with within the WTO framework. The committee is particularly keen to be informed about acts which may affect the level of protection in the areas of health, environment, labour market affairs, and consumer policy. Apart from this six-monthly information, the government regularly informs the committee about important work in the WTO. At present the European committee is preparing a report demanding a similar right of information regarding Schengen.

A final point that deserves mentioning, if only in passing, is the Danish European committee's recent involvement in the EU's comitology. In this respect, Denmark seems to be ahead of all other member states. The question remains, however, if the European committee has the capacity to process and make use of the huge amount of information emerging from EU committees. There is already a growing overload in the EU policy-making system which prevents an effective national democratic control.

The No in the first Danish referendum on the Maastricht Treaty provoked some soul-searching, prompting a number of government initiatives with a view to bringing EU politics closer to the people. A so-called Council for European policy was set up in 1993. It brings together a range of organizations and individuals with an interest in EU affairs, organizing conferences and hearings and producing policy papers. The secretariat of the Council is located in the Ministry of Foreign Affairs with the opportunities this gives for executive information steering.

Although the Danish system of democratic control is comparatively advanced, it still suffers from a number of weaknesses: first, as already indicated, the European committee suffers from a considerable overload and consequently a certain informal division of labour has developed between the individual committee members. One way of solving this problem is to involve the other sectoral committee even more closely in the EU policy-making process than is at present the case. Sources in the committee indicate that the trend points in this direction. One model which has been suggested foresees a substantive debate in the relevant sectoral committee capped by the production of a report, which would then go to the European committee.[35] Unlike the German Bundestag, the Danish Folketing does not collaborate very closely with the MEPs. The primary reason is probably that the members of the

[34] Interview with the EU consultant to the European committee, Apr. 1998.
[35] Interview, the European committee, May 1998.

European committee fear losing the 'monopoly position' they hold in the Danish parliamentarian EU debate.

In recent years other parliamentarian committees, notably those relating to the internal market such as the environment and planning committee, as well as the committee for health and foodstuffs, have been involved in the democratic scrutiny of EU legislation. Attempts have also been made to hold general debates in Parliament on select EU issues. Yet, experience has shown that it is difficult to attract the attention of ordinary parliamentarians.

A second weakness is that the European committee is involved at a rather late stage in the EU decision-making process. Although the committee is notified at the preparatory stage, it only becomes actively involved at the council stage, once the Danish negotiating position has been defined in COREPER. Often the European committee is only able to intervene at a late stage in the process, when intricate compromises have already been negotiated between the member states.

Thirdly, since most meetings in the council remain closed, the European committee has to rely on the government's own minutes for information about the negotiations. And fourth, the quality of the information which the government channels to the European committee is not always satisfactory, although it must be said that on this point the situation has improved in recent years. These reforms have mainly been provoked by the Foreign Ministry's unfortunate handling of the directive on additives. In this case the ministry 'forgot' to inform the European committee about the specific additives which the directive in question would allow. Nor did it assess the health risks involved.

Conclusion

Denmark's EU co-ordination emphasizes the general foreign policy expertise of the Foreign Ministry. It also puts a premium on consensus. But in addition, there is a significant element of sectorized specialization in Danish EU co-ordination in that sectoral ministries and the special committees with close ties to economic and other interest groups play a prominent role. Over the years the Foreign Ministry has lost some of its control over the EU policy-making process, but this does not necessarily imply a change of policy. Niels Ersbøll, the grand old man of Danish EU policy, has pointed out that the MFA has had an 'educational' role in relation to the sectoral ministries (1995: 81).

Normative co-ordination is of lesser importance in Denmark. In part this is probably due to the fact that foreign policy is normally not very personalized, although the incumbent Prime Minister may be an exception to that rule.

But it may also be of importance that Denmark has neither think-tanks or policy-planning units in the Foreign Ministry nor well-equipped political parties on a par with the German *Stiftungen*.

The presence of the parliamentary European committee in the EU co-ordination system has a considerable impact upon the system. It is a force for centralization in that the government has to get its act together before confronting the parliamentarians in the European committee. On the other hand, it would be wrong to interpret the strength of the European committee as a sign of 'government by the people' in the EU area. Not only are there a number of barriers to the effective use of the powers of the committee, notably the problem of overload. A considerable secrecy also surrounds the committee, the members of which soon come to see themselves as members of the government's 'privy council'. The sectorization and specialization that has been identified at the administrative level also creeps into the parliamentary sphere in that due to the heavy workload members of the European committee tend to specialize with a certain informal division of labour developing between members across party lines.

References

Christensen, J. G., et al. (1994), *Åbenhed, offentlighed og deltagelse i den danske EU-beslutningsproces* (Copenhagen: Udenrigsministeriet).

Ersbøll, N. (1995), 'Danmark fra EF til EU', in Nye Grænser (ed.), *Den danske Udenrigstjeneste 1970–1995* (Copenhagen: Udenrigsministeriet).

Grønnegaard, J., Germer, P., and Pedersen, T. (1994), *Åbenhed, offentlighed og deltagelse i den danske EU-beslutningsproces* (Copenhagen: Udenrigsministeriet).

Hagel-Sørensen, K., and Rasmussen, H. (1985), 'The Danish Administration and its Interaction with the Community Administration', *Common Market Law Review*, 22: 273–300.

Hennessy, P. (1990), *Whitehall* (London: Fontana Press).

Moravcsik, A. (1993), *Why the European Community Strengthens the State: Domestic Politics and International Co-operation* (Cambridge, Mass.: Harvard University Press).

Nedergaard, P. (1994), *Organiseringen af den Europæiske Union* (Copenhagen: Handelshøjskolens Forlag).

Nehring, N.-J. (1998), 'The Illusory Quest for Legitimacy: Danish Procedures for Policy Making on the EU and the Impact of a Critical Public', in G. Sørensen and H.-H. Holm (eds.), *And now What? International Politics after the Cold War* (Aarhus: Politica).

Page, E. C. (1997), *People Who Run Europe* (Oxford: Clarendon Press).

Pedersen, T. (1996), 'Denmark', in D. Rometsch and W. Wessels (eds.), *The European*

Union and Member States: Towards Institutional Fusion? (Manchester: Manchester University Press).

—— (1998), *Germany, France and the Integration of Europe: A Realist Interpretation* (London: Cassell Academic).

Taylor, P. (1991), 'The European Community and the State: Assumptions, Theories and Propositions', *Review of International Studies*, 17: 109–25.

Vad Torben, B. P. (1998), *Europeanisation of Standardisation* (Copenhagen: Institute of Political Science).

Wright V. (1996), 'The National Co-ordination of European Policy-Making: Negotiating the Quagmire', in J. J. Richardson (ed.), *European Union: Power and Policy-Making* (London: Routledge).

Conclusion

The National Co-ordination of EU Policy: Confronting the Challenge

Hussein Kassim

This book has investigated the domestic processes by means of which governments arrive at the position that they defend in EU decision making. The structures, organization, and action of national governments in Brussels—the European dimension of national co-ordination—form the subject of a companion volume (Kassim et al., forthcoming). Although it is not new to examine national administrations in the context of European integration (see, for example, Wallace and Wallace 1973; Siedentopf and Ziller 1988; Toonen 1992; Lequesne 1993; Metcalfe 1994; Page and Wouters 1995; Wessels and Rometsch 1996; Hanf and Soetendorp 1998; Harmsen 1999), much of the existing literature addresses the issue from the perspective of Europeanization. For the conveners of the current project, the deployment of Europeanization as an organizing concept was considered undesirable. Not only has this concept been used in such a variety of ways and to describe such different things that it no longer has a precise or clear meaning,[1] but as a problematic it construes the relationship between the Union and the member states in terms of a one-way, top-down relationship. The concept of co-ordination offers a broader focus, enabling exploration of both the administrative and institutional impact of European integration on the member states, and of how the way in which the member states organize their inputs into EU policy processes affects the functioning and capacities of the Union as a multi-level

My thanks go to the co-editors, Guy Peters and especially Vincent Wright, for their extremely helpful suggestions for this chapter. Anand Menon also read an earlier version and made a number of very useful comments. The considerable intellectual debt I owe to Vincent Wright (1996), and Jack Hayward and Vincent Wright (1998) is readily and gratefully acknowledged. All errors, of course, remain my own.

[1] Compare, for example, the definitions offered by Wessels and Rometsch (1996), Toonen (1992), Page and Wouters (1995), Ladrech (1994), Kassim and Menon (1996), and Harmsen (1999).

political system (Metcalfe 1994; Marks, Hooghe, and Blank 1996; Hix 1999). The use of co-ordination also introduces a comparative dimension, permitting instructive comparisons to be drawn between the way in which governments manage the demands arising from EU membership and their responses to other sources of co-ordination need (Hayward and Wright, forthcoming). Furthermore, co-ordination is preferred to Europeanization, because by narrowing the focus to this one aspect of the relationship between the Union and the member states it offers the possibility of producing a detailed examination rather than a necessarily superficial overview of the impact of the EU on all political activity.

This concluding chapter has three main aims: to identify the main findings that emerge from the case studies; to present an argument about the factors that shape strategies and structures of national co-ordination; and to draw attention to a number of wider issues on the basis of what the findings suggest. In so doing, it responds to the issues raised in the Introduction concerning the impact of pressures towards convergence and countervailing pressures towards divergence. The first finding is that European integration exerts a powerful need for co-ordination on the part of governments and that EU policy making has become an important locus of domestic co-ordination for governments. However, membership of the Union confronts the member states with very specific challenges, and meeting its complex demands is extremely problematic. Second, national responses to the demands of EU membership have led to a redefinition of the functions traditionally performed by some actors and a recasting or recalibration of interinstitutional relationships. The third finding is that there are important similarities between the way in which the member states co-ordinate their European policies. Prime ministers play an increasingly central role in EU matters, a tendency reflected in growing institutional support for the office, foreign ministries retain an important role, though in all the member states they are in a position of relative decline, and specialist bodies responsible for cross-departmental co-ordination have been established, to cite but three examples. However, diversity persists—a fourth finding. Institutional convergence is limited in scope and extent. 'Europeanization' in the sense that contact between national actors and European-level officials has grown more intense and spread over a wider range of policy fields, and 'fusion' in the form of continuous and permanent interaction between national systems and Brussels (Wessels 1997; Wessels and Rometsch 1996), are facts of life, but co-ordination is organized and operates very differently between member states, and any prospect that a single European administration might materialize seems very distant.

The principal argument of this chapter relates to this mixed picture. In the theoretical literature about institutional and organizational change and empirical scholarship on national administrations and the EU, two opposing approaches are advanced. Either it is contended that organizations in the same institutional setting will become increasingly similar in response to common stimuli from the environment and interaction with each other (see, for example, DiMaggio and Powell 1991), or it is argued that, when confronting external challenges, organizations respond on their own terms, mobilizing resources they have accumulated over time, and following pre-existing institutional logics and values (see, for example, March and Olsen 1989; Metcalfe 1994; Harmsen 1999). According to the first view, convergence is the inevitable outcome. The latter, by contrast, predicts continued diversity in changed circumstances. Common to both positions is the belief that a single overriding logic is at work, and that movement, either towards convergence or divergence, is inevitable. The argument presented here on the basis of the cases investigated in the preceding chapters is that the picture is more complex; that two imperatives are at work—pressure towards convergence and system-specific adaptation—that neither necessarily predominates, and that the outcome in terms of the organization of co-ordination is partial similarity combined with significant diversity.

Consideration of a number of general issues raised by the case studies is a further aim. These include: effectiveness, and the relationship between the efficiency of national co-ordination systems and the ability of member states to achieve favourable policy outcomes at the European level; the character of co-ordination as a process; the impact of national EU policy-making procedures on domestic politics and on the functioning of the EU as a 'political system' (Hix 1999); and the implications of national co-ordinating processes for the conceptualization of member states as actors in the EU policy process.

Co-ordinating EU Policy: A Cross-national View

The similarities

All ten of the countries considered in this volume have responded to the need generated by membership of the Union by putting into place specific arrangements for co-ordinating EU policy making: the responsibilities of existing actors have been adjusted and new ones created, co-ordination mechanisms have been introduced or developed, and special processes and procedures established. Six broad similarities emerge: heads of government have at their disposal specialist expertise and institutional support to enable them to carry out the increasingly routinized role they perform in EU decision making; foreign affairs ministries continue to occupy a central role in national processes, though they face challenges from several directions; interdepartmental co-ordination in EU matters is generally managed by mechanisms that have been specifically devised for the purpose; individual ministries have made adjustments to their internal organization and procedures; national parliaments usually have a formal role in EU policy making, but are rarely influential; and most member states have a junior minister for European affairs or the equivalent, but the office is not typically central to co-ordination.

Heads of government have historically played a crucial role in the European construction—Adenauer and de Gaulle in the 1960s, Giscard d'Estaing and Schmidt in the 1970s, and Mitterrand, Kohl, Thatcher, and Gonzales in the 1980s. In the past, however, their involvement was sporadic, and they were able to rely on a small number of advisers and the Foreign Ministry. Since the mid-1980s, their participation has become more frequent and wide-ranging. Heads of government assemble regularly for meetings of the European Council, for which the agenda can be lengthy and highly technical. They take the lead, assisted by their foreign and finance ministers, in IGCs. Moreover, as the EU has become a more salient issue in domestic politics, it has become necessary to develop early warning systems which alert them to possible dangers, as well as crisis management mechanisms which enable issues that become politicized to be dealt with effectively. This has led to the creation of new national bodies or the strengthening of existing ones at the national level in order to provide heads of government with the institutional support necessary to meet these demands. In the UK, for example, the Prime Minister is supported by the European Secretariat—and especially its head—the Foreign and Commonwealth Office, and advisers in the Prime Minister's Office or the Number 10 Policy Unit. In Germany, support for the Chancellor is provided by the Chancellor's Office, and in Denmark a special committee is convened to assist the Prime Minister in preparing for European Councils and IGCs. There is a close similarity in function and personnel between these offices.

The centrality of foreign affairs ministries in national EU policy making is a second similarity. In general, though Germany is an exception, foreign ministries are responsible for assuring the formal link between the capital and Brussels—both with the Permanent Representation and with the EU institutions—with national embassies throughout the Union, and with the embassies of the other member states. This function reflects its traditional role in providing and operating a communications infrastructure with the outside world (Spence 1995: 358–61). Finally, Permanent Representations are formally accountable to the Foreign Ministry, and draw a significant proportion of their staff from the diplomatic service to provide expertise about issues of 'high politics' (see Kassim et al., forthcoming).

Across the Union, however, the position of foreign ministries is steadily being eroded. As the importance of the EU in domestic politics has increased and the involvement of heads of government deepened, foreign ministers have increasingly been overshadowed by prime ministers. At the same time, the expansion of EU competencies demands technical rather than diplomatic expertise. Policy specialists have become familiar with the requirements of negotiating in Brussels and have developed the necessary skills and connections. As a Danish diplomat, quoted by Petersen in this volume, poignantly remarked, 'we are no longer the only ones who read French'. The spread of new technology has, moreover, weakened the control traditionally exercised by the Foreign Ministry over communications. Experts in home ministries can make direct contact with their European counterparts or officials in the EU institutions by fax or e-mail, and no longer channel all communication through the Foreign Ministry. Furthermore, though the Foreign Ministry is formally responsible for the Permanent Representation, the latter can use its strategic location in Brussels, its specialist expertise, and networks at home and abroad to influence the content of the instructions it receives from national capitals. Foreign ministries in countries with strong subnational authorities face a further challenge. The German *Länder* and Spain's Autonomous Communities have established their own independent offices in Brussels, enabling them to circumvent traditional diplomatic circuits.

The establishment of new mechanisms, or the adaptation of existing structures or procedures, to manage EU policy co-ordination is a third similarity. Specialist administrative units have been created in France (the SGCI), Spain (the SSEU), the UK (the European Secretariat), Italy (the Department for the Co-ordination of European Community Policies), and Portugal (the DGAC). Committees for managing interdepartmental relations in respect of EU policy exist at the official level in Germany (the Ausschuss der Europa-Staatssekretäre—the Committee of State Secretaries),[2] in Belgium (the P.11 Committee), in Denmark (the special committees and the EC Committee), in Italy (CIPE, the interministerial committee for economic planning), in Portugal (the CIAC), in Greece (the Economic Committee), and in the UK (EQ(O), the Cabinet Committee for European Questions). At the political level, Spain has an Interministerial Committee, Denmark a Foreign Policy Committee, the UK a subcommittee for European Affairs ((E)DOP), Greece an Interministerial Committee, Belgium the Interministerial Conference for Foreign Policy (ICFP), and Germany a Cabinet Committee for European Affairs. Special meetings are a further mechanism for carrying out co-ordination. In Austria, co-ordinators gather every Tuesday afternoon. On the same day in Germany, a committee of up to thirty civil servants from various

---

[2] The Committee is 'chaired by a Junior Minister in the Foreign Office and comprises representatives of that ministry as well as those from the Economics, the Finance and the Agricultural Ministries, from the German Permanent Representation in Brussels, the State Secretary in the Chancellor's Office responsible for European Affairs, and those State Secretaries whose departmental issues are under discussion' (Wright 1996: 158).

departments meets to discuss the items on COREPER's agenda and to send instructions to the Permanent Representation.

Adaptation by individual ministries is a fourth similarity. Government departments working in areas with an EU dimension—virtually all since the implementation of the Treaty of European Union—have reorganized their internal operation and structures, and introduced new procedures. With the exception of Spain (Molina, this volume), ministries have established special units to co-ordinate European business internally, to consult other interested ministries, and to represent national interests in negotiations in Brussels. They have also adjusted their personnel policies to support, for example, the 'recycling' of officials through Brussels, look to recruit officials with appropriate language skills, and have introduced special training programmes (Maor and Stevens 1996).

A fifth common feature that emerges is the limited role that national parliaments play in the process (Wessels and Rometsch 1996; see also Norton 1996; Katz and Wessels 1999). Parliamentary committees and special procedures have been put in place to handle European business in all ten member states, but few exercise a continuous influence on policy. This process of 'deparliamentarisation' (Wessels and Rometsch 1996) is explained partly by the volume of EU business, its technical character, and the speed at which business moves through the Council. Detailed scrutiny demands considerable time and investment of human resources, which are not in infinite supply and for which there is competition from many other sources. It also reflects executive dominance. Even where the legislature is in a strong formal position, the structure of the party system and the exercise of internal party or coalition discipline usually at least enables the government to get its way. The case of the EU Committee in the Folketing in Denmark, considered the most powerful of all West European legislatures in EU policy, is instructive. Its influence is limited, because it can intervene only at a relatively late stage in the process—when a dossier reaches COREPER—and the government does not need to muster a majority in support of each proposal, but must ensure only that there is no majority against.

The sixth—and final—similarity is the presence and status of a junior minister for European affairs. Such a post has been created in virtually all the countries considered, but only in France, and then only exceptionally, has the position been occupied by a political heavyweight. The post typically does not carry cabinet rank, may be a technical rather than a political appointment, and does not give its incumbent responsibility for a full-scale ministry or department. The minister usually lacks the authority to intervene in other departments and so to manage co-ordination, but may perform important diplomatic duties. Where a minister for European affairs has been an influential figure, as in the case of Élisabeth Guigou in France, this has usually been due to personal standing rather than the attributes of the office. Efforts to strengthen the position, however, would not necessarily make co-ordination any more effective. Establishing a 'proper' European ministry would lead either to the creation of a second diplomatic staff or to a super-ministry that reproduced in miniature the entire national bureaucracy, 'thus, turning the co-ordination requirement from an inter-departmental one into an intra-departmental problem' (Derlien, above).

Explaining the similarities

The similarity between domestic co-ordination arrangements can largely be explained by reference to two of the five factors identified in the Introduction to this volume. The dominant pressure is indeed that which derives from the institutional structure of the European Union. In common, member states confront processes and procedures at the European level that determine in which forums and under which decision rules, in what sequence and by which actors, business is to be transacted. By shaping the input that member states make in terms of where, when, and by whom decisions are taken, pressure is exerted on governments to organize their domestic arrangements accordingly. Two examples illustrate this point. First, the pre-eminent and growing role of the European Council, as well as the greater frequency of IGCs, has led at the national level to an increase in the institutional support available to prime ministers. Second, the various stages of Council deliberation are mirrored in virtually all of the member states with different actors coming into play, special procedures activated, or political intervention taking place when an issue moves from working groups to COREPER.

It is, however, important to emphasize that, although domestic procedures bear the imprint of EU structures and move to rhythms produced in Brussels, convergence operates by means of creating incentives to which member states may or may not respond. Union processes encourage organization of a particular kind, but do not require it.

The second factor is mimicry or learning (Rose 1991; Dolowitz and Marsh 1996; DiMaggio and Powell 1991). In the face of common problems, the member states have borrowed and learned from each other's experiences. New entrants have typically prepared for accession by examining how structures and procedures operate in existing member states (see Magone, this volume). Prior to its accession in 1973, for example, the UK dispatched officials to France to inspect the French system of co-ordination (Wallace and Wallace 1973). More recently, France has returned the compliment in its attempts to transpose elements of the UK model (Lequesne 1993).

Two qualifications need to be made with regard to lesson learning as a pressure towards convergence. First, the extent to which cross-national lessons have been learned, and the mechanisms used in one member state transposed to another, is limited. Mimicry and imitation is not a dominant pressure. Second, as the more general literature on institutional transfer and learning demonstrates (see, for example, Rose 1991; Dolowitz and Marsh 1996), lessons tend to be selectively drawn and imperfectly applied.

The remaining three pressures discussed in the Introduction have played little or no role in generating the similarities between national co-ordination systems. Coercion in the strong sense—force—can be discounted, but in weaker forms, particularly law, it is an important factor in the relationship between the EU and the member states. Action taken by the Union may necessitate adjustment on the part of national governments in a variety of ways (see, for example, Kassim and Menon 1996; Hine and Kassim 1998), and the development, implementation, and enforcement of EC law has been important in creating common policies. However, EU activity has been directed mostly towards substantive policy matters, rarely, if ever, touching on internal administrative domestic processes and procedures. So far as the subject of this book is concerned, coercion can be disregarded as a source of convergence.

Similarly, socialization, as a process whereby national officials become 'gradually socialized into the shared values and practices of the EU system' (Harmsen 1999: 84), is clearly at work in the functioning of institutions at the European level (see Kerremans 1996; Lewis 1998; Christoph 1993), but has not penetrated national systems, still less brought about their convergence. There is little evidence in the case studies to suggest that frequent contact between national officials, their counterparts in other member states, and officials in the European institutions, and the spread of common values, has brought about institutional change in national administrations. Moreover, theorists who have contended that socialization is a powerful factor in bringing about institutional change (see, for example, Haas 1958) have not explained convincingly how the spread of ideas can bring about structural change.

A final possible explanation as to why convergence may have come about rests upon what Harmsen describes as the 'assumption of optimization' (1999: 84). According to this view, which Harmsen strongly contests, 'there will be a gradual convergence of national practices around the most effective solutions to those common problems' (Harmsen 1999: 84), because governments face similar challenges deriving from membership of the Union. '[D]riven by a logic of optimization to adopt increasingly similar processes and structures' (Harmsen 1999: 84), national administrations will converge on a single model. This approach can be discounted. Not only does it exaggerate the extent of existing similarities, but it fails to recognize the existence of deeply entrenched and persisting national differences, and the strength of countervailing tendencies.

The differences

The broad similarities between national co-ordination arrangements described coexist alongside pronounced differences and specificities. Even in terms of the six features outlined above, the member states are not perfectly aligned. Though an important presence across the sample, the Foreign Ministry plays a different role in the ten countries examined in this volume. In some member states, such as Denmark, Portugal, and Spain, the Foreign Affairs Ministry is the dominant actor. In others, for example, responsibility is shared either with the Economics or Finance Ministry as in Germany and Greece, with the Prime Minister's department as is the case in Italy, or with the Cabinet Office as in the UK. In France it is the SGCI, responsible to the Hôtel Matignon rather than the Quai d'Orsay, that sends instructions to France's Permanent Representation.

The role of individual ministries in the overall process of co-ordination and the internal division of responsibilities offers a second example. In the UK, line ministries take the lead in EU policy. Each has a division responsible for internal co-ordination, which takes charge of horizontal issues, acts as troubleshooter, briefs ministers, and offers specialist advice inside and outside the ministry. It may also create or mobilize networks in Whitehall, Brussels, and beyond. In Italy, the ministries have assumed greater power within their fields of responsibility, largely as a consequence of a concerted effort on the part of successive governments to combat the country's poor implementation record (della Cananea, in this volume). By contrast, in Greece, co-ordination units in the ministries tend to be 'conveyor belts rather than think tanks' (Spanou, above) and EU policy is managed by technical experts rather than European specialists. In Austria, all ministries have an EU division which takes responsibility over from the technical officials once an issue reaches the Council and collaborates closely with the cabinet of the minister (Muller, above).

Beyond these differences lie more systematic divergences. First, member states have very different co-ordination ambitions. Some have far-reaching, strategic, and directive conceptions, and aim to construct an agreed position on every issue and to ensure coherent presentation by all national representatives at every stage of the EU policy process. Others have more modest ambitions that may be substantive—limited to particular policy types or issues—or procedural—filtering out policies that conflict with higher aims or ensuring that more important information is exchanged. These ambitions imply very different co-ordination strategies. The first calls for an organization with comprehensive coverage, the capacity to impose decisions 'by imposition or by negotiation, that reconciles potentially competing societal interests and departmental views' (Kassim, Peters, and Wright, this volume), and closely integrated horizontal and vertical procedures. The second suggests a less elaborate system where efforts are limited to ensuring that issues are dealt with by the appropriate department or disseminating information among relevant participants about each other's activities. Three countries stand out as examples that follow the first approach—France, the United Kingdom, and Denmark (Menon, Kassim, Pedersen, in this volume). EU policy making in these states is characterized by an all-encompassing and explicit co-ordination ambition, and a highly centralized co-ordination system. Even within this small group, however, significant differences are apparent.

France has an extremely ambitious co-ordination strategy, aimed at coherent defining and representing French interests.[3] The central body charged with responsibility for ensuring that this ambition is realized is the SGCI, a small elite unit of 150 officials, attached to the Prime Minister's Office—thereby, assuring its centrality and authority[4]—which is admired for its efficiency and expertise (Lequesne 1993, 1996; Guyomarch 1993). The SGCI monitors developments within the EU, 'receives and circulates EU documentation, disseminates information and invites preparatory studies on potential problems of harmonisation with national law' (Wright 1996: 156). Since 1986, it has also been responsible for overseeing the transposition of EU directives into national law. On receipt of proposals from the Commission and in advance of the Council, the SGCI convenes interministerial meetings which all interested departments attend. As Menon notes (above), 'the volume of Community legislation means that a virtually non-stop process of meetings takes place at the SGCI—around ten per day'. In most cases, a position is agreed, but if agreement cannot be reached, the matter is referred by the SGCI to the political level where it is discussed by the cabinets of the ministers involved, or in rare cases by the ministers themselves. The SGCI alone is authorized to send instructions to France's Permanent Representation, even when only a single ministry is involved.

The UK has similar ambitions,[5] but its system is less formalized and organized somewhat differently. The European Secretariat—the functional equivalent of the SGCI—is, with the FCO and the UK Permanent Representation, responsible for EU policy co-ordination. Each performs a distinct func-

---

[3] 'French positions in all the institutions of the European Union must be expressed with clarity and the greatest possible coherence . . . the unity of French positions is a necessary condition of the efficiency of our action. . . . [The] requirement of coherence in the French positions imposes the need for a strict respect of the procedures for interministerial concertation' (prime ministerial circular, quoted by Menon, above).

[4] This point was reinforced in the 1980s, following a three-year episode when it was transferred to the Minister for European Affairs.

[5] 'For any EU activity or proposal . . . agreement is reached on a UK policy in good time, taking account of identified UK interests and advancing or at least protecting those consistent with overall Government policy with realistic objectives taking account of the interests of other members of the EU and that the policy agreed is followed through consistently during negotiation, and put into effect once decisions have been taken in Brussels.'

tion, and the three bodies work closely together. The European Secretariat is also located close to the Prime Minister (in the Cabinet Office) and has similar mission and tasks to the SGCI, but is smaller—it has a staff of about twenty— and less interventionist. In the UK system, the lead in the development of national EU policy is taken by the relevant technical ministry, which has primary responsibility for consulting other departments. Although the European Secretariat maintains a watching brief, it intervenes only when a problem arises. Where it senses that guidance is necessary or is informed that interested departments cannot agree, its first response is to try informally to get the parties to reach a solution. If this is not possible, it may resort to more formal means by convening a meeting of the relevant cabinet committee, where it may be necessary to refer a matter upward in search of a solution (Kassim, this volume). In the UK system, subsidiarity is the governing principle, in contrast to the more coercive approach adopted in France.

Though also centralized, the Danish system is very different from both preceding cases. Co-ordination is achieved through a pyramidal structure of committees, the base of which is formed by the thirty-two special committees. Discussion on Commission initiatives begins in these technical committees that bring together both civil servants from interested departments and interest group representatives.[6] The committees are chaired by the lead department, which is responsible for preparing the position paper that provides the basis of discussion, and are always attended by a representative from the Foreign Ministry. Responsibility at the political level lies with two cabinet committees, the EC Committee and the Foreign Policy Committee, both of which are chaired by the Ministry for Foreign Affairs. Although it has lost power in recent years to its senior partner—the Foreign Policy Committee, which includes the Prime Minister, the Foreign Minister, and the eight ministers most affected by the EU—the EC Committee remains central (Pedersen in this volume). The Foreign Policy Committee meets (infrequently) to resolve highly sensitive political issues. The ubiquity of the Ministry for Foreign Affairs underlines its influence in the process.

The differences between the three systems are not restricted to the division of responsibilities within the core executive. The role of the national Parliament is markedly different. In France, the National Assembly is peripheral in EU matters. In the UK, Westminster has little influence in routine business, but has sporadically provided a focus for national debate, as, for example, during the ratification process of the Treaty of European Union. By contrast, the European Committee of the Danish Parliament has significant powers. It can veto the negotiating position proposed by the government, enjoys an unusual level of access to documents, and is involved in comitology.

---

[6] The committees can be quite large. Pedersen in this volume gives the example of the committee for environmental affairs which has seventy-five members.

Moreover, the circle of participation is drawn more tightly in France and the UK than in Denmark, where interest groups participate directly in co-ordination. In France, private interests are traditionally regarded as policy outsiders (Schmidt 1996), while in the UK, the views of interest groups are taken seriously, but interest groups do not participate in the formal co-ordination processes.

If the similarities between the three member states with far-reaching co-ordination ambitions conceal significant divergences, even greater diversity is apparent among those that take a more relaxed view. Concerning co-ordination aims, Spain has 'an explicit desire to speak with one voice' (Hayward and Wright 1998)—even if this tends to be realized only at the political level (Molina, this volume)—as does Portugal. In the latter case, efforts are concentrated on managing the Council presidency and in ensuring that Portugal's interests are effectively represented in decisions concerning the structural funds. Elsewhere—in Germany, for example—there is no explicit overall objective (Derlien, this volume), though, as in most member states, action concerning sensitive issues or areas is well organized and may involve the highest political level.

A second difference relates to the actors involved. In Portugal and Spain, the routine co-ordination of EU policy is the exclusive preserve of the Foreign Ministry. In Greece, however, the Ministry of the National Economy (formerly the Ministry of Co-ordination) has the task of co-ordinating domestic economic policy related to the EU and the actions of the technical ministries, as well as monitoring the adjustment of the economy to EC requirements, while the Ministry for Foreign Affairs is responsible for communication between individual ministries and the EU, and for the Permanent Representation. The former deals with the internal aspects of EU policy, the latter with external relations. Labour is divided somewhat differently in Germany's 'twin-track system' (Derlien), where the Ministry for Foreign Affairs co-ordinates treaty-related and institutional matters, and the Economics Ministry bears responsibility for economic and domestic policy issues.

A major difference separates those countries where central government determines policy unilaterally—for, example, Greece and Portugal—from those where subnational authorities are involved in decision making. The degree of participation and the form taken vary considerably. In Italy, the Joint Standing Commission of the State and the Regions is the main arena where subnational interests are articulated, but is only one among many forums for debating European policy, while in Spain, a special committee brings together representatives from all seventeen Autonomous Communities. In addition, the Basque Country and Catalonia have won the battle for additional bilateral channels to be opened with central government. Arrangements in Germany and Belgium, by contrast, are more elaborate and the involvement of subnational authorities detailed and far-reaching. In Germany, the influence of the *Länder* in EU policy has grown substantially in recent years. Their influence in the Bundesrat, as well as their role in policy implementation, has enabled them to secure a powerful position. *Land* governments also have in place 'foreign relations systems' (Derlien, this volume) that not only connect *Land* ministries with their counterparts and the Economics Ministry in Bonn, but also include representative offices in Brussels. In Belgium, meanwhile, the subnational governments, both regions and communities, negotiate EU policy on an equal footing with central government (Kerremans, this volume).

The *Länder* also participate in the co-ordination process in Austria, even if the failure of a reform effort aimed at maintaining their pre-accession position has left them in a weak position (Muller, this volume). *Länder* representation is assured through the Joint National Office. Although the Chancellery and the Foreign Ministry share responsibility for co-ordination in Austria, the system is very inclusive. All government departments, the national bank, the federation of local communities, and the major interest groups participate in the weekly Tuesday meeting that is the formal centrepiece of EU co-ordination in Austria. In terms of the number of actors involved only Italy surpasses Austria. The Ministry of Foreign Affairs was historically the main co-ordinator, acting through its Directorates General for Economic Affairs and Political Affairs, but its influence has progressively diminished. Its decline began in 1980 with the creation of the Department for the Co-ordination of European Community Policies, headed by a Minister for European Policy who reports directly to the Prime Minister. In recent years, the Treasury has become increasingly influential and has taken charge of co-ordinating financial matters. As noted above, individual ministries too have assumed greater responsibility. The influence of three parliamentary committees—the Foreign Affairs and EC Committee in the Chamber of Deputies, the Special Committee for EC policies, and the Senate's Foreign Affairs Committee and Junta for EC Affairs—should not, moreover, be overlooked.

A further difference relates to the mechanisms of co-ordination. The specialist units, committees, and meetings created for the interdepartmental co-ordination of EU policy have been identified above. Although they have similar names, however, their precise form, function, and standing differs markedly between the member states. The P.11 Committee in Belgium takes decisions, while the Tuesday meeting in Germany performs a 'postbox' function, agreeing decisions that have been taken elsewhere. The SSEU in Spain lacks formal authority. Its capacity to achieve co-ordination depends on its ability to mobilize informal networks. At a sectoral level, important differences are also to be found. In contrast to Austria, where broadly similar arrangements are in place across departments, the degree of organization elsewhere is more uneven across sectors. In Italy, for example, matters of finance are managed very effectively by the national bank and the Treasury, but the same is not true in other sectors, such as transport (della Cananea, this volume). Likewise in Belgium, there is considerable cross-sectoral variation in the arrangements for co-ordination (Kerremans, this volume).

More broadly, the repertoire of available mechanisms varies between member states, particularly if the three countries with a centralized co-ordination strategy are taken into account. In the UK, the government is able to draw on the principle of collective cabinet responsibility and can use party discipline to support co-ordination at the political level. Elsewhere, for example, in Austria and Germany, coalition agreements negotiated when a government is formed establish a general framework for European policy within which ministers operate and may serve as a point of reference in co-ordinating negotiating positions in Brussels.

Furthermore, the way in which mechanisms operate in practice may be at odds with the official picture. In some member states, the formal mechanisms are 'dignified' rather than 'efficient'. In Germany, the routine co-ordination of EU policy in technical areas largely bypasses the central structures and operates through sectoral networks that link specialists in Bonn, Brussels, and the *Länder*—hence Derlien's description of it as 'semi-centralized'. The division of responsibilities between the Foreign Ministry and the Finance Ministry has produced a two-track system. The first track, which links the foreign office with diplomats in the Permanent Representation and other capitals, handles 'polity' issues and is relatively short. The second track runs from the EU division in the Finance Ministry down to the *Länder* and up to technical experts in the Permanent Representation. In practice, contacts between specialists in Bonn, Brussels, and the *Länder* on this second track are strongly departmentalized—encouraged by the short distance between Bonn and Brussels, and by the principle of *Ressortsprinzip* (ministerial autonomy)—and produce what Derlien describes as 'vertical brotherhoods'. These networks, which bring together like-minded experts with similar professional training, enable domestic actors to negotiate the complexities of the multi-level game that confronts the federal state as the result of the deepening of the EU,[7] circumventing the formal machinery and increasing the autonomy of ministerial departments *vis-à-vis* the central co-ordinators. In Greece too, as Spanou argues (this volume), there is a disparity between what the presence of the formal structures implies and the reality of co-ordination. A fully-fledged formal apparatus is in place, but does not function. Co-ordination often occurs at the eleventh hour in Brussels, and involves the minister and an official at the Permanent Representation.

---

[7] Derlien uses a footballing metaphor to capture this complexity: 'bureaucratic professionals and (amateur) politicians are playing on three tiers these days: in the second division with sixteen teams (*Länder*), in the first division with fourteen teams (Bonn departments), and they join the European Cup competitions with fourteen other teams (Brussels), alternating between indoor and outdoor matches (interest groups, Bundestag and European Parliament)' (above).

A further example of differences in process relates to the way in which official and political levels are articulated. In Denmark, France, Germany, and the UK, the two are interconnected by well-established procedure. In most member states, even if co-ordination is fragmented at the sectoral level or is sectorally specific, coherent action is possible once an issue reaches COREPER. This is certainly true in Belgium and Spain. In other countries, co-ordination at the political level may be difficult to achieve. Spanou, in this volume, suggests that this was the case in Greece at least until 1993, which leads her to characterize the Greek EU co-ordination system as a 'truncated pyramid'.

Although a distinction emerges very clearly from the case studies between member states which pursue a strongly centralized and comprehensive strategy of co-ordination and those that adopt a more devolved and area- or issue-specific approach, it is important, as Wright has cautioned (1996: 157), not to exaggerate the difference. In particular, care should be taken not to overestimate the extent to which the co-ordination of EU policy is centralized. In France, for instance, the SGCI may be the central actor, but its monopoly is not absolute. In matters concerning the CFSP, monetary policy, and the CAP, the ministries for foreign affairs, finance, and agriculture have their own lines of communication and expertise, and can act with considerably autonomy (Menon, this volume; Wright 1996). As Wright observes (1996: 157), 'there are numerous examples of ministries resisting the centralising embrace of the SGCI: hence the need for a succession of circulars sent by Prime Ministers . . . insisting that departments had to refer European matters to the SGCI'. In preparing for IGCs, moreover, the SGCI often plays a surprisingly minor role. In addition, decisions that issue from the SGCI are often the 'product of micro-level negotiations' (Lequesne 1996: 114) that have taken place elsewhere or take the form of 'splitting the difference' (Menon, above)—a somewhat formulaic approach to co-ordination. In the UK, policies of low salience or which are the responsibility of only one ministry may be dealt with outside the Cabinet Office system (Wallace 1996; Kassim, this volume). Also, despite the fact that the European Secretariat has overall responsibility for co-ordination, the FCO plays an important role in areas of 'high politics' and the Treasury, though not formally a co-ordinator, has become an increasingly powerful actor at the centre. Even if co-ordination is more fragmented elsewhere, in Denmark, France, and the UK, sectorization is a powerful force.

Explaining national differences

Though subject to powerful pressures towards convergence discussed above, the member states have developed very different systems of co-ordination. The sources of enduring national distinctiveness lie, as the contributors to this volume have shown, and others have argued (Wright 1996; Peters 1999; Harmsen 1999), in five characteristics of the domestic polity: policy style; policy ambition; conception of co-ordination; the nature of the political opportunity structure; and the administrative opportunity structure. These values—the first three—and institutional structures—the last two—of the pre-existing political system, as countervailing forces, have shaped national responses to the demand for co-ordination exerted by the European Union (see Introduction, this volume).

National policy styles in this context—though see Richardson, Gustafsson, and Jordan (1982)—relate to whether the state characteristically adopts an impositional or a consensual approach to decision making, whether it is active or reactive in its approach to policy, and whether it consults widely, narrowly, or not at all in the policy process. The impact of policy styles on EU policy making is evident across the countries considered. For example, the inclusive approach to decision making that is a characteristic feature of politics in both Austria and Denmark is reproduced in EU policy co-ordination in which the social partners and other interest groups are integrated. Similarly, Belgium's style of consensualism, developed to govern a society segmented along lin- guistic, clerical, and socio-economic lines, informs the way that it makes EU policy. France's system of co-ordination, by contrast, reflects its statist and impositional policy style. Interest groups remain policy outsiders, at least until the implementation stage, and lobbying by private interests is regarded as barely legitimate by state officials (Schmidt 1996; Menon, forthcoming). The reactive nature of domestic policy making in Greece has also been transposed to its processes for formulating EU policy.

Policy ambitions—a second factor—concern the aims and objectives of governments with respect to the EU. They may be directed towards particu- lar types of policy, for example, polity (or institutional), redistributive or regulatory. They may also embody attitudes towards further integration, either supportive ('engine'), or opposed ('brake'), or indifferent ('spectator'). EU policy-making arrangements in Germany, characterized by the ability of the Chancellor to intervene in polity-level matters and a relatively relaxed atti- tude towards achieving cross-sectoral co-ordination, have been shaped by the primary objective of advancing integration. By contrast, suspicion of integra- tion and the desire to preserve national sovereignty lie behind the globalizing systems created in Denmark, France, and the UK. As Derlien (this volume) notes with respect to the latter two, 'the emphasis on *ex ante* central co- ordination can be explained by the more defensive nature of the two govern- ments towards European integration in the past'. Meanwhile, their concern with EU redistributive policies is reflected in the organization of co-ordina- tion in Greece, Spain, and Portugal (Magone, this volume).

A third factor is the conception of co-ordination that informs domestic practice (see also Introduction, this volume; Hayward and Wright 1998). Con- ceptions differ markedly from the strongly positive idea that the government should 'speak with one voice' to the less rigorous view that co-ordination means no more than ensuring that tasks are allocated to the relevant unit or that information should be exchanged between departments. These different approaches, moreover, are often tied to other values, such as the need to construct consensus to legitimize policy choices. They also reflect programmatic stances adopted by government, such as whether an emphasis is placed on positive and coherent action, monitoring or reviewing developments, or avoiding political disasters. These choices carry very different levels of commitment in terms of the mechanisms and procedures put into place, investment of resources, and effort by politicians and bureaucrats.

These conceptions have been readily projected onto the system for co-ordinating EU policy. In the UK and France, for example, the emphasis on unity at the centre of government generates a strongly positive conception of co-ordination, which is embodied institutionally at the centre by the Cabinet Office and the Secrétariat Général du Gouvernement, and by long-standing norms, conventions, and administrative procedures, has been extended to EU policy making. Consensus construction that is a central feature of politics in Austria and Belgium has been similarly transposed, as have the more relaxed attitudes towards co-ordination taken in Germany, Greece, and Italy.

Moving from values to institutions, a number of elements of the political opportunity structure clearly have an impact on the co-ordination of EU policy. The important elements are the nature of the party system, the structure of the executive, the role of Parliament, the balance of power between central and subcentral levels of government, and the dominant form of interest intermediation. The party system influences co-ordination strategy, the system put in place, and its operation. Majoritarianism makes possible the pursuit of positive co-ordination, since it allows 'more hierarchical inter-ministerial relations than does a coalition government' (Derlien, above). The combination of single-party government and strong internal party discipline in the UK, for example, is certainly consistent with the aim of policy coherence—though these were not always evident in the Major years. Coalition government may limit the set of feasible co-ordination options due to the fact that ministries are in the hands of different parties. In Austria, for example, the decision to share the responsibility for co-ordination between the Chancellery and the Foreign Ministry was motivated by the concern of each of the parties in the 'grand coalition', the ÖVP and the SPÖ, to institute a permanent check on its partner in government.

The structure of the executive is also influential. Where unified, as in the UK, the capacity for imposing decisions necessary for the operation of a strongly centralized system is likely to be present. Where divided or collegial, other co-ordination strategies may be necessary. In countries where the authority of the Prime Minister is limited (e.g. in Italy) or where ministerial autonomy is a key principle of government (e.g. in Austria and Germany), ministers can act with considerable independence in the European arena.

France usually falls under the first category, but its split executive means that the harmonious orchestration of EU policy may be disturbed. Although the Hôtel Matignon is the centre of administration, the President can use the foreign policy prerogatives and power of patronage of the office to intervene in European matters. During the first cohabitation, 1986–8, for instance, President Mitterrand's European adviser, Élisabeth Guigou, remained head of the SGCI, which led the Premier, Jacques Chirac, to attempt to circumvent her on some issues (Menon, this volume). Where opposing coalitions hold the two positions, the co-ordination of European policy can become more complex and difficult than is suggested by France's traditional image as a strongly centralized state.

As discussed earlier, the involvement of parliaments in EU policy making is generally limited. Here too the institutional features of the wider polity have shaped national responses to European integration, since national EU policy co-ordination systems typically reflect the dominance of the executive over the legislature that characterizes domestic politics. A more differentiated pattern, however, is evident in the impact of forms of subnational government. In the unitary states—Denmark, France, Greece, and, until 1998, the UK—co-ordination is the preserve of central government, while in the federal states—Austria, Belgium, Germany, and Spain—subnational authorities are necessary partners. Amongst the latter, the status accorded to subnational levels of government in EU policy typically reflects their domestic position and responsibilities. In Belgium and Germany, they are equal partners. In Spain, with its system of differentiated federalism, special status has been accorded to Catalonia and the Basque Country as noted above (Molina, this volume). In Austria, the *Länder* are less influential domestically and in the EU process. Similarly, patterns of interest intermediation—the final feature of the political opportunity structure—also exert an influence on EU policy making at the national level. This is illustrated in how widely the circle of participants is drawn. Austria and Denmark lie at the inclusive end of the continuum, reflecting the status of the social partners in domestic politics, while France is situated at the opposite end, its statist approach to domestic policy reproduced in its system for co-ordinating EU policy.

The fifth, and final, factor that shapes national co-ordination systems is the domestic administrative opportunity structure. Two elements particularly stand out from the case studies. The first is the extent of an administration's integration: are there are sharp vertical or horizontal divisions? Where is the frontier between political appointments and permanent officials? Is there a cabinet system, which may complicate the division of responsibilities? Do officials belong to a single cadre or to distinct corps? The second is the nature of the administrative culture. The co-ordination system in the UK reflects the unity of the administration and traditional civil service norms such as information sharing, mutual support, and co-operation. In Italy and Greece, by contrast, more differentiated structures and extensive political patronage help to explain why co-ordination is more fragmented in those countries.

The case studies show that the systems developed by the member states for the co-ordination of EU policy have been shaped primarily by pre-existing domestic institutional structures and values. This accounts for the pattern of enduring national distinctiveness in the face of common pressures that, it is often assumed, must lead inevitably to convergence. These findings are largely consistent with a new institutionalist perspective which interprets the development of national EU policy-making systems as a specific case of institutional change or reform (Olsen 1997; Peters 1999; see especially Harmsen 1999). In theorizing about reform, March and Olsen (1984, 1989: 53–67) argue that when compelled to adapt to changes in their environment, institutions have a preservative tendency, and endeavour to renew their position, identity, and status in the face of new challenges. Institutions conceive of change in terms of existing conceptions of legitimate political forms, as well as 'more diffuse values concerning the correct distribution and exercise of public power' (Harmsen 1999: 85). Collectively these constitute what March and Olsen term a 'logic of appropriateness' (1989: 21–39). Applied to the impact of European integration on national political systems, as Harmsen argues, the pressures exerted by EU membership 'are necessarily mediated through the existing institutional structures and values which characterise each national politico-administrative system' (1999: 85). The responses of the member states reflect the 'pre-existing balance of domestic institutional structures, as well as the broader matrices of values which define the nature of appropriate political forms in the case of each national polity' (1999: 81), and the outcome is a pattern of national differentiation.

Two notes of caution need to be struck, however, in relation to this assessment. First, although important differences exist between the member states, the presence of the similarities discussed above should not be overlooked. Thus, accounts which reveal a pattern of differentiation (Harmsen 1999) or 'uneven Europeanisation' (Metcalfe 1994) only describe half the picture. Second, national systems for the co-ordination of European policy are strongly influenced by features of the wider national polity, and institutions may seek to replicate their domestic standing in the EU policy-making structure. However, it should not be assumed that they will be successful. The national arrangements for managing EU policy are the outcome of interactions among national actors, institutions, and values, as well as between the latter and pressures from Brussels. For this reason, pre-existing domestic institutional structures and values are not isomorphically reproduced in EU policy co-ordination systems. European policy is an arena within which institutions battle for influence, drawing from the resources that they enjoy in the domestic arena and aiming to attain a similar or better position, but without are being certain of success. It confronts domestic actors with a new environment and privileges, in virtue of the demands that it makes, some institutions over others.

Concluding Remarks: Effectiveness, Co-ordination, Impact, and Theory

Examination of the way in which the member states co-ordinate their European policies raises a number of wider issues. Four are considered here: effectiveness; the nature of co-ordination; the systemic implications of domestic arrangements at home and at the European level; and the theoretical perspectives applied to the EU.

Effectiveness of national co-ordination systems

The question of effectiveness—what it means in an EU context and whether there is a recipe for success in the form of a particular national strategy— though undoubtedly an important concern, is extremely problematic. Wright (1996: 162–3) has suggested that effectiveness can be disaggregated into several distinct capacities. These are the abilities: to anticipate new EU legislation and its impact at the national level, to shape the EU policy agenda and tap the resources available in Brussels, to translate European legislation smoothly and quickly into national law, and to implement and monitor European legislation at street level. Reflecting on these criteria, it seems intuitive to suppose that member states with a strongly centralized co-ordination strategy would be the most effective in securing outcomes at the European level that are consistent with national preferences—a view reinforced by reputations for administrative efficiency enjoyed by France and the UK. In practice, however, this assumption cannot be sustained, as Wright again has observed.

First, the centre may be 'divided', 'paralysed', or 'inept' (1996: 161). Second, centralization is no guarantee of quality. The latter depends on resources such as adequate personnel, expertise, and linguistic skills. While available in France and the UK, they are obviously not only present in these two countries. Experienced, expert officials in member states with a more decentralized approach to co-ordination may form networks that enable co-ordination to be achieved even in the absence of formal institutional mechanisms. Third, centralized systems often lack flexibility (Menon and Wright 1998). Once a position has emerged as the result of delicate compromise between domestic ministries or a decision-making process laid down by the centre, it is not easy to modify to take account of fast-moving negotiations in Brussels or the appearance of problems late in the day.

A centralized strategy may not, moreover, be best attuned to the complexity or consensual 'policy style' (Kassim and Wright 1991; Mazey and Richardson 1995) that characterizes EU decision making. A more flexible or selective approach may ultimately prove more effective. Derlien (this volume) contends that 'the German pattern of *ex post* co-ordination, a policy style resembling management by exception, is ultimately superior to a practice of *ex ante* co-ordination of all policy matters regardless of their salience. . . . [Centralization] is counter-productive, for it leaves little room for the recurrent, multi-issue bargaining process at the European level and the informal norm of reciprocity.' Germany's 'fire brigade' approach to co-ordination 'might be less spectacular [than the "police patrol" approach exemplified by France and the UK], but its reactive style and management by exception might be well suited to the kind of incremental decision making in a multi-level game'. Distinguishing between 'sprints' and 'marathons', Derlien argues that the 'short-term maximization of benefits or minimization of costs may be detrimental in the long-run when optimization of multiple issues in sequential, recurrent deals eventually counts'. In a context where games are repeated and decision making is continuous, flexibility and a willingness to compromise are essential. On the one hand, as Peters (1992) has argued, 'you cannot always win, what matters is to stay in the game' (cited by Derlien). On the other, 'a sophisticated poker player should allow the beginner to win occasionally; otherwise he'll lose a partner'.

Centralization may, furthermore, ultimately offer fewer rewards than a sectorized approach. Under conditions of imperfect information such as those that prevail in Brussels, decentralized systems may be at an advantage: 'hundreds of arrows may be more effective than one shot with Big Berta' (Derlien). Although sectorization limits the ability to construct package deals across sectors, it makes available political capacity to mobilize the support of sectoral interest groups, as well as, in the German case, the *Länder*. On the other hand, determination to produce an integrated position may lead 'to non-negotiable packages, to blocking policy or opting out of specific European policies altogether' (Derlien). Although Derlien perhaps exaggerates the effectiveness of a decentralized approach, his arguments certainly serve as a powerful antidote to the sense of superiority exuded by advocates of centralization. Implicit in his discussion is the highly plausible assumption that national success is dependent on the conditions that prevail at the EU level. A similar point is made by Wright (1996: 163–4), who argues that, in addition to 'political clout', the determinants of a member state's success in Brussels include: 'constitutional congruence', or the extent to which national policy coincides with the logic of the EU's basic principles or aspirations; 'policy congruence', or the degree to which domestic policies are in line with the *acquis communautaire*; 'policy climate congruence', which relates to the extent to which a national policy objective accords with the climate in Brussels; and 'administrative congruence', or the 'extent of the match between the administrative procedures and the policy style of a country with the procedures and policy style at EU level'.

A final point, also made by Wright, is supported by the case studies. Success may be largely determined by external conditions, but it is important that it be measured against national ambitions. The individual studies reveal a wide range of objectives. The UK, driven by its preference for intergovernmental solutions and a concern to keep EU expenditure at a minimum, is almost uniquely concerned with all aspects of EU action. For France and, especially, Germany, however, the advancement of integration is a primary interest. All member states, moreover, have special arrangements for dealing with policy areas that are salient or which serve domestic interests. Thus, Portugal and Spain are especially concerned with the structural funds and cohesion policy, Italy with EMU, France with the CAP, and the UK with the CFP. For this reason, Wright concludes that 'the effectiveness of a country's domestic EU co-ordinating capacity must be judged according to the issue, the policy types, the policy requirements and the policy objectives. Merely to examine the machinery of co-ordination is to confuse the means and the outcomes' (1996: 165).

Co-ordination as a process

The case studies provoke some tentative conclusions about co-ordination as a process. They suggest, first, that co-ordination need is strongly contextual. Pressures for co-ordination are interpreted in terms of existing values and practices. Co-ordination ambitions and arrangements are shaped similarly by understandings of what is possible, desirable, and appropriate. Co-ordination is justified, and strengthened or weakened, by other values. These include system goals, policy ambitions, the pursuit of consensus, consultation, and unity of purpose. Moreover, co-ordination is traded off against other 'desirable goals, including organisational harmony, transparency, flexibility, and accountability' (Hayward and Wright 1998: 1). For this reason, perhaps, despite the strong demands emanating from Brussels, positive co-ordination is an ambition that is rarely pursued. Such a conception is extremely demanding. The requirements imposed on participants at all levels of the system are stringent: vertical and horizontal relationships must be well defined and tightly integrated, and the importance of overall co-ordination must supersede departmental, sectional, or technical preferences. It must, in addition, be supported by a co-operative administrative culture. Furthermore, positive co-ordination is prone to particular pathological forms. Foremost is the tendency of junior officials to abdicate responsibility and to refer matters up the hierarchy. The result is a loss of flexibility and overload at the top (Hayward and Wright 1998: 16).

The systemic implications

The findings suggest that the way in which national co-ordination is arranged has important implications for each of the domestic polities and for the EU as a whole. At the domestic level, the development of co-ordinating structures has altered the pre-existing institutional balance. Executives have, for example, been strengthened *vis-à-vis* the legislature (see also Moravcsik 1993, 1994). Within national administrations, the relative position of foreign ministries, ministries of agriculture, and, more recently, finance has been enhanced. The territorial balance has also been affected. While the 'Europe of the Regions' may not have materialized, subnational authorities in the federal states have been largely successful in their efforts to ensure their participation in domestic co-ordination processes (Hooghe 1996).

The organization and operation of national processes have important implications for the EU as a political system. Most obviously, the individual styles and strategies of the member states influence the quality and speed of decision making at the European level. Governments that have centralizing co-ordination systems tend to adopt rather intransigent positions that can make the search for agreement problematic. On the other hand, they introduce clarity and predictability which can facilitate negotiations. Member states that take a more relaxed approach towards co-ordination may facilitate compromise by bringing latitude to the bargaining table. Wright (1996: 165) conjectures that '[p]oor national co-ordination may even be functional for the EU itself, since it does facilitate interstate bargaining', while Wessels (1997) goes so far as to suggest that the lack of co-ordination in Bonn may have been a prerequisite for advancing the European cause. The decentralized approaches do, however, have a dysfunctional aspect. Issues that negotiators considered to have been satisfactorily resolved may reappear at a later stage, representatives of the same member states may adopt contradictory positions, thereby introducing uncertainty about possible solutions, and an early flexibility adopted by a national delegation in the early phases of negotiations may give way to rigidity on the part of the same member state as the dossier moves to a higher level.

The quality of implementation and enforcement of EU legislation depends, moreover, on national administrations and domestic processes in the absence of a federal administration or field services Metcalfe (1994). As the case studies in this volume, as well as Metcalfe's earlier findings, show, many do not perform well, thereby producing the EU's 'management deficit' (Metcalfe 1994). Metcalfe argues that any improvement in the EU's institutional capacity is necessarily dependent upon the preparedness of national governments to undertake domestic administrative reform. As he asserts, 'internationalisation requires more of national governments rather than less' (1994: 271), and criticism of the EU's administrative capacities should be interpreted as a displaced response to unresolved problems at national level. Various initiatives taken at the EU level to improve implementation by publicizing national performances, such as the Single Market Scoreboard, are only likely to succeed if they spur governments into action.

The implications for democratic control and accountability are a further concern. There is not enough space here to undertake even a cursory summary of the literature on the so-called 'democratic deficit', but two observations can be made.[8] First, the general weakness of legislatures in the EU policy process at the national level, which is regarded in some diagnoses of the deficit as the principal cause of the Union's democratic failings, is confirmed by the case studies. Parliaments have a very little ability to scrutinize Union proposals, still less to influence their content, and are able only in very exceptional cases to direct the actions of their respective governments. The case studies are instructive with respect to a second concern about accountability, namely, the view that the EU system is a 'mandarins' paradise'. From this perspective, appointed officials rather than democratically elected politicians control the policy process. In the literature, the fault is located either within national systems of co-ordination or in the decision-making methods of the Council. According to the first, national EU policy is largely managed by officials on an automatic or autonomous basis (see, for example, Bulmer and Paterson 1987), while the second emphasizes the high percentage of decisions that are taken without deliberation by ministers, by agreement reached at lower levels of the Council (Van Schendelen 1996). The findings presented here suggest that both claims need to be qualified. The studies of Germany and the UK show, at least in two cases, that officials do not operate on 'auto-pilot' (Rose 1985), determining policy independently of their governments, but act within general policy orientations or on specific instructions laid down by the minister. In Germany, as in the UK, 'an internal departmental reporting system keeps a minister informed on all matters of political importance. Policy proposals are elaborated in an iterative process between experts in the sections and the hierarchy' (Derlien, above). Under these circumstances, legitimacy and accountability are more or less assured.

Theoretical issues

Empirical investigation of national co-ordination systems also raises a number of conceptual or theoretical concerns. One relates to the way that

---

[8] See, for example, Weiler, Haltern, and Mayer (1995), Chryssochoou (1998), Williams (1991), Bogdanor and Woodcock (1991) for representative sample.

member states are conceptualized as actors within the EU. Much of the literature proceeds on the assumption that there is symmetry between the member states, a homogeneity in form, structure, and interest at the national or unit level. Against this view, the case studies in this volume reveal the presence of important differences in ambition, processes, and institutional arrangements. These factors not only suggest that the belief that the differences between member states are insignificant is mistaken, but go a long way in explaining why governments act differently from each other at the EU level (see Menon, forthcoming). This supports the argument, made long ago by Bulmer (1983), that an understanding of how the EU functions requires knowledge of domestic systems (see also Menon and Hayward 1996) and an appreciation of the distinctiveness of national polities.

Another concerns the relevance of domestic co-ordination to understanding the process of national preference formation EU policy.[9] The findings of this volume challenge both the 'classical' version of intergovernmentalism (see, for example, Hoffmann 1966, 1982) and the more sophisticated liberal intergovernmentalist variant (Moravscik 1993, 1998). Neither offers a satisfactory account of how governments formulate their positions. Both depend on what Metcalfe (1994: 276), writing about conventional realist international relations theory, has called 'an over-organized concept of the state'. According to this view 'effective systems for the internal management of external relationships enable "states" to arrive at the international bargaining table fully prepared to take part in negotiations' (Metcalfe 1994: 276). Liberal governmentalism attempts to provide a fuller account by 'factoring in' the role played by societal interests in shaping the state's preferences. However, even this view treats the state executive as a 'black box' or 'cipher'. It ignores the way in which the organization of the state affects the representation and articulation of interests, and discounts any impact co-ordination arrangements may have on the definition of the position presented and defended by governments in Brussels. What is clear from the foregoing chapters is that the policies that governments pursue at the European level are the outcome of often complex processes of intragovernmental bargaining, bureaucratic politics, and co-ordination of variable quality. The failure to appreciate what this implies for the formation of national preferences inevitably leads to an overly simplified view of member state action and the EU policy process.

References

Baker, D., Gamble, A., and Ludlow, S. (1994), 'The Parliamentary Siege of Maastricht', *Parliamentary Affairs*, 47/1 (Jan.).

[9] See Forster (1998) for a discussion of this point in relation to the UK negotiating team at Maastricht.

Bassompierre, G. de (1988), *Changing the Guard in Brussels: An Insider's View* (New York: Praeger).

Bender, B. (1991), 'Whitehall, Central Government and 1992', *Public Policy and Administration*, 6/1: 13–20.

—— (1996), 'Co-ordination of European Union Policy in Whitehall', lecture delivered at St Antony's College, 5 Feb.

Bogdanor, V., and Woodcock, G. (1991), 'The European Community and Sovereignty', *Parliamentary Affairs*.

Buller, J., and Smith, M. J. (1998), 'Civil Service Attitudes towards the European Union', in D. Baker and D. Seawright (eds.), *Britain for and against Europe* (Oxford: Clarendon Press).

Bulmer, S. (1984), 'Domestic Politics and EC Policy-Making', *Journal of Common Market Studies*, 21/4: 261–80.

—— and Paterson, W. E. (1987), *The Federal Republic of Germany and the European Community* (London: Allen & Unwin).

Butler, M. (1986), *Europe: More than a Continent* (London: Heinemann).

Christoph, J. B. (1993), 'The Effect of Britons in Brussels: The European Community and the Culture of Whitehall', *Governance*, 6/4: 518–37.

Chryssochoou, D. N. (1998), *Democracy in the European Union: A Journey into Theory* (London: IB Tauris).

Cram, L. (1994), 'The European Commission as a Multi-organisation: Social Policy and IT Policy in the EU', *Journal of European Public Policy*, 1/2: 194–217.

Di Maggio, P. J., and Powell, W. W. (1991). 'The Iron Cage Revisited: Institutional Isomorphism and Collective Rationality', in W. W. Powell and P. J. DiMaggio (eds.), *The New Institutionalism in Organizational Analysis* (Chicago: University of Chicago Press).

Dolowitz, D., and Marsh, D. (1996), 'Who Learns What From Whom: A Review of the Policy Transfer Literature', *Political Studies*, 44: 343–57.

Edwards, G. (1992), 'Central Government', in S. George (ed.), *Britain and the European Community: The Politics of Semi-Detachment* (Oxford: Clarendon Press).

European Commission (1995), *Report on the Operation of the Treaty of European Union*, SEC (95) 731 Final, 10.5.95.

Flynn, G. (ed.) (1995), *Remaking the Hexagon: The New France in the New Europe* (Boulder, Colo.: Westview).

Forster, A. (1998), 'Britain and the Negotiation of the Maastricht Treaty: A Critique of Liberal Intergovernmentalism', *Journal of Common Market Studies*, 36/3 (Sept.).

Guyomarch, A. (1993), 'The European Effect: Improving French Policy Co-ordination', *Staatswissenschaften und Staatspraxis*, 4/3: 455–78.

Haas, E. B. (1958), *The Uniting of Europe* (Stanford, Calif.: Stanford University Press).

—— (1990), *When Knowledge is Power: Three Models of Change in International Organizations* (Berkeley and Los Angeles: University of California Press).

Hanf, K., and Soetendorp, B. (1998), *Adapting to European Integration: Small States and the European Union* (London: Longman).

Harmsen, R. (1999), 'The Europeanization of National Administrations: A Comparative Study of France and the Netherlands', *Governance*, 12/1: 81–113.

Hayes-Renshaw, F., and Wallace, H. (1997), *The Council of Ministers* (London: Macmillan).

Hayward, J. E. S., and Wright, V. (1998), 'Policy Co-ordination in West European Core Executives', End of Award Report, unpublished mimeo.

—————(forthcoming), *Governing from the Centre* (London: Macmillan).

Henderson, D. (1998), 'The UK Presidency: An Insider's View', *Journal of Common Market Studies*, 36/4 (Dec.): 563–72.

Hine, D., and Kassim, H. (eds.) (1998), *Beyond the Market: The European Union and National Social Policy* (London: Routledge).

Hix, S. (1999), *The Political System of the European Union* (London: Macmillan).

Hoffmann, S. (1966), 'Obstinate or Obsolete? The Fate of the Nation State and the Case of Western Europe', *Daedalus*, 95/4: 862–915.

——(1982), 'Reflections on the Nation State in Europe Today', *Journal of Common Market Studies*, 21: 21–37.

Hooghe, L. (ed.) (1996), *European Integration, Cohesion Policy and Sub-national Mobilisation* (Oxford: Oxford University Press).

Howe, G. (1990), 'Sovereignty and Interdependence: Britain's Place in the World', *International Affairs*, 66/4.

Kassim, H. (1997), 'The European Union and French Autonomy', in special issue of *Modern and Contemporary France*, ed. Vincent Wright, 5/2 (May): 167–80.

——and Menon, A. (1996) (eds.), *The European Union and National Industrial Policy* (London: Routledge).

——and Wright, V. (1991), 'The Role of National Administrations in the Decision-Making Processes of the European Communities', *Revista trimestrale di diritto pubblico*, 3: 832–50.

——Menon, A., Peters, G., and Wright, V. (eds.) (forthcoming), *The National Co-ordination of EU Policy: The European Level* (Oxford: Oxford University Press).

Katz, R. S., and Wessels, B. (1999), *The European Parliament, the National Parliaments and European Integration* (Oxford: Oxford University Press).

Kerremans, B. (1996), 'Do Institutions Make a Difference? Non-institutionalism, Neo-institutionalism and the Logic of Common Decision Making in the European Union', *Governance*, 9/2: 216–40.

Kirchner, E. (1992), *Decision-Making in the European Community: The Council Presidency and European Integration* (Manchester: Manchester University Press).

Knill, C. (1998), 'European Policies: The Impact of National Administrative Traditions', *Journal of Public Policy*, 18/1: 1–28.

Ladrech, R. (1994), 'Europeanization of Democratic Politics and Institutions: The Case of France', *Journal of Common Market Studies*, 32/1: 69–88.

Lequesne, C. (1993), *Paris–Bruxelles: Comment se fait la politique européenne de la France* (Paris: Presses de la Fondation Nationale des Sciences Politiques).

——(1996), 'French Central Government and the European Political System: Change and Adaptation since the Single Act', in Y. Mény, P. Muller, and J.-L. Quermonne (eds.), *Adjusting to Europe* (London: Routledge).

Lewis, J. (1998), 'The Institutional Problem-Solving Capacities of the Council: The Committee of Permanent Representatives and the Methods of Community', Cologne: Max-Plank-Institut für Gesellschaftsforschung, Discussion Paper 98/1.

Lord, C. (1992), 'Sovereign or Confused? The "Great Debate" about British Entry to the European Community Twenty Years on', *Journal of Common Market Studies*, 30: 4.

Lowi, T. J. (1964), 'American Business, Public Policy, Case Studies and Political Theory', *World Politics*, 16/4: 677–715.

Ludlow, P. (1991), 'The European Commission', in R. O. Keohane and S. Hoffmann (eds.), *The New European Community* (Boulder, Colo.: Westview).

Maor, M., and Stevens, H. (1996), 'Measuring the Impact of New Public Management and European Integration on Recruitment and Training in the UK Civil Service 1970–1995' (European Institute, London School of Economics and Political Science).

March, J., and Olsen, J. P. (1984), 'The New Institutionalism: Organizational Facts in Political Life', *American Political Science Review*, 78: 734–49.

——— (1989), *Rediscovering Institutions: The Organizational Basis of Politics* (New York: Free Press).

Marks, G., Hooghe, L., and Blank, K. (1996), 'European Integration from the 1980s', *Journal of Common Market Studies*, 34/1: 341–78.

Mazey, S., and Richardson, J. (1993), *Lobbying in the European Community* (Oxford: Oxford University Press).

——— (1995), 'Promiscuous Policymaking: The European Policy Style?', in C. Rhodes and S. Mazey (eds.), *The State of the European Union: Building a European Polity* (Harlow: Longman).

Menon, A. (1996), 'France and the IGC', *Journal of European Public Policy*, 3/2.

—— (forthcoming), 'France', in H. Kassim, A. Menon, G. Peters, and V. Wright (eds.), *The National Co-ordination of EU Policy: The European Level* (Oxford: Oxford University Press).

—— and Hayward, J. (1996), 'States, Industrial Policies and the European Union', in H. Kassim and A. Menon (eds.), *The European Union and National Industrial Policy* (London: Routledge).

—— and Wright, V. (1998), 'The Paradoxes of "Failure": British EU Policy Making in Comparative Perspective', *Public Policy and Administration*, 13/4: 46–66.

Metcalfe, L. (1994), 'International Policy Co-ordination and Public Management Reform', *International Review of Administrative Sciences*, 60: 271–90.

Moravcsik, A. (1991), 'Negotiating the Single European Act: National Interests and Conventional Statecraft in the European Community', *International Organization*, 45/1: 19–56.

—— (1993), 'Preferences and Power in the European Community: A Liberal Intergovernmentalist Approach', *Journal of Common Market Studies*, 31/4: 473–524.

—— (1994), 'Why the European Community Strengthens the State: Domestic Politics and International Co-operation', Centre for European Studies Working Paper Series, Centre for European Studies, Harvard University.

—— (1998), *The Choice for Europe: Social Purpose and State Power from Messina to Maastricht* (New York: Cornell University Press).

Norton, P. (ed.) (1996), *National Parliaments and the European Union* (London: Frank Cass).

O'Nuallain, C. (ed.) (1985), *The Presidency of the European Council of Ministers* (London: Croom Helm).

Olsen, J. P. (1997), 'European Challenges to the Nation State', in B. Steunenberg and F. van Vught (eds.), *Political Institutions and Public Policy: Perspectives on European Decision Making* (Dordrecht: Kluwer).

Page, E. C., and Wouters, L. (1995), 'The Europeanization of the National Bureaucracies?', in J. Pierre (ed.), *Bureaucracy in the Modern State: An Introduction to Comparative Public Administration* (Aldershot: Edward Elgar).

Peters, B. G. (1992), 'Bureaucratic Politics in Institutions of the European Community', in A. Sbragia (ed.), *Euro-Politics: Institutions and Policy-Making in the 'New' European Community* (Washington: Brookings Institution).

—— (1997), 'Escaping the Joint-Decision Trap; Repetition and Sectoral Politics in the European Union', *West European Politics*, 20: 22–36.

—— (1999), 'Institutional Isomorphism, but Which Institution? The Politics of Policy Co-ordination', unpublished paper.

Pierson, P. (1996), 'The Path to European Integration: A Historical Institutionalist Analysis', *Comparative Political Analysis*, 29/2 (Apr.): 123–63.

Pollack, M. A. (1996), 'The New Institutionalism and European Community Governance: The Promise and Limits of Institutional Analysis', *Governance*, 9/4 (Oct.): 429–58.

—— (1997), 'Delegation, Agency and Agenda Setting in the European Community', *International Organization*, 51/1: 99–134.

Putnam, R. (1988), 'Diplomacy and Domestic Politics: The Logic of Two-Level Games', *International Organization*, 43/2: 427–60.

Richardson, J., Gustafsson, G., and Jordan, G. (1982), 'The Concept of Policy Style', in J. J. Richardson (ed.), *Policy Styles in Western Europe* (London: Allen & Unwin).

Rose, R. (1985), 'Steering the Ship of State', mimeo, 85/46.

—— (1991), 'What is Lesson Drawing?', *Journal of Public Policy*, 11: 3–30.

Scharpf, F. W. (1994), 'Community and Autonomy: Multi-level Policy Making in the European Community', *Journal of European Policy*, 1/2: 219–42.

—— (1996), 'Negative and Positive Integration in the Political Economy of European Welfare States', in G. Marks, F. W. Scharpf, P. C. Schmitter, and W. Streeck (eds.), *Governance in the European Union* (London: Sage).

Schmidt, V. A. (1996), *From State to Market? The Transformation of French Business and Government* (Cambridge: Cambridge University Press).

Siedentopf, H., and Ziller, J. (eds.) (1988), *Making European Policies Work: The Implementation of Community Legislation in the Member States*, 2 vols. (Maastricht: European Institute of Public Administration).

Spence, D. (1995), 'The Co-ordination of European Policy by Member States' in M. Westlake, *The Council of the European Union* (London: Cartermill).

Toonen, T. A. J. (1992), 'European of the Administrations: The Challenges of '92 (and Beyond)', *Public Administration Review*, 52: 108–15.

Van Schendelen, M. C. P. M. (1996), ' "The Council Decides": Does the Council Decide?', *Journal of Common Market Studies*, 34/4 (Dec.): 531–48.

—— (1999), *EU Committees as Influential Policymakers* (Aldershot: Ashgate).

Wallace, H. (1996), 'Relations between the European Union and the British Administration', in Y. Mény, P. Muller, and J.-L. Quermonne (eds.), *Adjusting to Europe* (London: Routledge).

—— (1997), 'At Odds with Europe', *Political Studies*, 45: 677–88.

—— and Wallace, W. (1973), 'The Impact of Community Membership on the British Machinery of Government', *Journal of Common Market Studies*, 11/3: 243–62.

Wallace, W. (1973), *National Governments and the European Communities*, European Series No. 21 (London: Chatham House).

Weiler, J. H. H., with Haltern, U. R., and Mayer, F. C. (1995), 'European Democracy and its Critique', *West European Politics*, 18/3 (July).

Wessels, W. (1997), 'An Ever Closer Fusion? A Dynamic Macropolitical View on the Integration Process', *Journal of Common Market Studies*, 4/1 (Mar.): 128–45.

——and Rometsch, D. (1996), 'Conclusion: European Union and National Institutions', in D. Rometsch and W. Wessels (eds.), *The European Union and the Member States* (Manchester: Manchester University Press).

Westlake, M. (1995), *The Council of the European Union* (London: Cartermills).

Williams, S. (1991), 'Sovereignty and Accountability in the European Community', in R. O. Keohane and S. Hoffmann (eds.), *The New European Community: Decision-making and Institutional Change* (Oxford: Westview Press).

Wright, V. (1996), 'The National Co-ordination of European Policy-Making: Negotiating the Quagmire', in J. J. Richardson (ed.), *European Union: Power and Policy-Making* (London: Routledge).

Young, H. (1998), *This Blessed Plot. Britain and Europe from Churchill to Blair* (London: Macmillan).

INDEX

References in **bold** refer to figures and those in *italic* to tables.

administrative structures:
 forms of 17–18, 252–3
 specialist units 239
Austria:
 cabinet, role of 201–2, 204, 207, 208,
  209, 217
 coalitions 201–2; co-ordination
  between parties 209
 council for integration policy 202–3
 European Council: preparations for
  presidency of 207
 interest groups 202, 203, 215–16
 Länder, role of 214–15
 membership of EU 201, 202, 203, 216
 ministries, role of 204–5, 207, 209;
  Chancellery 205, 206; co-ordination
  meetings 205, 206; EU divisions 207;
  Foreign Ministry 205, 206
 'negative' co-ordination 209, 210
 Parliament, role of 201, 207–8, 210–13,
  216, 217
 Permanent Representation 206
 political structure 201, 202, 203
 'positive' co-ordination 209
 President, role of 213–14
 shift of power 217

Belgium:
 approach towards EU policy 182
 Co-operation Agreement 189, 190, 191,
  196
 Concertation Committee 190, 191
 division of society 184
 European Council: representation in
  191, 192, 193
 formalization of co-ordination 196–7,
  198–9
 implementing EU legislation 182–3,
  185, 194
 Interministerial Conference for Foreign

 Policy (ICFP) 190, 191
 ministries, role of: European
  co-ordinators 194, 195, 197–8, 199;
  federal correspondents 194, 195, 199;
  'P.11 meetings' 187, **188**, 188, 189–90,
  191, 193–4, 196
 'on-the-spot co-ordination' 191, 192,
  193
 Permanent Representation 195
 political culture: consensus building
  183, 184, 185, 186, 187, 190–1;
  informal and ad hoc decision making
  185, 186; ministerial autonomy 184,
  185, 186, 198
 state reforms 189
 subnational governments 191, 192

cabinets
 role of: Austria 201–2, 204, 207, 208,
  209, 217; France 82, 89–90, 97;
  Germany 57, 60–1, 71; Italy 109; UK
  27, 34–7, 244–5
centralization:
 effectiveness of 254–5
 extent of 249
co-ordination:
 ambition 243–4, 245–6
 assessment of 164, 254–6
 chain of 6
 conceptions of 13 15, 162–4, 250–1,
  256–7
 cross-sectoral variation 247–8
 failure 110
 formal mechanisms, circumventing of
  248
 impact of 257
 importance of 164–5, 220
 need for 3–6, 236
 political level 249
 problems of 6–10